Witness to the German Revolution

Victor Serge

Witness to the
German Revolution
Writings from Germany 1923

Translated from the French
by Ian Birchall

Haymarket Books
Chicago, Illinois

Printed with permission from the Victor Serge Foundation.
Translation © 1997 Ian Birchall

This translation first published in 1997 in London by Redwords.
This edition published in 2011 in Chicago by Haymarket Books.

Haymarket Books
PO Box 180165
Chicago, IL 60618
773-583-7884
info@haymarketbooks.org
www.haymarketbooks.org

ISBN: 978-1-60846-085-4

Distributed to the trade:
In the US, Consortium Book Sales and Distribution, www.cbsd.com
In Canada, Publishers Group Canada, www.pgcbooks.ca
In the UK, Turnaround Publisher Services, www.turnaround-uk.com
In Australia, Palgrave Macmillan, www.palgravemacmillan.com.au
All other countries, Publishers Group Worldwide, www.pgw.com

Cover design by Eric Ruder.

This book was published with the generous support of Lannan Foundation
and the Wallace Global Fund.

Printed in Canada by union labor on paper containing 100 percent
postconsumer waste in accordance with the guidelines of the Green Press
Initiative, www.greenpressinitiative.org.

Library of Congress Cataloging in Publication data is available.

Entered into digital printing January, 2023.

Contents

Introduction

A successful workers' revolution in Germany in 1923 would have changed the entire course of the century's history. A second workers' state—in one of the most advanced industrial countries—would have made nonsense of Stalin's slogan of "socialism in one country" and enormously enhanced the chances of spreading the revolution to France, Britain and Italy. And Adolf Hitler, even if he had escaped summary execution, would have found it hard to make any impact on events. The two great tyrannies of the century, Stalin's Russia and Hitler's Germany—with their host of imitators and would-be imitators—would have been aborted. Of course, there would have been other dangers, other possibilities of defeat still to face. But the scales would have been shifted significantly in favor of socialism.

One person who had the opportunity to observe and analyze the events of 1923 at first hand was Victor Serge. Serge was still a young man—32—in 1923, but he had an extensive revolutionary past behind him. Born in Brussels to Russian revolutionary parents in exile, he went to Paris while still in his teens and became active in anarchist journalism. He spent the years 1913 to 1917 in jail after defending the anarchist bank robbers of the notorious Bonnot Gang. He went next to Spain, where he participated in the unsuccessful 1917 Barcelona syndicalist uprising. Then he made his way to revolutionary Russia, where he soon decided to become a member of the Communist Party (though he never abandoned political dialogue with his former anarchist comrades). His experiences in revolutionary Russia are described in his *Memoirs of a Revolutionary*,[1] and in the pamphlets he wrote at the time.[2]

By 1922 Serge was feeling considerable disillusion at the way events were developing in Russia. He believed that only by spreading could the revolution survive: "Relief and salvation must come from the west. From now on it was necessary to work to build a Western working-class movement capable of supporting the Russians and, one day, superseding them."[3] With Zinoviev's assistance he got a job in Berlin with the Comintern [Communist International] press agency Inprekorr (*Correspondance internationale*), which provided reports for the Communist press around the world. He spent most of 1922 and 1923 in Berlin, then worked in Vienna and elsewhere before returning to Russia in 1926. He became a supporter of the Left Opposition, and was sent into internal exile before being expelled from the USSR. Back in the West he continued to be an intransigent anti-Stalinist writer, who also produced a series of outstanding novels. With the German occupation of France, he left Europe for Mexico, where he died in 1947.

In his *Memoirs* Serge gives only a relatively sketchy account of his activities in Germany.[4] Even before the major clampdown of November 1923 his activity was at best semi-legal. Many articles under his name appeared in the Comintern press of the time, but they generally dealt with Russian affairs. It was doubtless useful to let the German authorities think "Victor Serge" (itself a pseudo-nym; he was born "Kibalchich") was in Russia. But for German matters, on which Serge wrote a weekly column between July and December 1923, he adopted the pseudonym "R. Albert." As a result, Serge's writings on the German revolution lay for many years ignored and forgotten in the files of Comintern publications.

Albert was first identified as Serge by Richard Greeman after a study of the style and content of more than 20 articles in *Correspondance internationale* and the *Bulletin communiste*.[5] And in 1990 the French Trotskyist historian Pierre Broué,[6] in collaboration with Serge's nephew Bernard Némoz, published a collection of Serge's writings from 1923.[7] The selection in this book is inspired by Broué's edition, but I have added eight additional pieces not included by Broué (see the appendix for details of the comparison between the two books). In fact, on close study Serge's authorship becomes obvious. His style, his eye for significant detail, are un-mistakable. Even his characteristic punctuation—the way in which he frequently, and often irritatingly, ends a sentence with three dots—is there. Doubtless the German police did not employ experts in literary analysis.

Much that has been written on Germany in 1923 has focused on the relations between the German Communist Party (KPD) and the Russian leadership of the Comintern. Serge tells us nothing new on this—even if he had been aware of such discussions, they would not have been suitable matter for publication. What he does give is a vivid account of events in Germany during 1923, and in particular a picture of the consciousness and mood of the working class, the crucial factor in evaluating any revolutionary situation. Serge is describing the German events for an audience abroad—and especially for the French left—his former comrades and the people whose solidarity would be crucial if German workers made a bid for power.

Working in a press agency, Serge read the entire range of the German press from far left to far right. He also had access to the KPD's internal channels of communication. But on top of that he found time to walk the streets and observe daily life. He documented the inflation of 1923 with lists of figures that sometimes become wearisome. But he always quickly returned to the concrete—what did it mean for a worker with two children who wanted to buy some bread and an egg? The major events of the year—the French occupation of the Ruhr, the rise of Hitler, the creation of "workers' governments"—were followed through week by week.

But, despite their fragmentary appearance, Serge's reports were not just random impressions. Serge's account was in fact structured by a rigorously Marxist, materialist method. At the very core was the theme to which he returned again and again—the need for German capitalism to restore its profits. There was only one way it could achieve this—by increasing the level of exploitation. Hence the key aims of cutting real wages and extending the working day from eight to ten hours (reversing the one real gain of the 1918 revolution). It is this that makes sense of the otherwise confusing political fluctuations of the period. Would the bourgeoisie opt for parliamentary democracy (with or without the social democrats), for military dictatorship, or for the Nazis? The answer: whichever would best enable it to increase exploitation and raise profits.

Around this central core Serge accumulated a mass of detail which illuminated the crisis. A trial verdict made clear the balance of class forces. An art exhibition revealed the way in which capitalist decline dehumanized. (It is hard to know which is more surprising: that art exhibitions still took place in 1923, or that Serge found time to attend them.) When he observed a policeman watching a bread queue and looking miserable, he speculated that the cause of the misery was the fact that his wife was in the queue. In one sentence Serge said more about the contradictory nature of the bourgeois state than many learned tomes.

For many years Serge's reputation has rested on his novels and his *Memoirs*. But his earlier writings from his period as a Bolshevik activist show that before being a remarkable novelist he was a remarkable journalist.[8] At a time when we have seen so many journalists, during the recent Balkan War, acting as mere transmitters of the government line, it is important to remember that revolutionary journalism has a quite different history—that it can combine passionate commitment with honest observation. Serge wrote with wit, humor and irony, but above all it was anger that motivated his writing—anger at a system in which the rich got richer while, over ten years, working people faced first slaughter in the trenches, then armed repression, and finally starvation. It is Serge's anger, controlled but never suppressed, which makes this book such a striking testimony to the experience of a revolutionary year.

Serge could not tell all he knew in these articles. He was writing under the gaze of the enemy, and the KPD's secret activity (especially its plans for insurrection in October 1923) was not a matter for the public press. Nobody could blame Serge for being deliberately misleading. But, as he made clear in the later articles, a major defeat had taken place. It was the responsibility of a revolutionary party to exercise the most rigorous self criticism. Lenin was on his deathbed, and the Comintern was now in the hands of Zinoviev, a man Serge aptly described as "Lenin's biggest mistake."[9] But the tradition of honest accounting had not yet been destroyed, and Serge's attempts at evaluating the causes of failure were in marked contrast to the blustering, triumphalist style that characterized the Comintern in the Stalinist epoch.

Serge wrote as an activist working with the KPD, and as such he brought out the party's heroism, its resolute opposition to the corruption and injustice of crisis-ridden capitalism, the dedication of its rank and file. But, reading between the lines, it is also possible to see the fundamental weakness of the KPD. The year 1923 was a frantic one. From demonstration to strike, and from crisis to arrest, militants scarcely had time to sleep. The preceding years since 1918 had been equally hectic. Amid such frenetic activity it was not possible to build a stable and consistent leadership, and to establish the necessary relations of intelligent trust between leadership and rank and file activists. The KPD had come into existence only in 1917; no organization had been built in advance of the crisis. Hence the rapid changes of leadership, the hesitations and tactical zigzags that marked the years of upheaval.

In retrospect it is easy to point to things that Serge missed. He was far too pessimistic about the cultural decay of postwar Germany. While he was very much aware of the rise of anti-Semitism, he tended to see it as a throwback to a more backward society like tsarist Russia rather than as a grim portent of much worse to come.

It is also possible to detect a certain ultra-leftism in Serge's account, perhaps deriving from his anarchist past, but also reflecting a continuing weakness of the German revolutionary tradition. He was quite right to denounce the cowardice and betrayals of the SPD—the party of Ebert, Scheidemann and Noske had since 1918 pursued a policy that was not only treacherous but murderous. But denunciation was not enough. No revolution could be made in Germany without winning over the mass of workers still under the influence of social democracy, and although Serge described the various attempts to implement a united front policy he sometimes underestimated the need to win over social democratic workers.

Like so many Marxists before and since, Serge compressed the timescale. Often he wrote as though German capitalism had no way out in 1923. In fact, the Wilhelm Marx government did achieve temporary stabilization—there was even a brief period of prosperity in the mid-1920s. But on the essential point Serge was all too right—the choice was socialism or fascism, and the failure of socialism, in 1923 and later, as the KPD lurched into Stalinism, left no alternative to the triumph of Hitler. An understanding of the failure of 1923 is essential to seeing why and how Hitler came to power, and Serge was a lucid witness of that failure.

In some ways the world of the Weimar Republic may seem very remote to modern readers. Yet there are many features of Serge's account that remind us we are still confronting the same bankrupt social system. The starvation that haunts large parts of the Third World, the disintegration of 1990s Russia, the economic sabotage that preceded Pinochet's coup in Chile, the sheer lunacy of the international money markets—all these have their counterparts in Serge's account.

History does not repeat itself, but a knowledge of the past arms us for the future. Serge himself summed it up beautifully in his novel *Birth of Our Power*, when he reflected that defeated revolutionaries could look forward to the success in the future of others, "infinitely different from us, infinitely like us."[10]

Ian Birchall
January 1999

---

1 Oxford, 1967.

2 *Revolution in Danger* (London, 1997).

3 *Memoirs*, p155.

4 *Memoirs*, pp157-175.

5 In his 1968 Columbia University doctoral dissertation *Victor Serge: The Making of a Novelist (1890-1928)*, University Microfiches, Ann Arbor, MI.

6 In 1971 Broué had suggested that "in all probability" Albert was in fact Serge. See P Broué, *Révolution en Allemagne* (Paris, 1971), p597.

7 *Notes d'Allemagne* (Montreuil, 1990).

8 See in particular the writings from the Russian civil war period collected in *Revolution in Danger.*

9 *Memoirs*, p177.

10 *Birth of Our Power* (Harmondsworth, 1970), pp65-66.

Note on Translation

A collection of Serge's writings on Germany—*Notes d'Allemagne*—was published in French by Serge's nephew, Bernard Némoz, and Pierre Broué. I am deeply indebted to their work, but I have arranged the material in a different way (see appendix). I have also added eight further pieces not included in the Broué edition. Serge wrote copiously at this time under his own name and under pseudonyms. Even for 1923 I have translated only a selection of his work. There is still plenty more material for others to discover and translate. Correspondance internationale, for which Serge wrote, was a press service designed to provide material for the Communist press around the world. Hence it is possible some of Serge's articles appeared in English at the time. However, apart from some short extracts in *Revolutionary History 5/2* (1994), none of it has appeared in English in recent years.

Serge was working in a difficult and hectic situation. He, and his printers, obviously made mistakes, and on occasions he may have received faulty information. I have corrected obvious misprints but have not otherwise changed any details, preferring to leave the reader with Serge's view at the time he wrote. Thus his reference to "Colonel Hitler" gives an interesting insight into how little was known of Hitler in 1923. I have used the most recognizable forms of place and personal names—thus "Gdansk" and "Aachen" rather than "Danzig" and "Aix-la-Chapelle." I have not attempted to check or correct Serge's arithmetic, which occasionally seems shaky. All notes have been added by the translator except where specifically indicated as "Serge's note."

Acknowledgments

I am grateful to Richard Greeman for encouragement and advice on this project, to Sharon O'Nions for critical comments on the translation and notes, and to the late Peter Sedgwick, who first made me aware of Serge over 30 years ago.

I thank staff at the British Library and the LSE library for their assistance. I was working at the British Library during the period of the campaign against the proposed introduction of charges for use of that library. Fortunately the campaign succeeded, otherwise independent socialist historians like myself would be unable to gain access to our socialist heritage.

I was unable to consult material at the Bibliothèque Nationale in Paris because of the collapse of the computerised system at the aptly named François Mitterrand site. But I salute the staff there who took strike action against unacceptable working conditions.

Chronology

1914

August 4 War begins. SPD deputies vote for war credits.

1917

April 5 Spartacist conference, founding of organization that was to become KPD.

1918

November 9 Proclamation of republic.

1919

January 15 Murder of Luxemburg and Liebknecht.
April 13–May 1 Soviet Republic in Bavaria.

1920

March 13–22   Kapp putsch blocked by general strike.

October 12–17   Halle conference of USPD. Majority votes to join KPD.

1921

March 18–30   March Action.

1923

January 11   French and Belgian troops occupy Ruhr.

July 29   Anti-Fascist Day called by KPD.

August 9–11   General strike brings down Cuno government.

August 13   Stresemann Great Coalition formed, including SPD.

October 10   Workers' government formed in Saxony.

October 13   Workers' government in Thuringia.

October 21   Chemnitz conference fails to back general strike.

October 23–24   Hamburg insurrection.

October 29   Reichswehr removes Saxon government.

November 2   SPD ministers leave Stresemann government.

November 8   Hitler's beer hall putsch.

November 6–12   Fall of Thuringian workers' government.

November 23   KPD made illegal.

November 30   Wilhelm Marx government formed.

Abbreviations and German Terms
Used in Text

ADGB: Allgemeiner Deutscher Gewerkschaftsbund—main (SPD-linked) trade union federation.

AfA: Allgemeiner freier Angestelltenbund—main white collar union federation.

DDP: Deutsche Demokratische Partei—German Democratic Party (liberal).

DNVP: Deutschnationale Volkspartei—German National People's Party (right wing conservative).

DVP: Deutsche Volkspartei—German People's Party (liberal/ nationalist).

KPD: Kommunistische Partei Deutschlands—German Communist Party.

SPD (or *VSPD*): (Vereinigte) Sozialdemokratische Partei Deutschlands—German Social Democratic Party after reunification with USPD.

USPD: Unabhängige Sozialdemokratische Partei Deutschlands— Independent Social Democratic Party (only a small group in 1923 after bulk of party fused with SPD).

Landtag: Parliament of one of the constituent states (Länder) of the Reich.

Reich: From 1918 to 1933 the republic. Refers to the federal government as opposed to the constituent states (Länder) which had their own governments and considerable autonomy.

Reichsrat: The upper house of the federal parliament, with representatives from the various constituent states.

Reichstag: The federal parliament.

Reichswehr: Armed forces of the republic.

Reichsbank: National Bank.

Rentenbank: National Mortgage Bank, established October 1923, basing German assets on industrial and agricultural land rather than on gold (of which Germany had little).

Rentenmark: Temporary currency (November 1923 to August 1924) replacing marks made worthless by inflation.

Stahlhelm: Steel Helmet. An ex-servicemen's association which became a far right organization.

*This article has been selected out of sequence as a suitable introduction setting
the tone for the whole collection. Serge, who had been politically active in
France before 1914, and had many contacts there, was addressing an appeal
for international solidarity to French workers. The Versailles Treaty (June 28,
1919) had imposed a heavy burden of reparations on Germany, which had to
pay the victorious Allies twenty billion gold marks. French troops were already
occupying the Rhineland, and as the economic crisis made Germany unable to
pay the reparations, the threat of an occupation of the Ruhr became more real.*

Letter from Germany to a French Comrade

Correspondance internationale, September 23, 1922

Thirty five million workers, on the right bank of the Rhine, are anxiously awaiting the "winter that kills poor people." In less than two months the average cost of living in Germany has more than tripled, the prices of essential goods (shoes and clothes) have gone up five times. As from October 1 rents go up five times, the cost of postal communications three or four times (a letter abroad which today needs a six mark stamp will cost 20 marks), and the price of telephone calls, railway and tram tickets are going up at a preposterous rate. It has been announced that the price of bread will be quadrupled!

These are the facts. As for wages, the increases are always slow and inadequate, lagging far behind the rise of prices. The most fortunate wage earners have seen their wages doubled since the calamity of the mark. That means that in relation to food prices they have lost a good third, and in relation to the price of clothing more than two thirds...

And this is continuing, it comes on top of years of undernourishment, constant hardship, deep poverty for many. Our comrades Ludwig and A. Friedrich from *Die Rote Fahne*[1] have calculated that out of a total annual wage bill for working Germany[2] of between 100 and 120 billion[3] paper marks,[4] taxes of at least 40 billion are deducted, that is more than 40 percent. Our comrade Varga[5] has published figures based on scientific statistics drawn up by bourgeois experts showing that German workers are eating half as much bread and meat as they ate before the war. Hence the productivity of their labor is falling. And hence in the streets of Neukölln and Moabit[6] you see so many ashen young faces, bearing the marks of tuberculosis and hunger.

People have noted in Germany "the man with no shirt," the worker who conceals the absence of garments behind a miserable shirt front. They have noticed the children with no shoes: in the working-class districts the great majority of children, even in wind and rain, go to school with bare feet and bare heads. This winter they won't go to school. A certain percentage will die of bronchitis... You've heard about those suffering from shell shock, the pathetic disabled ex-servicemen wearing the macabre ribbon of the Iron Cross,[7] who sell matches in the wealthy thoroughfares of Berlin and are insulted by the police. And the beggars who swarm round the approaches to cafés, shabby, humiliated, jeered at in this country of order where all the doors to respectable homes have an enamel

---

1 *Red Flag*: main daily paper of the KPD.
2 Calculation made three months ago. [Serge's note.]
3 The term billion is used to mean a thousand million (10^9); likewise trillion is used to mean a million million (10^{12}) and quadrillion a thousand million million (10^{15}).
4 Figure for all German workers—this was before the massive inflation.
5 Eugene Varga (1879-1964), leading Comintern economist.
6 Working-class districts of Berlin.
7 German war medal.

plate reading, "No beggars, hawkers or musicians." These are the shocking but superficial aspects of an immense, incurable poverty.

There are others, more tragic, which you only see if you live in Germany. The countless prostitutes, at the doors to every café, in all the dark streets at night, in all the apartment buildings; and they're hunted down, cooped up, put on a register, and persecuted with methodical ferocity... The corruption of hungry minor civil servants who are willing to sell any imaginable export license to a cosmopolitan speculator for a piece of bread... The proletarianization of a whole working class made up of former petty bourgeois whose prosperity was once the pride and the strength of the nation... Speculation drives out trade, business becomes stock exchange gambling, credit is impossible, since the slightest article no longer has a fixed exchange value but is the object of frenetic outbidding. And the big stores get visibly more and more impoverished, week by week. —And the feasting, the feasting of the rich amid this social decay, every night lighting up the windows of the restaurants where you can dine modestly for 2,000 marks (more than a week's wages for a working woman in Berlin), while the American bars and the cafés with musicians are filled with revellers and expensive whores in fur coats, a rich harvest of assignations. Just as on decaying corpses you see flourishing hosts of enormous black and green flies, so on the corpse of German society you see swarming and also flourishing, a whole rabble of those fishing in troubled waters, of crooked capitalists, of organizers of trusts, of thieves, of international spies, from the Marquis de Lubersac[8] to Stinnes and from Stinnes to the grocer from round the corner.

Such is Germany, comrade.

---

8 Wealthy French banker involved in negotiations on reparations with Stinnes.

II

Of course all the misfortunes of capitalist Germany in decay fall only on the working classes. The others live ruthlessly—and consume greedily. There is plenty to be found in a shipwreck—so long as you are a good predator.

Now the German working class, whose growing poverty is exhausting its strength and killing its children, is—second only to the Russian working class—the one which in the last few years has done the most for the liberation of humanity. If it had not risen up in 1919, generously spilling its blood on all the public squares of its great cities, what foul reaction would now be ruling over capitalist Europe? What rival "national blocs" would be carving up the world in fraternal hatred?

On November 9, 1918, the German working class overthrew the rule of the Kaiser. In January the following year it courageously tried to make its social democratic government take the major industries into public ownership—in other words to commit central Europe to embarking on the socialist road. Workers' blood flowed in torrents. Liebknecht and Rosa Luxemburg fell on the threshold of the future which had been postponed. In March 1919, a second rising, put down by the Socialist Noske, in the style of a Galliffet.[9] Jogisches was murdered. So much blood, so much blood! But in March 1920 the German working class broke the back of reaction, during the coup by von Kapp and his ruffians.[10] Immediately afterwards SPD ministers had them shot at.[11]

---

9 General Gaston de Galliffet (1830-1909), one of the commanders responsible for crushing the Paris Commune of 1871.

10 The Kapp putsch, an attempted right wing military coup defeated by a general strike called by all the workers' organizations.

11 When the SPD-led government supported the army's crushing of workers' insurrectionary movements after the Kapp putsch.

In March 1921, a third insurrection, deliberately provoked so it could be drowned in blood.[12]

Do we have to recall here some of the other great men and women who died in the German revolution—Leviné, Gustav Landauer, Sylt, Dorrenbach—or give numbers, which run into tens of thousands? Must we remember that hundreds of brave revolutionaries are every day walking in circles in the courtyards of German prisons, under the eyes of a warder from the old regime, who takes pleasure in bullying these defeated men? Must we remember the thinker Erich Mühsam,[13] in prison—the poet Ernst Toller[14]—in prison—the intractable Max Hoelz,[15] imprisoned for life? We must certainly do so, although it is unjust to pick out a few individuals from so many brave men.

The living and the dead, fighters from three revolutionary years, prove what great potential for violence and sacrifice the German working class has. And they remind us of our duty towards it—that is, towards the revolution that is ripening within it.

Now here is the vital question:

Will this German working class, energetic and combative, with great revolutionary experience, whose wounds from the civil war have not yet healed, will it allow itself to be debased, weakened and exploited in times of famine and social disintegration, without reacting with all its strength?

---

12 The March Action of 1921 was a response to police action in central Germany ordered by the social democrat Horsing; but Serge is disingenuous not to mention that the KPD was guilty of irresponsibility in launching this adventurist action.
13 (1878-1935): anarchist, songwriter and playwright; imprisoned for his role in the Bavarian Soviet Republic; released 1924; imprisoned and killed by Nazis.
14 (1893-1939), leader of Bavarian Red Army in 1919, and well-known expressionist playwright.
15 (1889-1933), organizer of a guerrilla army during March Action.

III

What is certain is that the status quo in Germany—and in Austria, where the problem is exactly the same—*cannot last.* No conservative power has the ability to prevent the unfolding of events. There are three possible outcomes:

On the one hand, the German proletariat, contrary to everything that its past leads us to foresee, contrary to its vital interests, will, betrayed by the social democracy, remain generally passive, will work itself to death, undernourished, in order to produce badly. All we can glimpse at the end of this road is irreparable degeneration, the end of a race.—But isn't it absurd to admit that the most powerful proletariat in continental Europe could end up like this?

Or else reaction will break all resistance, will behead the revolutionary party, will tame—with a whip—the accommodating social democracy, and establish a dictatorship of hunters protected by a firing squad. And that would mean for some years the triumph of white terror in central Europe, with the consequence of perpetuating the victory of fascism in Italy, and in France the omnipotence of a military caste in the service of a handful of financiers.

Or else revolution.

Since German reaction could triumph only by beheading the revolution, in the two most likely hypotheses we are facing the German revolution.

And that, comrades, is what we must turn our minds to. Tomorrow, perhaps, red flags will be flying over Cologne; the orgesch[16] of Germany, in cooperation with the black troops of the army occupying the Rhineland,[17] will try to put down the fourth

---

16 Organization Escherich, an armed body created by the far right Bavarian Interior Minister Escherich.
17 The French used colonial troops from Senegal and North Africa in the occupation of the Rhineland and, later, the Ruhr. Morgan Philips Price, who visited the

rising of German socialist workers. What will you do, comrade, when that day comes?

Do you know that last February, during the magnificent general strike by German railway workers, the command of the occupying forces on the left bank of the Rhine intervened to stop the strike in the occupied regions?

Do you know that in April 1918 French troops "restored order" in Luxemborg?

Do you know that the reformists in Germany have no better counter-revolutionary argument than the threat of foreign intervention, French invasion and repression?

Do you know that as of now the occupied territory is treated as conquered territory; that newspapers considered to be subversive are suppressed (among other things, for publishing birth control information); that "suspect" inhabitants are driven out; that our publications are banned; that postal censorship is in operation; that a reactionary separatist movement is being deliberately encouraged by the occupiers so that when the time comes red Germany will be the victim of the same blow as was struck against Soviet Russia from white Estonia, Latvia, Lithuania, and Georgia?

Do you know, comrade, and do the people you are in contact with know it?

When the barricades go up in Berlin, what will you do, knowing that the defeat of your German brothers will confirm, perhaps for another generation, your enslavement? When you are called up either to co-operate with their capitalist masters in making an exhausted people "pay," or to put down their revolt, what will you do?

Rhineland in November 1921, reports that while there was racist feeling against the black troops among the middle classes, working people were often dehumanized with the African troops.

You must prepare yourself for these possibilities. One who knows what Germany is like at present has the duty to tell you. The fate of the whole European working class will depend on the struggles developing there.

Are you a Communist, a syndicalist or a libertarian? I haven't enquired, for in the face of the practical conclusions—or better to call them obligations—imposed by this situation, I don't think that your personal opinions are of any great importance.

On the day when the action starts, whatever your political alignment, you must support with all your strength the German Communists: because they will be, as they always were, the first to face the danger. To act yourself, you will need an organization that is strong, large, flexible, disciplined, and clearly aware of its aims and its methods. It's obvious that this is the condition necessary for victory. For you cannot hide from yourself the real strength of your enemies: the bourgeois state, the bourgeois army, bourgeois justice, the bourgeois press—all formidably organized for repression, and disciplined by centuries of religious and secular education backed up by frequent applications of the military law.

Build the strong revolutionary organization which tomorrow will enable the French proletariat to save the German revolution—that is the urgent great task to which you must contribute with all your strength, if you don't want to play into the hands of international reaction by your passivity or your incompetence!

One of Serge's first journalistic assignments on arriving in Germany was to report on the Conference of the Three Internationals. This was a response to the Genoa Conference of April 1922, the first post-war conference to bring together nations from both sides in World War I. It was part of the Comintern's strategy of seeking a united front around concrete demands with the various reformist and centrist parties that still had the support of a significant section of the working class. The three internationals were the Comintern (Third International), the Second International, which had failed to oppose the war in 1914, and the International Union of Socialist Parties (known as the Two and a half International), consisting of parties (including the British ILP) to the left of the Second International but which refused to join the Comintern.

Conference Impressions

Bulletin communiste, April 29, 1922

The Social Democrats are still at home in the republic of Stinnes and Noske. Which explains why the Conference of the Three Internationals met in one of the rooms of the Reichstag.

In the government offices of the Entente,[1] the last preparations are being made for Genoa, where the job is to strangle simultaneously victorious red Russia and defeated workers' Germany. Meanwhile here, meeting around these three tables arranged in the shape of a T, are the representatives of the three socialist internationals, in whom are embodied the consciousness and the will of hundreds of millions of the oppressed.

Socialism! Marx, his labors, his strong, sure doctrine; the First International and the wave of enthusiasm which passed over the

---

1 Originally the alliance of Britain, France and Russia before and during World War I; after 1917 the alliance of Britain and France.

world; the murdered Commune, then the renewal of ideas, the great congresses; 1914, when everything collapsed; 1917—and the revolution... Now there are three internationals. And here they are.

At the far end of the room a fleshy, bald Vandervelde, cupping his hand to his ear, a small compact face with a beard and pince-nez.—Vandervelde, steeped in ministerial gravity, who just now was talking about democracy and the rights of small nations.—Do you know, minister, what it is they call red rubber? Once upon a time you had a charming visit to the Congo. You were the apostle of democratic colonialism, well fed and covered in honors. And 17 million blacks are still slaving, sweating and bleeding in your immense equatorial jail, minister. So you made war. Do you sometimes think of the number of soldiers executed (by mistake) who are now being rehabilitated? Not many, it's true, amid the hecatombs you have presided over, with your spine respectfully bent before your king. Then after the war you achieved victory and signed the Treaty of Versailles. What do you think, minister, of the poverty, famine and despair of the workers of Germany? What do you think of the death of Vienna?

But you can see by the serenity of his short sighted gaze that M. Vandervelde is thinking of less bitter topics. This socialist is thinking about how to judge the instigators of the Russian revolution. That is why he is here.

His international is that of the ministers. Scheidemann, Ebert and Noske all belong to it. Herr Radbruch, who has just handed over Luis Nicolau Fort and Joaquina Concepcion[2] to the inquisitors

---

2 Luis Nicolau Fort was one of the Spanish anarchists responsible for the assassination of the Spanish prime minister, Eduardo Dato, in March 1921. He and his wife, Joaquina Concepcion, were extradited from Germany to Spain in early 1922, despite the fact that the extradition treaty between Spain and Germany excluded political prisoners.

of Madrid, is also one. And there is, at M. Vandervelde's table, a former Georgian minister... As for Mr. Ramsay MacDonald, we can have no doubt that he will be a minister.[3]

Mr. Chernov[4] ought to belong to this international, and it is unforgivable forgetfulness, error or omission if he isn't a part of it. Was he not more than a minister, almost president of the republic? Mr. Chernov carries with satisfaction, amid the wizened faces of worn out petty bourgeois, a fine head like an old actor's, crowned with white hair. He is well: terrorism and civil war (after all, it is always other people who die) have not encroached on his robust health. He is still ready to demand penalties against the Bolsheviks. And he is the man of the hour: two internationals are going over and over his list of accusations as though they will never be finished.

Formerly, Mr. Chernov pronounced sentence on grand dukes, imperial governors—and with them, to the same death, students, workers full of faith, heroes. These are long forgotten stories. From very high up, Mr. Chernov, assisted by an agent provocateur who has remained notorious, directed terrorism; and when, hungry, betrayed, arrested, sold out, hanged, the revolutionaries of his party felt they had been dupes of some sinister manipulator, Mr. Chernov used his high authority to cover for Azev,[5] defended him and saved his precious skin. Then he was a minister and, like all ministers, repressed. Then he had Volodarsky[6] killed and had the mur-

---

3 MacDonald was to become the first Labour prime minister after the December 1923 election.
4 V. M. Chernov (1876-1952), formerly Russian Social Revolutionary leader, lived abroad after 1920.
5 Evno Azev was a police spy who penetrated the Social Revolutionary organization.
6 V. Volodarsky, a leading Bolshevik, was assassinated by the Social Revolutionaries in June 1918.

der disowned the very same day. Then he organized civil war... But we can't mention all the details of such a full career. Besides, it would only produce a futile nausea.

In fact the other socialist international, the one based in Vienna, is rather better! Adler,[7] round shouldered, rests his wearied intellectual's moustached head on the table. Wretchedness of Vienna where they weren't able to make the revolution, where the socialism of the waverers was not even able to defend the worker's last piece of bread, wretchedness of weak-willed socialism which does not dare to will either the revolution or the re-establishment of capitalism. It is a heavy burden to bear when one has weak shoulders and fumbling hands.

So if the London international is that of ministers and bourgeois repression, the Vienna international is that of weaklings. To be convinced of this you only need to see at the same table Adler—so old, so tired, alongside Clara Zetkin,[8] brave and vigorous—Longuet,[9] Martov,[10] and not far from them, Serrati[11]... They have all had, they still have vague revolutionary desires, but when it comes to breaking with Renaudel, whom he despises, Longuet cannot bring himself to do it; when he has to break with Turati, Serrati can't do it; and when he should break with the counter-revolution whose infamous deeds he is aware of, Martov cannot do it... So what will they be able to do today?

---

7 Friedrich Adler (1879-1960), Austrian socialist leader who assassinated the prime minister in 1916; later secretary of the Second International.
8 Zetkin was in fact 22 years older than Adler!
9 Jean Longuet (1876-1938), son of Marx's daughter Jenny; member of the French Socialist Party; opposed affiliation to the Comintern.
10 L. Martov (1873-1923), Russian Menshevik leader; opposed Bolshevik revolution; emigrated 1920.
11 G. M. Serrati (1872-1926), leader of left of Italian Socialist Party; refused to join Italian CP in 1921, but joined in 1924.

Speeches and statements. What is at stake? Is it the united front? In England two million unemployed and a million locked-out workers are waiting for socialism to defend them.

Throughout central Europe, people who have been methodically starved are in despair. In a few days from now the victorious powers are going to meet at Genoa to try to impose on red Russia the law of the strongest bourgeois... And 30 million people are dying of hunger from the Volga to the Black Sea. What concerns can socialists have at such times, if not to finally confront the aggressions of the enemy class with all the strength of labor? The war for justice has borne fruit; it seems that the most ministerial of socialist ministers can no longer evade their elementary duty...

Nonetheless! Speeches and statements: in all this the united front, the defence of the proletariat, the strangling of workers' Germany, the ambush against red Russia, don't have much of a place. These socialists, of whom not one lacks comfort and security in bourgeois society, are at this moment in history *imposing conditions on the Russian Revolution.*

Journalists, lawyers and members of parliament from London, Vienna, Paris and Brussels seem to have assembled here with the sole aim of judging a guilty party. And this guilty party is the Russian Revolution. It's Lenin, whose crime is to have made the imperialist democracies tremble on their foundations and to have survived the bullets of the Social Revolutionaries.[12] It's you, peasant from the Volga, whose land has been devastated by the Czechoslovaks and Mr Chernov's party, you who, under the five pointed red star and with your rifle in your hand, drove the British out of Baku and Tbilisi![13] It's you, workers and peasants of Russia, who, by de-

---

12 In August 1918 the Social Revolutionary Fanny Kaplan shot and seriously wounded Lenin.
13 Baku, capital of Azerbaijan, oil producing center; Tbilisi (Tiflis), capital of Georgia.

fending for five years your revolution and your right to life against war, blockades, cold, hunger, ignorance, sabotage and conspiracies, have infringed so many sacred principles! Vandervelde accuses and MacDonald repeats. Almost universal approval.

The crucial question, you see, is not the fate of the Russian Revolution, nor that of the employers' offensive in every country, nor even reparations: it is knowing whether Mr Chernov's friends, all of whose base deeds will be unveiled in Moscow, quite openly before a revolutionary court,[14] will be judged with all the desirable guarantees!

But someone has stood up, at the Communists' table. Here the delegates are younger, more vigorous, they don't have the prosperous appearance of long-serving parliamentarians, nor the pampered appearance of socialists with ministerial office who are used to living in armchairs. These are revolutionaries and you can see it. Someone has stood up: a hard bony figure, with a face that jars, a grey complexion, vehement gestures and a biting voice: Radek.[15]

Radek replies to Vandervelde. And the whole meeting is immediately turned round. You don't accuse the revolution, he declares, when you have been a minister of war, when you signed the Treaty of Versailles, when you are the political friend of Scheidemann and Chernov! That is pushing irresponsibility beyond the limits of demagogy. In five minutes Radek has shown what terrible accounts the revolution has to settle with the socialists who are there. But the time for that debate has not yet come. Today:

"Do you or do you not want to defend wages, fight unemployment and obstruct the criminal intentions of imperialism?"

---

14 The trial of the Social Revolutionaries began in Moscow in June 1922. Vandervelde and other Western social democrats acted as defense lawyers for the accused. The trial ended with 14 death sentences which were suspended.
15 Karl Radek (1875-1939), Bolshevik leader who played an important role in Germany on behalf of the Comintern in the 1919-23 period.

In this New Year article Serge reviewed the situation at the start of 1923. Reactionary forces were advancing in Europe, notably in Italy, where Mussolini was strengthening his position. In Germany inflation was already a major problem, though it had not yet reached the disastrous level it was to attain later in the year. Meanwhile in Russia the New Economic Policy was beginning to show results.

Balance Sheet of a Year

Correspondance internationale, January 3, 1923

It is a good thing that, from time to time, a person concerned about the future should turn round and look critically at the road already traveled. Shall we take a retrospective look at 1922, the fourth year of peace since the unatonable slaughter of peoples? Does the experience of this year condemn our hopes to frustration and legitimize the old society which we are fighting to overthrow? So many people whom up to yesterday we still thought of as comrades are going round saying with a knowing smile, "It's still intact, this old building which the prophets from Moscow have so often predicted was about to collapse!"

And perhaps they believe it, for there are none so deaf...

Nineteen twenty-two also dawned with fields of corpses. If humanity in our time had really had a social conscience, it would have been enough to damn the social order. Nineteen twenty-two dawned on the great famine in Russia, on millions of men, women and children dying amid the snows of the Volga, while maize was being burnt in Argentina, while wheat was being piled up—"It can't be sold, you understand, because of the low prices"—in America, and the excessive number of boats available in Britain and America was causing a grave shipping crisis. Christian bourgeois humanity, enlightened with science and philosophy, looked on dispassionately as Russian mujhiks died, while calculating that these piles of corpses would allow them to extort profitable concessions from the soviets...

The statesmen of the victorious powers meanwhile devoted all their ingenuity to rationally imposing starvation on Austria and then on Germany. With the assistance of the obliging German-speaking bourgeoisie, who for the time being look on the end of Europe as being good for business, remarkable results have been achieved in this direction. Austria is no more than a diplomatic fiction. A hundred thousand unemployed are quietly rotting of hunger there. And 500,000 workers are waiting for their turn to die under the care of Friedrich Adler.[1] In Germany the cost of living has increased fortyfold; unemployment looms; black bread is getting blacker; there are hordes of tubercular children, and of mutilated beggars, thieves, prostitutes, state officials who have been bought by *Schieber* (racketeers), or are simply on sale to whoever wants to buy... The Social Democratic Party (SPD) has dropped the defense of the eight-hour day; strikes begun in desperation are ending in defeat: for the big companies are growing rich from the appalling poverty of nearly fifty million people. And every day you can feel it getting closer, like a shadow already looming over everything, the catastrophe of tomorrow.

---

1 Serge seems to be blaming Adler as a representative of international social democracy. Adler was a leading figure in the Austrian Social Democracy, which took power at the birth of the republic in 1918, but he did not hold any major governmental responsibility.

The German mark has joined the Austrian crown. The French franc and the Italian lira, whose artificial stability is to a great extent based on gold marks,[2] which, it is true, are ever more hypothetical, have shown worrying fluctuations in value.

Financial crash, selling off by auction, undernourishment, excessive exploitation, massive financial inflation in Germany. The strangling of Vienna. Unemployment and industrial slump in Czechoslovakia. Stagnation and poverty in Poland (whose mark is worth three times as much as the German mark) and in Horthy's[3] Hungary. So much for the economy.

In internal politics, it's the rule of the man with a truncheon and the executioner. The year started with massacres of miners in Johannesburg. Childers[4]—and a good many others—were hanged in Ireland. The Communist Kingissep was shot in Tallinn, the Communist Purin in Riga, and there are still hangings (after seven years of repression!) in the Rand.[5] There is legal terror established in "independent" Egypt on behalf of a British governor. Repressive laws in Yugoslavia. Terror in Hungary and Romania. In Poland and Estonia, Communist members of parliament are wearing convicts' uniform. In Italy, Benito Mussolini, a renegade from socialism, is being borne towards dictatorship with no difficulty by those who burn down trade union buildings; their so called "revolution" has mainly consisted of hunting down the disarmed and decimated class enemy and of administering castor oil to prisoners, doubtless in order to emphasize the depraved aspect of things.

---

2 Gold coins had circulated freely before the war, but were collected in during the war. They retained value when paper marks became worthless.
3 Admiral Miklós Horthy headed an authoritarian regime in Hungary from 1920 after the overthrow of the short lived Communist regime.
4 Erskine Childers (1870-1922), executed as a member of the IRA.
5 Over 200 were killed in the South African miners' strike.

In international politics, it is the comic aspect that is dominant. Endless discussion and more discussion! The diplomats carry their anxious bald heads from one conference to another. Washington, Cannes, Genoa, the Hague, Paris, London, London again, Lausanne—long journeys, long discussions, long machinations, leading to fiascos and more fiascos. In a whole year the question of the Interallied debt has not come a millimeter closer to a solution. As for disarmament, better not to speak of it. The question of reparations has got so much worse that nobody can try to conceal the latent state of war in capitalist Europe. Sometimes the results obtained by statesmen are exactly the opposite of what they were trying to achieve. At Genoa, the aim was to subjugate the Soviet Republic: but the sole result was the Rapallo Treaty[6] which re-established the USSR's relations with Germany. At the Paris conference the aim was to patch up the Sèvres treaty, which the new Turkish regime chopped to pieces the very next day—irrecoverably—with a hefty bayonet blow.[7] At Lausanne, the object was to put a noose around the neck of the new Turkish regime which would resist any challenge. Nothing was achieved. Fire is smoldering in the East. Every day the financiers in the City of London assess the growing danger facing Mosul[8] oil and the route to India…

—Yes, but there is still socialism!

Socialism, alas, is also continuing down the same path that it took on August 2, 1914. There are hangings in the Rand, shootings in Ireland, massacres in India: the Labour Party keeps silent. M. Vandervelde, signatory of the Versailles Treaty, blusters against

---

6 April 16, 1922.
7 The treaty of Sèvres was signed between the Allies and the Ottoman Empire in 1920, but revised in 1923 following Turkish victories.
8 An Iraqi city.

the soviets. When fascism triumphs, Jules Destrée,[9] another former minister, and one of the king of Belgium's socialists, expresses his great pleasure at the fact. Paul Levi, formerly a Communist and one of the first rebels against the "tyranny of Moscow," has completed his unplanned evolution by falling into the arms of Scheidemann and Noske. The Independent Social Democrats,[10] unable to pay their full-timers, have fused with the SPD which is ready for anything—and old Ledebour has departed... After proletarian Italy has shed its blood every day for 18 months, defeated because it was divided and betrayed, Serrati has made due apology and is seeking readmission into the Communist International. Democratic socialism, for so long bound to the fortunes of bourgeois society, seems to be decaying along with it. In 1922 it waged only one major campaign, against the Russian Revolution, and in support of the counter-revolutionary Socialist Revolutionaries. It rejected the Communist proposal for a united front. Now, at the Hamburg conference, it is preparing to solemnly reconstruct the socialism of ministers and dilettantes, by uniting the internationals of London and Vienna.[11]

In all the social battles of the year, its complicity has secured victory for the employers' offensive. Over the railway workers and the miners in the USA—thanks to Mr. Gompers[12] and the reformists who allowed the export of European coal—over the Rand

---

9 (1863-1936): Belgian Socialist.

10 The Independent Social Democrats (USPD) split from the SPD in 1917; in October 1920 the majority voted to fuse with the KPD; in September 1922 most of what was left of the USPD reunited with the SPD, leaving a small splinter group including the veteran revolutionary Georg Ledebour (1850-1947).

11 That is, the Second International (of which the British Labour Party was a major constituent) and the International Union of Socialist Parties (Two and a half International), founded in Vienna.

12 Leader of the American Federation of Labor.

miners, the German railway workers and, very recently, over the Ludwigshafen strikers.

Thus goes the old world, thus goes "socialism," a living insult to true socialism! This is the sphere of what is dying and rotting in a society whose decline, even if it has slowed down, is nonetheless still undeniable. Now we should look at what is being born, amid the pain, toil, effort and uncertainty that accompanies every birth.

Despite the immense sufferings caused by famine and the aftermath of civil war, despite the crushing ills of a period of transition to socialism in a backward country, which is bankrupt, decaying and encircled by the capitalist powers, nonetheless Soviet Russia ends the years with the following balance sheet:

Nationalized production, which in 1919-20 fell to 6 percent of normal production, has risen in 1921-22 to around 25 percent. During the same year, the real wages of Russian workers, although their privations are still great, more than doubled. The countryside is at peace, and the tax in kind has been collected in full. At the cost of admittedly heart rending sacrifices, the famine has been almost overcome. At Genoa, at the Hague, at Lausanne, the red republic has conceded nothing of its dignity or of its legitimate entitlements. In the face of the world powers, it has proclaimed the right to revolutionary expropriation. A striking victory, moral much more than military, enabled it to regain the whole of the Siberian far east, obliging Japanese imperialism to end its grip on Vladivostok. And the year's end found it still at work, with the Tenth Congress of Soviets completing its internal unification...

Let us turn our eyes towards that which is being born!

This article was written for the fourth anniversary of the deaths of Luxemburg and Liebknecht. The KPD organized annual rallies on the anniversary of their death; demonstrators carried Käthe Kollwitz's picture of Liebknecht on his deathbed with his head in a bloodstained bandage.

The Anniversary of January 15: Karl Liebknecht and Rosa Luxemburg

Correspondance internationale, January 10, 1923

Since 1919, January 15 has become a day of mourning for revolutionaries all round the world.

On January 15, 1919, the young German revolution was beheaded and the fate of the European revolution was compromised by the double murder of Karl Liebknecht and Rosa Luxemburg.

Nothing of that day must be forgotten. The class war goes on. We must remember what the enemy did, what it is still capable of. Here are the proofs: a file of the SPD daily paper *Vorwärts*, official statements... We should reread this, comrades, at the time of the occupation of the Ruhr, while starvation is establishing itself in the homes of 30 million German workers.

On January 13 and 14, 1919, the Spartacists[1]—the German Communists of the proud Spartacus group which, not long before, had been alone in its defiance of the Kaiser and of Ludendorff—were fighting in the streets of Berlin against the troops of a socialist government. This government had provoked the rising by removing from office the red police chief of Berlin, our comrade Eichhorn.[2] The working class were determined to keep power in the capital. They went over from the defensive to the offensive, and the struggle for power was engaged.

On January 14, the SPD government, obviously alarmed, issued an appeal to the population... "We must defend our frontiers against the new military despotism in Russia"—this was written in 1919, at a time when several historical miracles seemed necessary to save Communist Russia, encircled and starving, under attack from Kolchak, Denikin and Yudenich![3]—"Bolshevism means death to peace, death to freedom, death to socialism..." wrote the very people who, two days later, would make holes in the skulls of Karl and Rosa! "The present government is composed of social democrats [...] representatives of the working class [...] The present government is defending the cause of democracy and socialism..." The appeal was signed: Ebert, Scheidemann, Landsberg, Noske, Wissell.[4]

On January 15, the victory of socialist order was confirmed. Liebknecht, recognized and informed on, was taken prisoner in a suburb of Berlin, Mannheimerstrasse 43, in Wilmersdorf. *Vorwärts* rejoiced: on this very day the paper had returned to its old

---

1 Split from the SPD led by Liebknecht and Luxemburg which became the original core of the KPD.

2 Emil Eichhorn (1863-1925), member of USPD. On November 9, 1918 he occupied Berlin police headquarters with a group of workers and soldiers and became police chief. His removal from office, on January 5, 1919, led to workers' rising and repression.

3 Admiral A.V. Kolchak (1873-1920), General A.I. Denikin (1872-1947), General N.N. Yudenich (1862-1933): leaders of the white forces in the Russian civil war.

4 Otto Landsberg and Rudolf Wissell were, like Ebert, Scheidemann and Noske, SPD ministers and people's commissars in 1919.

premises, from which Noske's police had driven out the Spartacist "bandits." Then, a day of silence. That's order.

On January 17 at dawn, the workers of Berlin learned from their newspapers the abominable tragedy which had been kept from them for 48 hours. For 48 hours Karl and Rosa had been dead, "victims of the civil war which they themselves sparked off," wrote the anonymous member of the *Vorwärts* staff detailed to clean the pavement after the murder.

An official statement from the police headquarters—they call it the *Polizeipräsidium*—described the crime in terms of such administrative lunacy that you feel ashamed for the murderers. Just listen.

"Having been arrested during the evening at Wilmersdorf, Dr. Karl Liebknecht was taken to the Eden Hotel, where the headquarters of the Horse Guards division had been set up. From there, he was due to be transferred to the Moabit prison.

"At 9pm a large crowd was blocking the exits to the hotel. Dr. Liebknecht was got out through a back door and made to get into a car; he was warned that if he made any attempt to escape, the guards would use their weapons." (This clumsy confession of premeditation is emphasized in the text.) "The crowd surrounded the car. An unknown person gave Dr. Liebknecht a violent blow on the back of the head. He began bleeding copiously. The driver accelerated. To avoid the mob, it was decided to make a detour by way of the zoo. Near the New Lake the car stopped; the engine was out of order because of the excessive speed, and needed to be fixed. Dr. Liebknecht was asked if he felt well enough to walk to the Charlottenburger Chaussée, where it was hoped they could find a taxi. The prisoner replied in the affirmative. But they were scarcely 50 yards from the car when Dr Liebknecht broke free of his escort and began to run straight ahead. A man who tried to stop him got a knife wound on the right hand." (Again, this is emphasized in the original text.) "As Liebknecht did not stop running, despite repeated warnings, several shots were fired at him. He fell, killed on the spot."

The Berlin zoo is a huge park situated in the middle of the city, and deserted in the evening. Liebknecht was taken there "to avoid the mob." Liebknecht didn't have the presence of mind to throw himself into the thickets which run along both sides of all the paths. He "ran straight ahead," knowing very well that he would be shot at. This prisoner had been warned he would be killed, but he was not handcuffed. At the guards' headquarters, they had even left him with a knife. Scrupulously, Noske's soldiers repeated their warnings before shooting him and killing him on the spot, a man running through a darkened wood at 11pm!

To cobble together this inept account the authorities needed no less than 48 hours. They had to find some explanation of why, having been arrested without offering the slightest resistance at 9:30pm, Liebknecht was killed in a deserted place two hours later!

At the same time Rosa Luxemburg was also dying.

"The threatening crowd surrounding the Eden Hotel had several times tried to seize Frau Rosa Luxemburg. Her guards succeeded in taking her as far as the running-board of the car which had been prepared for her. At this moment there was a scuffle. Frau Rosa Luxemburg became separated from her escort, and when they snatched her back from the crowd she was unconscious. They stretched her out on the front seat of the car. As the car was moving off, an unknown man leaped onto the running-board and fired a pistol shot at point blank range into the unconscious Frau Rosa Luxemburg.

"The car went along the Kurfürstendamm towards the center of Berlin. When it reached the canal, unknown persons shouted, 'Halt!' The driver, believing this was a patrol, obeyed. The crowd surrounded the car, shouting: 'It's Rosa!' The body of Frau Rosa

Luxemburg was snatched and dragged off into the dark."

The murdered woman's remains were thrown in the canal.

In all of contemporary history, which is not short of assorted horrors, there are few scenes so revolting as that of this bourgeois crowd, bent on lynching a prisoner, a white haired woman who had fainted, and who was one of the most powerful minds of world socialism. You would have to go back to the Paris Commune to find anything comparable. The women of Versailles[5] used the tips of their parasols—doubtless with a little pout of disgust—to touch the bodies of those atrocious *Communards*. The Berliners of 1919 dragged Rosa Luxemburg's body, still twitching with life, along the pavement to the canal.

And the next day *Vorwärts* wrote: "Social democracy, despite all the aberrations of left and of right, is defending order, human life, the rule of law against force. That is what it is fighting for! No one should believe it can be disarmed!" In the very same issue we can pick out the following headlines and subheadings: "The end of Bolshevism"—"Petrograd at death's door"—"Counter-revolution in Russia"—"Gorky reported to have fled to London."

Four years have gone by since then. Liebknecht's chief assassin died accidentally. Rosa Luxemburg's murderers are known but have not been prosecuted. One of them, Runge, confessed; he got six months in jail for being indiscreet. The gaoler Tamschick from the Moabit prison who killed Leo Tychko and then Dorrenbach[6] was promoted.

Four years have gone by. Now we have tasted the fruits of victory, won at this price by the German social democracy.

Thanks to it, the proletarian revolution, which could have suc-

---

5 The troops which crushed the Commune of 1871 were sent in from Versailles, outside the Commune's territory.

6 Heinrich Dorrenbach (1888-1919); revolutionary and sailors' leader in 1918. Arrested 1919 and shot "trying to escape."

ceeded in central Germany, did not triumph. The likes of Stinnes, Thyssen, the aniline millionaires[7] and those of many other industries enjoyed prosperity. Herr Cuno of the Hamburg-America Line is in power.

The Germany of the workers, which the SPD threatened with famine and blockade in 1919 if it dared to make its revolution, did not make its revolution and it is starving nonetheless. Germany of the workers, which Scheidemann and friends threatened with Allied intervention, is perhaps at this very moment seeing the Senegalese[8] invade the Ruhr. Fascism is looming. Erzberger and Rathenau,[9] leading bourgeois with mildly radical views, have been killed; Ludendorff is left in peace and Colonel Hitler is peacefully organizing his counter-revolutionary assault troops in Bavaria.

"Order, respect for human life, rule of law, socialism" were the key themes of the social democrats during the days when Karl and Rosa died—a peculiar cynicism. Reality has other names: famine, colonization of Germany by foreign capital, triumph of large scale speculation, the rule of profiteers, the employers' offensive, the arming of reactionary forces.

As Communists, we do not look at history fatalistically. In the class struggle, there are no inevitable defeats or victories. Material,

---

7 The Badische Anilinund Soda Fabrik, a major chemical company.

8 French use of black African troops in the Ruhr occupation posed particular problems for the KPD, since some sections of the left responded in a racist manner. The KPD line was to reject racism while agreeing that black troops should not be there. A special leaflet was issued for Senegalese troops, which stated, "You are here to pillage and steal in favor of the same French imperialists who murder and rob you in your homeland."

9 Walter Rathenau, the Jewish foreign minister of the Reich, was murdered on June 24, 1922 by an extreme right organization because of his support for paying reparations.

intellectual and moral forces come into conflict, and the stronger breaks the weaker. In January 1919, although in mortal danger, the Russian Revolution in its struggle with reaction reached the peak of its potential to expand and create. Hungary was progressing towards soviet rule. The revolutionary wave was rising in Italy. In the victorious states, demobilization had not been carried out: armed workers were returning from the trenches, scarcely restraining their powerful anger; everywhere the fearful, cowardly bourgeoisie which had stayed in the rear retreated before them. Proletarian Germany wanted to carry through its program of public ownership, to follow the great Russian example. It still had those four remarkable minds: Franz Mehring,[10] a scholar and a bold thinker, the very heart of the Spartacus group; Leo Tychko (Jogisches), the best of organizers, the most skillful of conspirators; Karl and Rosa. Proletarian Germany could have won.

The bourgeois and socialist counter-revolution struck down three of these thinkers; then old Franz Mehring died in the sudden dark despairing twilight of defeat. Social democracy understood only too well that a class that has been beheaded is halfway to defeat. Its killers finished off the work of demoralization that had been begun by the SPD's treachery. If, instead of that, it had carried out its most elementary socialist duty, what a future would have been opened up to the working class of Europe—certainly after a hard struggle; but the bleak present serves only to delay and to prolong! Let us think of this on the day of Karl Liebknecht and Rosa Luxemburg. We must remember what the enemy is capable of. In the crime of January 15, 1919, there is a great historical lesson.

---

10 Franz Mehring (1846-1919), veteran socialist closely associated with Rosa Luxemburg.

On January 11 French and Belgian troops occupied the Ruhr, following the
dispute about unpaid reparations. The German government launched a
campaign of "passive resistance," refusal to cooperate with the occupying forces.
Meanwhile the French Communist Party, in association with the KPD,
embarked on a major campaign of opposition to the occupation. The Ruhr crisis
worsened Germany's already difficult economic situation.

News from Germany

Correspondance internationale, February 9, 1923

What is happening to German finances? An eminent economist who took on the job of predicting their development would be a brave man. Bankruptcy is a fact. Every day it is more ruinous, more complete. How far will it go?

From January 17 to 23 (according to an official report) the national bank issued new banknotes to a value of 217,000,000,000 (nine zeros) marks. And at the beginning of February, large financial establishments in Berlin paid out no more than 150,000 marks, for paper money was in short supply!

In recent days the issue of 50,000 mark notes has been announced, to be followed shortly by 100,000 mark notes.

On January 23 there were in circulation banknotes for 1,654,600,000,000...—in words, one thousand six hundred and fifty-four billion...banknotes...

The state presses are still functioning. And the most bald-headed statesmen are studying the problem of stabilizing the mark.

The rise in prices or, more accurately, the automatic reduction of wages, continuing to infinity, naturally keeps step with the issuing of banknotes. Make your own judgment.

On the evening of February 3, a pound[1] of good quality butter cost 6,900 marks; on February 5, 7,200 marks. In the same period, second rate margarine, poor people's butter, rose by 10 percent, from 4,200 to 4,500; potatoes went up 15 percent, from 26 marks a pound to 30; lard went from 6,000 to 7,200 marks per pound (20 percent); an egg from 380 to 420 marks (11 percent).

It should be noted that it is the most commonly consumed items that are rising the fastest.

Meanwhile, subsequent wage increases are under discussion. By the time they happen, prices will have doubled or tripled again.

A hundred or so cases of poisoning from bad flour have been reported in the area surrounding Berlin, and several cases involving rotten horse meat. There have been several deaths. From these miscellaneous news items you can see how the poor of Germany are being fed.

In January 116,574 homeless people, including 9,135 women, were accommodated in the Berlin night-shelters. In January last year, the number of Berlin homeless was only 78,263—an increase of 38,211 in one year. Who is paying the...reparations?

We reported earlier the death of a Communist deputy in the Bavarian Landtag: Hagemeister, one of the courageous prisoners from the soviet revolution in Munich.[2] He died on January 16 in the Niederschönenfeld fortress, where he was serving a long sentence of imprisonment with forced labor.

---

1 A metric pound—half a kilogram.
2 Communists played a leading role in the short-lived Soviet Republic in Bavaria in April 1919, and were afterwards victims of savage repression.

The truth, which has been revealed by the Communist fraction in the Reichstag, is that Hagemeister died as a result of ill treatment. When he was sick he was refused medical assistance. He spent nights of despair, wholly isolated in his cell, suffering from a fever which alternately froze and burnt him. The prison administration knowingly left him to die, a doomed, defenseless class enemy.

That is how people are put to death in the prisons of German democracy. We should note that the genuine death of Hagemeister caused much less stir in the European socialist press than the fictitious death[3] of the Social Revolutionary Timofeyev in Moscow, not long ago...

There is a fair amount of killing going on in the Ruhr. The poor wretches shot down by French and Belgian sentries—who have been brutalized by their vicious instructions—are now being counted by the dozen. At Düsseldorf a schoolboy was killed: perhaps he gave the troops in the square an impudent look. A little girl next to the murdered boy got a bullet in the stomach. M. Poincaré has called for the "peaceful (!) protection of his engineers." He makes an ingenious use of euphemism. Basically he is simply treating the inhabitants of the Ruhr as he did the strikers of Le Havre.[4] It's his job. But when he faces a firing squad, he will have got what was coming to him.

---

3 Timofeyev was one of 14 Social Revolutionaries sentenced to death in Moscow in 1922, but the death sentences were suspended.
4 In Le Havre, on August 25, 1922, workers striking against a pay cut clashed with police who killed three and injured 15.

From July to December 1923 (with the exception of two weeks in August–September) Correspondance internationale *carried a weekly column by "R. Albert" under the heading "Reports from Germany." These columns are all reproduced here, together with a few additional pieces that appeared in the bi-weekly edition. The Ruhr occupation was still continuing, but the French and German ruling classes recognized that they had a common interest in restricting the development of working-class opposition.*

A Document on German Patriotism

Correspondance internationale, July 1, 1923

The Communist press in France and Germany has just been enriched by a contribution which was as valuable as it was unexpected. It came from Herr Lutterbeck, deputy to the chief district official of Düsseldorf, the author of a letter to General Denvignes,[1] certain passages of which deserve to be preserved in the annals of working-class literature. This official from Düsseldorf is asking for the favor of assistance from the French commander in order to repress the working-class movement. It would be impossible for us to express better than he does the necessities and reasons for international capitalist solidarity. The recall of the events of 1871[2] takes on

---

1 Joseph Cyrille Magdalaine Denvignes, French general who spent six years in Germany. He described his experiences in *La guerre ou la paix* (Paris, 1927).
2 The assistance given by Bismarck and the Prussian troops in the crushing of the Paris Commune.

a very particular flavor when a senior Prussian civil servant is writing to one of Foch's officers. We will quote from the text:

> Events such as those at Gelsenkirchen are liable to encourage elements hostile to the state. Further disturbances will occur, and order, the necessary basis for civilization and production, risks being shaken for a long time to come.
>
> There would be great risks if France imagined that, in the present circumstances, it could easily re-establish the normal state of affairs. The industrial region is so complex that it is possible for a spark in one city to become a flame in another, and the flame will be such that the force of arms cannot control it, and that neither the Rhine nor the German frontier beyond the Rhine can stop it. This threat hangs over the whole world. And if the French command waits passively until the rising attacks it, then it will appear as if France wishes German authority to be shaken in the Ruhr at any price, even if it be the price of a rising which would threaten European civilization by putting the Ruhr in the hands of the rabble. This is a dangerous game for France itself. The army of occupation is not made up of inanimate material, rifles, machine-guns and tanks. The weapons are borne by men who have eyes and ears. There is a danger that they will carry from the Ruhr a seed destined to take root in French territory. In face of such dangers, may I take the liberty of stressing the heavy responsibility which would be incurred by the French command if it were to show itself as being indulgent in the face of anarchy. If it does not act itself, then at the very least its obligation is to leave the German authorities with their hands free in order to do their duty. Prime Minister Poincaré recently told a Socialist deputy called Auriol that incidents in the occupied territory are not inevitable, citing the precedent of 1871-72. At that time in France there were no conflicts in France between the population and the occupying forces. May I recall in this respect that at the time of the Paris Commune the German command did its best to anticipate the needs of the French authorities as far as repression was concerned. I am under an obligation to request you to observe a similar attitude if, in the future, dangerous clashes cannot be avoided.

This senior Prussian civil servant is not embarrassed by patriotic scruples. The pursuit of revenge against France, which is doubtless dear to him, in no way obscures his clear judgment as a class conscious bourgeois. He is the sort of person who will get on well with those clearsighted French bourgeois who, in 1918-19, when the dead of the Great War had scarcely been buried, bluntly declared that Ludendorff was better than Liebknecht.

By July the continuing economic crisis was causing serious political tensions. In the Rhineland demands were growing for independence from the German republic. The government of the shipping magnate Wilhelm Cuno, based on the parties of the center, was increasingly unpopular.

Amid the Collapse of Bourgeois Germany

Correspondance internationale, July 14, 1923

The revolutionary situation is ripening in Germany. The remarkable and rapid growth of Communist influence is perhaps the best indication of it. After having remained for several months with an average print run of 25,000 copies, *Die Rote Fahne* of Berlin is now printing 60,000, more than *Vorwärts*. And it is, after all, only one of the KPD's 30 daily papers. The growth in the party's membership is also noticeable, as is the extension of its trade union influence, its moral leadership within the factory committee movement—the most active current in Germany's proletariat—its key role in the political life of Saxony and Thuringia, and its striking electoral successes in such a backward area as Mecklenburg-Strelitz. All these facts are evidence that the masses' will for action is awakening. When a Communist Party develops in this way, it is because it is approaching a historical turning point. The German revolutionaries are well aware of this.

On July 12 *Die Rote Fahne* published a document whose style and tone take us back to just before the great days of 1919. It is an appeal from the KPD central committee to the party members. The gravity of the political situation is set out in precise terms—bluntly and with no bombast. The conclusions are formulated with the sober energy of a challenge issued after mature consideration to the reactionary elements which are biding their time just outside the frontiers of legality. The KPD central committee mentions the preparations being made in the Rhine region to proclaim a Rhineland republic, under the aegis of the occupation authorities and with their financial assistance. The Bavarian fascists used to get French money; some Rhineland fascists are still getting it. The government, and the social democrats who are members of it, are quite well aware of the preparations for a reactionary violent coup and for foreign intervention. Fascist action could also begin as a result of measures by the Reich against red Saxony and Thuringia; or else it could be the unexpected result of a simple wage struggle. To quote the document itself:

> Our party must raise the combativity of its organizations to such a level that they will not be surprised by civil war wherever it may be launched.
>
> [...] If legal communications are interrupted by a general strike in the railways and postal services, or by military operations, we must make sure of all our lines of communication in advance.
>
> [...] The fascists count on winning in civil war by the most resolute use of violence and of crushing brutality. Any workers who resist them and are then taken prisoner will be executed. To break strikes, they will go so far as to shoot every tenth striker. Their violent coup can only be stopped by meeting white terror with red terror. If the fascists, armed to the teeth, shoot our proletarian fighters, they will find us implacable and determined to destroy them. If they put every tenth striker up against the wall, the revolutionary workers will kill one fascist in five.
>
> The fascist associations have arms and military equipment.

Those workers who are not yet in possession of arms must know
where and when they can obtain them if they are needed.

It is in the Ruhr and the occupied region that the working-
class faces the greatest threat. The KPD considers armed struggle
against French imperialism to be impossible, and envisages a general strike there if necessary.

Why?

German corn is more expensive inside Germany than American and Argentinean corn. At Hamburg at the beginning of July
100 kilograms of cereals cost (including freight for foreign corn):

La Plata wheat	11.5 guilders[1] or 730,000 marks
American wheat	11.7 guilders or 737,000 marks
Russian rye	8.35 guilders or 530,000 marks
German rye	610,000 marks
German wheat	850,000 marks

The consequence is that within one week the price of a loaf has
risen from 7,000 to 20,000 marks on the free market, and from 4,200
to 10,000 (from July 23) on ration cards for the poor. From June 29
to July 5, the minimum subsistence level for a household with two
children has risen by 147,000 marks a week, to a total of 919,668 according to the official index. Between July 10 and 11 in Berlin, the
cost of living rose by 22 percent in 24 hours. A pound of margarine
went from 34,000 to 38,000 marks, an egg from 3,400 to 4,400, a
pound of bacon from 35,000 to 48,000 (that is, 37 percent increase).
It is true that there is talk of raising wages—every ten days.

Such are the results of the combined efforts of a government in
the service of big capital, the landowners and French imperialism.

In working-class Germany, statistics reveal that since the new
falls in value of the mark, unemployment has gone down slightly.

1 Netherlands currency.

In May there were only 6.2 percent unemployed among trade unionists as against 7 percent in April. In the tobacco industry, the worst affected, there were only 21.5 percent as against 32.3 percent. The number of unemployed receiving assistance from various organizations (far from all of them) has fallen, in the same period of time, from 279,135 to 244,742. Industries affected by limitations on the number of hours worked employ 5,400,000 workers of whom 1,159,963 (21.7 percent) are only working shortened weeks (shoemakers, metalworkers, textiles, clothing, tobacco).

When we remember that German workers long ago exhausted their savings and any money put aside, and that they earn a pittance even when they work full weeks, we can image the sum of wretchedness embodied in these figures. It is easy to understand the disturbances in the Rhineland and Saxony, in the course of which a certain number of unemployed have been killed by the police force of the democratic order.

The dollar continues its dance. The Reich is devoting millions of gold marks to "stabilize the mark," that is, to prevent it from vanishing into thin air too rapidly, and thus to favor the stock exchange speculations of the barons—or bandits—of finance. On this point, the Communist fraction in the Reichstag are asking Herr Cuno the following tricky questions: "Has the Hugo Stinnes steamer company (shipping line) been exempted from the compulsory surrender of foreign currency? Why? Is it the only one?"

It isn't the only one. And who can fail to understand why?

But on the evening of July 10, the dollar, quoted at 256,000 or 266,000 marks at Gdansk, and at 276,000 marks at New York, was, thanks to government action, only at 187,000 marks at Berlin. The difference between the official and the real rate of exchange is paid by the people on small fixed incomes—the only ones affected—to the big financial establishments. That's what they call "stabilization."

The Reich's floating debt doubled in June, reaching the splendid figure of 24.9 billion marks. On June 30, there was paper money in circulation to the value of 17,291.1 billion marks.

But if the Reich's finances are expressed by such fabulous—negative!—figures, if the bankruptcy of the state becomes a little clearer every day, then the big financial establishments for their part seem prosperous enough. Take a look. The Diskontogesellschaft, the third largest bank in Germany, has published its accounts. It's ending up with a net profit of 4.8 billion marks, that is to say, 24 times higher than last year. It is paying 250 percent dividends to its fortunate shareholders. And all these figures are doctored so as not to be too startling to people with no bread and no shirts, but who nonetheless read the papers.

For its part the *Dresdner Bank* is only paying 200 percent dividends for 1922. Its profit and loss account is closed with a net profit of 18,227,522,795 marks.

Inflation caused by lack of confidence in paper money has obviously swollen all these figures, which, if they were reduced to 1914 proportions, would still be very respectable. Above all, in a land with tubercular children, with the most wretched wages, and where begging and prostitution are very widespread.

Here we have merely set out figures, well known facts that have been published and are unquestioned. They will show you, comrade, what a capitalist society looks like when it is breaking down on the eve of some formidable crisis... They explain why the German Communists, the only ones to look reality in the face amid the shipwreck, are using the determined language quoted above while demanding the seizure of the real values[2] of the bourgeoisie.

---

2 The Communist demand was that the part of the nation's real wealth (land, buildings, factories) which was not eroded by inflation should be confiscated by the Reich to enable it to balance its budget.

By mid-July the crisis was leading to polarization of left and right. Hermann Ehrhardt, one of the leaders of the Kapp putsch and involved in the murder of moderate Jewish cabinet minister Rathenau in 1922, had escaped from jail with official complicity. The KPD moved onto the offensive with the call for a national Anti-Fascist Day on July 29.

Reports from Germany
Disturbances at Wroclaw and Frankfurt

Correspondance internationale, July 28, 1923

In the course of the last month, the situation in Germany has become more tense to an unimaginable degree. And for a very simple reason: no wage any longer enables you to stay alive. You know in the morning that the dollar will certainly be worth 50,000 marks more by the evening. There is now no brake or limitation on rising prices; the cost of living goes up by the hour, and often by 20 to 30 percent in the course of 24 hours, while the slightest increases in wages and salaries must be negotiated over a week. Housewives are driven crazy and retailers are beginning to be afraid. The population is trying to lay in stocks, foreseeing that "something" is coming; the shopkeepers are rationing them. Sometimes the insane rise in prices prevents them from restocking their shops. Others, knowing very well that one day they will be looted and strung up, are hiding their stocks and fitting iron bars on their doors.

Eight days ago hunger riots suddenly broke out in Wrocław,[1] sparked off, it seems, by young fascists who called on the crowd to loot Jewish shops. The police intervened brutally, supported by the reformist trade union leaders.—*Order must come first!*—The result: six dead, 15 wounded, 150 proletarians in jail, 750 billion marks of material damage. For the hungry crowd had nonetheless given a good lesson to some vicious grocers.

On July 23, at Frankfurt-am-Main, a large anti-fascist demonstration, *organized jointly by the SPD and the KPD*, mobilized all the hungry in the city. On the route of the march was the home of the public prosecutor Haas, who ran out with his revolver in his hand to shut the iron gate to his garden. The appearance of this armed bourgeois in the street was enough to unleash the terrible latent anger of thousands of people. In a few moments prosecutor Haas was knocked down, stabbed and his house completely ransacked. Remember the anger in the streets in Paris in 1789 and the fate of those who caused starvation, Foulon and Berthier[2]...

Yesterday (July 25) at the Berlin food markets, housewives were queuing up at the stall of a potato seller.—For there is a spud crisis: you can't find them anywhere, speculators are hiding them. Think about it! They'll be worth twice as much tomorrow. The first women to arrive got them at 5,000 marks a pound. Those who arrived half an hour later were already paying 6,000 marks a pound. To those who came last the worthy trader offered his potatoes for 7,000. They nearly beat him up. The municipal police—in green uniforms[3]—intervened with the greatest brutality. One poor

---

1 On July 23 there had been violent clashes between demonstrating workers and police in these two cities. Wrocław was formerly known as Breslau.
2 Louis XVI's minister Foulon and his son-in-law Berthier, the *intendant*, were killed by the Paris crowd on July 22, 1789.
3 German police wore green or blue uniforms according to which force they belonged

woman was literally trampled underfoot by three uniformed brutes. Afterwards she was carried for first aid to *Die Rote Fahne*, whose offices were nearby. And that is significant.

These people feel condemned, that they can't go on living like this, and that the authorities are quite ready to give them bullets rather than bread.

July 29

It is in these conditions that everywhere in Germany preparations are being made for the Anti-Fascist Day of action on July 29, in which the KPD is calling for the participation, not only of workers, but of the *working middle classes, civil servants, small investors, peasants,* in short all the ruined, all the hungry, all the infuriated, precisely all those whom fascism is asking to fight against the proletariat on behalf of high finance…

After long hesitation, the government, greatly embarrassed, has made its mind up. The Reich minister of the interior, Herr Oesel, has proposed that all the states in the Reich should ban all open air demonstrations and disperse them, if necessary by force. Citizen[4] Severing, social democratic minister of the interior in the bourgeois Prussian government, the Severing of the odious provocations of March 1921,[5] immediately banned the demonstration on July 29. His colleague Noske, social democratic president of the Hanover government, had anticipated him by doing the same some days earlier.

---

to. The Schutzpolizei—municipal police—wore green; the national *Sicherheitspolizei*, under direct control of the minister of the interior, wore blue.
4 Serge refers to SPD members as "citizen"—a form of address current in the French bourgeois revolution—rather than using the Communist "comrade."
5 At the time of the March Action.

The demonstration will go ahead nonetheless. Peacefully or otherwise—that depends entirely on the government's attitude—it will now, in any case, have a doubly revolutionary impact. Will Herr Cuno dare, if the situation arises, to use the troops against the proletariat and middle classes determined to demonstrate their willingness to struggle against fascism which, for its part, is mocking the Leipzig high court, defying the republican government and counting on the support of the Reichswehr and the police? When the Bavarian reactionaries disregard the republican laws of the Reich, the central government puts up with the blow and does not react in any way. The KPD today is strong enough not to submit to the decrees of ministers who are protecting fascism. On July 29 shall we see the police and the army mobilized alongside the fascist gangs, forming a common front with them? To tell the truth, it would be no surprise. But then the government of the "republic" would decisively discredit itself in the eyes of the backward working-class elements who still have illusions in it. And that would be a big step forward.

The fascist organizations in Berlin are preparing a counter-demonstration for July 29. Their appeal is signed by the DNVP, the People's Party of National Freedom (officially banned, but this detail is unimportant to it), the National Union of German Officers and the United Patriotic Associations. The fascist game is clear. If the government acts against the proletariat, make a bloc with it, impose vigorous repression, and then grab all the advantages from the situation. We are on the brink of civil war.

Ehrhardt and Noske

Naturally Ehrhardt is still on the run. There are even good reasons to believe that at this moment he is the darling of the smartest salons in Budapest. There is nothing more revealing of the complicity of the republican regime towards reaction than the escape of this commander in chief. The Saxon government has published some very interesting material on this subject. A cousin of Ehrhardt from Hamburg, a friend of various ministers and of Herr Cuno, was able to discuss freely in private in Leipzig jail with the man charged by the high court. The latter enjoyed all conceivable freedoms in prison. His escape still remains mysterious. Not a single door was forced. The prisoner evaporated leaving no trace. Good Lord! Benevolent jailers opened the doors for him. They expect to receive promotion—after the fascist coup. One detail: a few days before Ehrhardt's escape I noticed in the *Deutsche Allgemeine Zeitung,* the paper of Stinnes's press trust, a thoroughly pro-fascist organ, a very ambiguous note in which it was observed, though without any conclusion being drawn, that Ehrhardt's imprisonment on remand was being excessively prolonged... Opinion was being prepared for his escape.

The Leipzig high court has just (July 23) passed judgment on one of his accomplices, the young Princess of Hohenlohe. She has been sentenced to six months in prison for giving false evidence to assist Ehrhardt. She's only a stooge, and the affair is without importance. But it produced a delicious statement in evidence from Noske. The social democrat Noske came before the court to testify that Ehrhardt had been able "by methods which were admittedly inhumane' to form an élite corps[6] which had been highly useful in restoring order in Germany and in repressing Bolshevism. "I had to use these troops because I had no others." This scoundrel of a socialist had no others! At the time of von Kapp's coup in 1920, Ehrhardt offered military dictatorship to von Kapp. Do you know why? "Because," Noske tells us, "despite his repeated requests, I had refused to be dictator." What a great citizen, believe me! And

---

6 The Freikorps, used to crush the working class in 1919.

to think this bloody reactionary scum still belongs to a Socialist Party, to a Socialist international, to the same one as Fritz Adler and Jean Longuet. Which of these men has sunk the lowest?

As the economic crisis got worse and the Cuno government became more unpopular, the KPD faced a major problem. There were threats to ban the anti-fascist demonstrations called for July 29. The KPD sought advice from Moscow and got contradictory and inconsistent replies. In most parts of Germany the demonstrations were replaced by mass meetings; not a complete climbdown, but a withdrawal to a more defensive stance.

Scarcity in Berlin

Correspondance internationale, August 4, 1923

It must be possible to measure, day by day, the progress of Germany, this great capitalist country, so wonderfully organized, as it slides towards the abyss.

What is new this week? The paper money crisis, the scarcity—publicly acknowledged—of potatoes and fats, the enormous rise in the cost of living and the proportional fall in wages. The Reichsbank is issuing billions of paper marks every day: but on the New York stock exchange, the mark is falling ever faster. By the time they have been printed, German banknotes are worth no more than what they cost in paper and ink. Over the last few days there has been a shortage of notes. Private printshops had to be rapidly called into service to print notes of one, two, five and ten million marks... They were not even in circulation when the dollar, which five days ago was worth 400,000 marks, was quoted at 1,000,000 (on the evening of July 28). They had to hurry and print notes of one, five and ten billion!

Between July 20 and 26, the cost of living rose by 50 percent. From July 25 to 27, in two days, the price of foodstuffs leaped by... 107.7 percent (butter, from 70,000 a pound to 180,000; margarine from 50,000 to 80,000; pork from 60,000 to 120,000, etc.). The Reich statistical department is deliberately falsifying the cost of living index. On July 23, it registered an increase of 36.1 percent for the previous week. *Die Rote Fahne* checked and found it was 50 percent. Housewives check even better.

And what they find is worse... The shopkeepers simply refuse to sell to them. They are waiting for next week's increase so as to make better profits or to run less risk. So potatoes—the basic food of the German worker—butter, margarine and milk have no longer been on sale in Berlin for the last four days. The days before revolution are always the same! The monopolist is one of the last products of an exploiting society in disintegration.

But all our figures mean nothing unless they are compared to wages. I know a well paid skilled worker who last March was earning around 500,000 marks; at the time the dollar was "stabilized" at 20,000, which gave him around 25 dollars a month. In July his wage rose to around four million, or, if we accept an average rate per dollar of 300,000, between 13 and 14 dollars (in other words a net reduction of 11 out of 25). At the end of 1922, he tells me, he was earning 3,000 marks a month, which was worth over thirty dollars. In two years his real wages have fallen by half. He's a social democrat, but he's started reading *Die Rote Fahne*. When he sees there that wages are rising in Russia, he frowns and looks thoughtful.

The bourgeoisie are afraid

The *Kreuz-Zeitung*, the very moderate paper of the Catholic Center Party, recently wrote that "we see in the population the same mood as just before November 9, 1918," that is, at the time of the fall of the Kaiser. Agreed, but what could fall today? Herr Cuno? That wouldn't be much. Why are the bourgeoisie so worried?

In fact it is quite likely that Herr Cuno will fall, but that isn't what matters. His brilliant operation to stabilize the mark cost the Reichsbank some 200 million gold marks; it brought fabulous wealth to certain financial sharks and swindlers. On July 25, shares in the Siemens-Rheinelbe-Schuckert Union (Stinnes) rose by 60 percent in a single day. Some bonds reached two million percent of their face value. But they can't go on fleecing the poor like this in-definitely. The mayor of Berlin went, on the instructions of his mu-nicipal council, to make a bitter protest to Herr Cuno. "There is a storm cloud hanging over the capital. If the events in Frankfurt and Wroclaw were to be repeated in Berlin, they would take on the shape of a revolution. The fate of our country is being played out in our streets."[1] These points were repeated at the municipal council on June 27. The councillors nonetheless decided to increase charges for water, gas and electricity...

All this explains the alarm caused by the announcement of anti-fascist demonstrations on July 29. Herr Severing banned them. The KPD insisted they would go ahead, thus revealing the state of disarray of the enemy, and obliging minister Severing to show his hand. It worked. We are in possession of a secret circu-lar addressed by the minister to all police units, both in the crim-inal police and the Reichswehr. They are instructed to be prepared for all eventualities, and not to permit any unlawful as-semblies. They must act energetically, resort to armed force and, if the police cannot handle the situation, the troops must be sent

---

1 In June we saw a sharp increase in the crime rate and in suicide. In Berlin alone, there were 2,700 crimes against property in the course of the month, and over 150 suicides. [Serge's note.]

into action. In other words, the socialist minister for plutocrats, troublemakers, monopolists and speculators, realizing the enormous danger, and fearing the great popular demonstration which would have united on the streets the starving and the enemies of reaction—in short, the whole poverty-stricken population—took the desperate decision that he would unite the armed forces and the fascist gangs in order to drown the whole movement in blood immediately. The party has thwarted this provocation. It can congratulate itself on having made the rulers of the republic tremble. And it could not call off its demonstration; the open-air march in Potsdam has been replaced by 23 mass meetings in Berlin and the suburbs.

The SPD—to which Severing belongs—is profoundly embarrassed. It has clumsily absolved itself of all responsibility for the Frankfurt events. Contrary to its normal practice, it has kept almost complete silence with regard to the preparations for the anti-fascist demonstration. Breitscheid has spoken up to demand an end to benevolent neutrality towards Herr Cuno and the adoption by the party of a policy of outright opposition. For the moment one thing stands out a mile, even to the most retarded social democrats: the KPD is the only party to speak out against everything that has gone wrong, to call everything by its proper name, and to show the solutions: seizure of real values, workers' government,[2] rapprochement with Soviet Russia.

---

2 Since 1921 there had been much discussion of the demand for a "workers' government," that is, a KPD-SPD coalition within the existing parliamentary framework. Such a demand flowed from united front policies yet risked encouraging reformist illusions. As Serge shows, the "workers' governments" established in Saxony and Thuringia later in 1923 were conceived as short term measures, and as springboards for insurrection and civil war.

Herr Cuno leaves...

Herr Cuno has not yet resigned at the time of writing, but he has got himself into such an impossible position that people are talking of nothing but his departure. Who will replace him? Today, Monday, July 30, the food shortage has got worse. Many stalls in the open-air and covered markets are closed: there is no food. A bourgeois newspaper *Neue Berliner Zeitung*, writes, "We are facing a catastrophe much more serious than a cabinet crisis." Herr Cuno, the skillful businessman from the Hamburg-America Line, has squandered a large amount of public funds, brought the Reich close to bankruptcy, destroyed the mark he aimed to "stabilize," left the country facing famine and massively discredited the bourgeois government. A wonderful achievement for democratic institutions! This minister—"responsible to parliament," as they all are—having created this pretty mess, makes his bow and departs. But who will replace him? Nobody wants to pick up the terrible inheritance. People are talking of a "Great Coalition," to include right wing bourgeois elements, Herr Stresemann, and the SPD. The reality is that in order to carry on imposing on the German people a policy of ruin and starvation—to the advantage of a few plutocrats and a rabble of speculators—they absolutely must have the cooperation of the SPD. And one way or another that cooperation is guaranteed. We shall assuredly soon see the official social democracy attempt one last supreme effort to save this wretched bourgeois state as it crumbles...

Comparing Germany and Russia

There are some curious controversies taking place here and there between Communists and nationalists, fascists or National Socialists. The proletarianized intellectuals, young people from the middle classes who have fallen into poverty and who are haunted by nostalgia for the great prosperous Germany of the Hohenzollern,[3] are not completely blind and deaf. They remember that, together with the social democrat Noske, they have put down three attempts at revolution.[4] And what is the result after five years of order, democratic perhaps, but certainly bourgeois? The Ruhr, hunger, bankruptcy, and the fear of worse to come. Germany is no longer a great power, nor even a small one: a French soldier can trample it underfoot. It is easy for our Communist comrades to show their opponents the example of red Russia, which has indisputably become one of the great powers of Europe and Asia, holding the diplomats of all bourgeois nations at bay, strengthening its Red Army, developing air transport, organizing trade fairs and great exhibitions, reorganizing its transport services, preparing, less than two years after the famine, to export corn, creating new banknotes *(chervonets)*[5] which are perfectly stable and are quoted on the exchanges at London, Stockholm and Copenhagen like the pound sterling, increasing workers' wages and paying them—as has just been done in various Petrograd factories— in *chervonets!* The evidence is powerful. It is true that Russia has suffered enormously. But what tribulations are still ahead for Germany? It is a proven fact that peoples who have been slaughtered, ruined and thrown into chaos by imperialist wars can be saved only by revolution. It is a proven fact that from now on the bourgeoisie is unworthy to rule nations. The Russian bourgeoisie allied itself with foreign intervention against the revolutionary nation, looted public funds (Kolchak), sold off the fleet (Wrangel, Merkulov), mortgaged the

---

3 The royal family of Prussia and subsequently of the German Empire.
4 November 1919; the general strike following the Kapp putsch in March 1920; the March Action in 1921.
5 A bank note (1922) and gold coin (1923) issued by the Russian state bank, worth ten roubles.

national wealth and ended up by collapsing ignominiously. While Germany has been in a state of collapse, the German bourgeoisie has invested funds abroad, speculated, sold to the French the secrets of its chemical industry *(Badische Anilin)*, plotted in Bavaria with Poincaré's agents and squandered the Reich's gold reserves... Since the world war the internationalist proletariat is the only true representative of the vital interests of the nations.

In early August the Cuno government was clearly on its last legs. It was unable to deal with the inflation which was reaching catastrophic proportions and there was growing working-class discontent. The SPD leadership, however, was more interested in a return to governmental office than sticking the knife in.

Phynances,[1] the gold loan, etc.

Correspondance internationale, August 15, 1923

Morally bankrupt, resigned, driven out—take your pick how you describe it—the Cuno cabinet is still in power because nobody has been found to take over. It's not a happy inheritance to pick up—and bourgeois democracies have a horror of taking responsibilities. So, while it is in process of being buried, the Cuno government is concerning itself with phynances. Through what alchemy can it transmute into gold the worthless paper money of the Reichsbank? It has just invented a gold loan, payable in paper money on the basis of the value of the dollar on the day of the subscription, guaranteed with all the assets of the nation: banks, industry, commerce, agriculture, in short everything which can be taxed. To pay the interest,

---

1 Serge uses a comic misspelling of "finances," borrowed from the dramatist Alfred Jarry, author of *King Ubu.*

the government will have the right to deduct 500 million in gold marks from income tax, which will be increased if necessary. The notes will be for one, two, five, ten dollars, etc. The loan will be exempted from the taxes on stock exchange dealings and on inheritances, and therefore will be a profitable investment: it will pay 6 percent. The small denomination notes will have to be reimbursed in 1935 at 50 percent above their face value. Until then, they will pay nothing. The aim of the loan is to provide the German public with a stable German value[2]: an official admission that the mark is dead. But…1935 is a long way away! I should be very surprised if the possessing classes in this country, who are very skillful at thwarting all measures of taxation—which in fact are only instituted for demagogic reasons—will subscribe enthusiastically. They will certainly find it less risky to continue purchasing real dollars…

As for the Reichsbank, it has just decided (August 3) to give credit only on stable values. Don't ask it for credit on the basis of the marks which it itself issues! At the same time it has raised the bank rate to 30 per cent, a completely derisory measure. In wholesale trade, transactions are now only carried out in foreign currency. The mark is used only for paying wages; it is the counterfeit coin which every Saturday is slipped into the workers' hands, and which, for them alone, is the obligatory currency.

But let's come back to the bizarre "finances" of the Reich. All the measures taken by the Cuno government against speculation have had the sole consequence of scandalously encouraging speculation. The regulation of currency dealing—which in fact cannot be verified by a bourgeois government that is both weak and indulgent towards the big banks of which it is in fact the tool—led on July 19 to a complete and irreversible fiasco. The Reichsbank, claiming that

---

2 The term "stable value" meant, in effect, inflation-proof.

it was checking the receipt of foreign currency by German exporters, took on the job of providing currency for importers. That day, on the Berlin stock exchange, they asked it for 20 billion marks in foreign currency. The Reichsbank could provide only 14 percent of that sum. The demand was massively increased by those true patriots which we know all businessmen to be. There was a huge conflict between the banks and the Reichsbank. The regulation collapsed.

The establishment of an official exchange rate for the dollar on the Berlin stock exchange had a no less colorful outcome. At Gdansk,[3] Cologne and London, a dollar bought in marks was worth noticeably more than in Berlin. As a result, businessmen bought dollars cheap in Germany and exported them to...Gdansk, thus making fortunes at the expense of the state and of the holders of small sums in foreign currency. The good bourgeois always shows such patriotism, such a feeling for the national interest!

A bourgeois government, that is, one that represents the interests of high finance, of the large employers, of large landed property, in other words of those who, amid the shipwreck of the nation, are still enriching themselves and who think, with the blindness of doomed classes, that they can go on enriching themselves indefinitely from the collective poverty—those who, belonging to international capitalist organizations, actually believe they can grab a large part of their wealth even from the hands of a revolution, and who are, after all, those directly responsible for the catastrophe which has been caused exclusively by their selfishness as a rich class determined to yield nothing of its property (sooner let the universe perish!): such a government is obviously condemned, in a crisis of this sort, to the most ludicrous impotence...

---

3 Part of Prussia 1893-1919, then a free city, known in German as Danzig.

The evaporation of wages continues

From July 23 to 30, the cost of living officially rose by 31.7 percent. From July 27 to August 2 beef went from 58 and 109,000 marks a pound to 130 and 180,000; an egg went from 6 and 17,000 marks to 12 and 25,000[4]; a 1,200 gram loaf on the free market from 31,000 to 58,000, 100 bricks of compressed coal which, on July 27, were worth 60,000 had risen to 98,000 on August 2 and to 218,000 on August 4. As for wages...

In the social democratic union bureaucracy they are talking, they are demanding, or rather preparing to demand, wages calculated in stable values. At present wages are revised—not without difficulties, struggles, hard work and repeated failures—every week or every ten days or every fortnight, according to what trade one works in. And automatically they go down every day... From July 27 to August 2, the weekly cost of living index for a working-class family with two young children rose by 93 percent and reached the minimum figure of 5,158,912 marks, just about the monthly wage of many households.

To make it worse, wages are not always paid at all! In Munich, for the last ten days, there has been a shortage of paper money, and the banks are not issuing more than 500,000 marks (2.5 French francs at pre-war value) per person, per week. Workers get vouchers which will be cashed later—if it's even three days later they will already have lost half their value. There's a similar crisis in Cologne. In Mecklenburg, metalworkers are having to wait for their wages...

There are disturbances at Oberhausen, in the Ruhr: the police opened fire on workers who took to the streets to shout that they were without bread: two killed, eight wounded. Disturbances at Wiesbaden. Disturbances at Munich. Disturbances at Dresden.

---

4 Unfortunately Serge does not make clear what the two separate figures refer to.

Disturbances in the Erzgebirge. The basic question is as follows: for how long can the lead bullets of bourgeois order continue to take the place of bread in a country of 60 million inhabitants, of whom nine-tenths are in a situation of wretchedness?

The last defender of the German bourgeoisie

At last social democracy has noticed that things are not going very well. The big bourgeois parties have dropped Herr Cuno in as far as it's possible for them to drop him; the SPD hesitates, deliberates and…gives him a vote of confidence. On July 30 thirty opposi-tional SPD deputies met at Weimar; Kurt Rosenfeld, the former member of the USPD,[5] and Paul Levi, the former Communist, are airing their views. Opposition to the Cuno government (it's about time…), rejection of a great ministerial coalition from Stinnes to the SPD, in preparation (you don't say!) for collaboration with the Communists…(nothing more, nothing less). It is touching to see Paul Levi wanting collaboration with the Communist Party that he betrayed, abandoned, tried to infiltrate, abused and insulted[6]… So this abominable Muscovite party has some good features in his eyes, when the hungry, despairing proletariat is beginning to aban-don the likes of Paul Levi and Rosenfeld just as it is abandoning the likes of Stampfer and Wels.[7] All these former USPD members are still above all the party of hesitation and empty protest; their present attitude simply shows that they are aware of the growing disaffection of the masses with regard to social democracy. If they

---

5 The Independent Social Democrats—USPD—split from the SPD in 1917. The majority fused with the KPD in 1920. The remainder voted in September 1922 to return to the SPD.
6 Levi had been expelled for public criticism of the disastrous March Action of 1921.
7 Leading figures in the SPD.

really had any revolutionary dynamism there could only be one consequence: an immediate break with the wretched reformist SPD, the party that is guilty of every betrayal and despicable action, the party which tomorrow will try again, with Stinnes, to save German capitalism. On August 4, according to reports, the SPD fraction in the Reichstag decided by 120 votes to 60 to effectively maintain its previous attitude and prepare a great cabinet coalition, for which citizen Stampfer in *Vorwärts* has taken on the job of enthusiastic advocate... The social democrats in Hesse have already come out clearly for ministerial collaboration. In Germany the reformist SPD is the last, most tenacious, and most influential of defenders of bourgeois society in total bankruptcy...

In early August strikes—including one by printers producing the new banknotes made necessary by the galloping inflation—spread into a general strike. On August 12 Cuno resigned and the following day Gustav Stresemann announced the formation of a "Great Coalition," representing everything except the KPD and the extreme right. His government contained four SPD ministers, three from the Center Party, and two each from the DDP and the DVP.

The General Strike in Germany
The Great Coalition: Stinnes-Stresemann-Noske-Hilferding
Correspondance internationale, August 18, 1923

On Thursday August 9, Chancellor Cuno, the man of bankruptcy and famine, the man whom the whole of the press and public opinion believed to be on the way out, appeared before the Reichstag, asked for a vote of confidence and got it: the SPD observed benevolent neutrality towards him. Throughout this memorable session he looked just like a man who was finished, overwhelmed by his responsibilities. He began his speech with the words: "In a few days..."—he was interrupted by a shout of, "In a few days the dollar will be worth ten million!" Faced with jeers from the Communists, he put his head down and mumbled that "the government will be ruthless in quelling disturbances." The majority gave him his vote of confidence and the next day the *Berliner Tageblatt* announced that "from now on there can be no question of a cabinet crisis." Stinnes' paper, the *Deutsche Allgemeine Zeitung*, published an editorial praising him for speaking "so clearly, so strongly, so determinedly." Herr Cuno was still there. It was Friday… And on Saturday Herr Cuno went.

All the bourgeois parties had told this bankrupt—the SPD nodding its approval—"You can stay in power!" The working class shouted: "Get out!" And he got out.

He acted wisely. For two days the courtyards of the Reichstag were besieged by innumerable delegations from the factories which had come to demand Herr Cuno's resignation. On Friday, August 10, there was virtually a general strike throughout Germany. The big factories in Berlin began passive resistance, systematic go-slow and then more vigorous action. Berlin metalworkers stopped work. Printers too—in particular those working for the Reichsbank; a tube strike had just been ineffectively stifled. In Hamburg, work stopped in the docks. At Lübeck in Saxony, at Emden, at Brandenburg, at Gera, at Lausitz, at Hanover, at Lea, huge mass movements stopped production, brought massive crowds onto the streets, sometimes turned into rioting, and confronted shopkeepers and capitalists with the immediate threat of a revolution.

Thereupon the SPD convened its parliamentary fraction to revise its decisions of two days earlier. Three bourgeois parties, the Catholic Center, the German Democratic Party and the German People's Party, immediately endorsed the SPD program for a coalition (vigorous financial measures, revision of taxation policy on the basis of stimulating real values,[1] struggle against inflation, orientation towards the re-establishment of the gold mark, wages based on stable values, purging of illegal organizations from the Reichswehr, a solution to the problem of reparations compatible with the unity and sovereignty of the German people, membership

---

1 Amid the massive inflation, there was much concern to base money on "real values"—
Sachwerte—that is, actual goods exchanged for bills in the bank's portfolio.

of the League of Nations). The Stresemann cabinet was formed. The leader is an ambitious old businessman, with a reputation for energy, former leader of the National Liberal Party and now leader of the German People's Party, at the service of Herr Stinnes. His Great Coalition means an alliance between the plutocracy and the social democracy, from Stinnes to Noske, to overcome bankruptcy and fight against revolution.

Stinnes's man, the former business agent of the association of Saxon industrialists, the "progressive" former monarchist, has united, in order to govern this Germany of starving and exhausted workers, with the eminent "Marxist" of the Austrian school, Hilferding, formerly of the USPD, author of *Finance Capital*, former editor of *Freiheit*,[2] the greatest theoretician, after Kautsky, of reformist socialism—and one of the benevolent gravediggers of the Socialization Commission[3] in 1918. As minister of the interior, he has kept the social democrat Oeser, and at the ministry of justice he has reinstalled the social democrat Radbruch, notorious for outrageous extraditions. While this brilliant coalition was being established in power—uniting all the parties of a ruthlessly selfish bourgeoisie, which has just driven the nation to the brink of the abyss, with a social democracy which crawls on its belly to it—workers' blood was flowing almost everywhere in Germany… For there have been 50 deaths, 50 murders of workers in three days…

Some causes and effects of bankruptcy

The Great Coalition has a fine mess to deal with. In less than a week, the economic crisis has worsened in unbelievable proportions.

---

2 *Freiheit* was the USPD's main daily paper from 1918 to 1922.
3 This was set up at the time of the November Revolution to examine proposals for public ownership. It achieved little or nothing.

On August 7 the dollar was quoted at New York as worth 2,127,600 marks; on August 9 it was worth 6,500,000 marks. The same day a bushel of corn cost 2.08 dollars at New York and 2.45 dollars at Berlin. Corn was noticeably more expensive at Berlin than in the land of the dollar. Prices rose prodigiously. From August 7 to August 8, they doubled or tripled (a single egg went from 15,000 marks to 30,000; a pound of potatoes from 15,000 to 30,000; a pound of flour from 70,000 to 150,000; rice from 50,000 to 200,000; coffee from 600,000 to 1,800,000). In three days the price of bread tripled, going from 82,000 to 160,000 marks, then to 240,000. From August 7 to 8 the price of clothing and shoes leaped even higher still. The cheapest men's shoes went from 3,500,000 to 9,500,000. A tram ticket cost 20,000 and a newspaper 30,000. Now the *Frankfurter Zeitung*'s wholesale trade index for July already showed an increase of 617 percent. For these startling figures to have any precise meaning, they must once more be compared to wages. At the beginning of August, wholesale prices were 286,248 times what they had been before the war; wages were 87,000 times pre-war wages. So workers of 1923 have lost two thirds of their 1914 wages. In general German workers' wages vary between five and 25 (pre-war) centimes[4] for an hour's labor. As for those with retirement or invalidity pensions, we know some who in July got a monthly payment of 10,800 marks (one tram journey). In the face of this prodigious daily price rise, retailers—themselves grabbed by the throat by the wholesalers—limited or stopped sales, afraid of not being able to replenish their stocks. The working woman had her money refused by the cautious grocer. A shortage of milk, butter, eggs, potatoes, vegetables. On Thursday, August 9, retailers

---

4 A centime was a hundredth of a French franc. Serge several times gives comparative figures in French money, clearly expecting many of his readers to be French.

went on strike and the big stores shut in solidarity, demanding from the government that they should be allowed to fix prices in gold marks—for a working population paid in paper marks! To make things worse, the Reichsbank shut its doors, overwhelmed by the demand for paper money. For eight days there had been a shortage of notes. They had been ceaselessly printing notes of five, ten and 20 million marks—now they are even using private printshops to print *assignats*[5] for 50 and a 100 million. The city of Berlin is putting old notes in circulation overprinted so as to increase the value by a thousand times. The banks were issuing checks for five million marks, sometimes typewritten ones which few people accepted.

The report by the minister of finance, Hermes, to the Reichstag, brought some staggering revelations. The Reich's public debt, which on January 1 stood at 1,629 billion on August 4 reached 210 million gold marks. In the first ten days in August the state debt rose by 40 percent while its income, at the end of July, scarcely covered 4 percent of expenditure. In the last few days, they didn't cover more than 2 percent. In other words, the German state no longer had any income.

How well a capitalist state functions! Manufacturers and traders calculate in dollars, and only do business in dollars and other stable foreign currencies. The mark, as we have said before, is only the counterfeit money which the boss slips into the workers' hands every Saturday—and which the boss, the financier and the speculator also hand over to the taxman, when they agree to pay their taxes after six months or two years delay. The Reichsbank has given credit in gold to commerce and industry which has been repaid in paper money that had declined in value. In a year, it has thus given the capitalists nearly 50 million gold marks—and this

---

5 Serge is comparing the paper money to the *assignats,* paper currency issued during the French Revolution from 1790 on, which were notorious for rapid loss of value.

impoverishment of the state is one of the main causes of the death agony of the mark. When the head of the Reichsbank, Herr Haverstein, was asked what proof of the extent of need was provided by those asking for foreign currency, the worthy financier answered coldly: "A businessman's word."

The state coffers no longer contain a single coin of any value. The gold reserve has been given to the bandits of high finance. No more food in the towns, no more wages, not even any more paper money available to give the appearance of wages.—The social democracy has in fact betrayed, lulled and enfeebled a part of the working-class population. French militarism has crushed it in the Ruhr, and is now willing to unite with Stinnes and Noske against a working class rising. But all the same, things cannot go on in this way. Under the pressure of an irresistible strike movement and of food riots, the Cuno government, before collapsing, made the Reichstag vote for a series of laws which finally obliged commerce, industry and the banks to pay something: a 400 percent increase on company tax, a new tax on large incomes, varying between 200 percent and 1,600 percent of the old rate; a requirement for industrialists to pay double the deductions from workers' wages (taxes on wages); a tax in gold on agriculture (1.5 marks per month for a property worth 2,000 pre-war marks). The terrified bourgeoisie had understood the necessity to make sacrifices.

The general strike

As I write, the general strike, called throughout Germany by the factory committees, seems to be spreading, despite the formation of a new government and the repeated calls from the leaders of the ADGB for a return to work. The factory committees have, in the present situation, a role which is in some ways reminiscent of that of the soviets at the beginning of the February Revolution in Russia in 1917. They bring together the most vigorous elements from all the workers' parties, and they constitute a genuine proletarian power in the face of the government. Now the whole of Berlin stops when confronted with their little red posters; there is excitement and discussion, but nobody dares deface them. The spontaneous strike movement of the last few days, marked by strikes of metalworkers in Berlin, of miners in Saxony and dockers in Hamburg, has been channeled, led and united by the factory committees. Everywhere the movement has been formally condemned and sabotaged by the reformist union leaders. Everywhere the social democracy and the police lined up together against it. On Saturday in Hamburg, there were several killed. At Wilhelmsburg on Monday, six died. At Hanover, Noske, the social democratic chief official, gave the order to fire on the crowd: 20 deaths. At Greiz, 15. At Aachen, 10. At Zeitz (near Halle), 20. At Jena, the fascists and the municipal police went into action together, and there were some 30 killed and wounded. At Wroclaw, there are reports of one killed and 30 wounded. At Kulmbach one was killed, at Krefeld four, at Ratibor four, at Strassfurt one. But it is impossible to list all these events which keep on happening, in ever greater numbers, hour after hour. Everywhere there are reports of attempts to ransack shops, of the looting of stocks of potatoes from markets by housewives, of large demonstrations by strikers, of vicious attacks by police, of dead—workers—and wounded. At Halle and Leipzig, strikers have confiscated the cattle belonging to landowners in the surrounding area, killed some and distributed the meat.

At Halle, the fascists of the Stahlhelm attacked the newspaper offices, and there was a pitched battle. Not far away, at Helmstedt, Young Germans[6] attacked Communists and left one dead.

---

6 The Jungdeutscher Orden, a right wing paramilitary organization.

In accordance with a new press decree, signed by Cuno and Ebert on August 10, which provides for the suspension and confiscation of newspapers calling for violence against the republic, the Berlin edition of *Die Rote Fahne* in Berlin has been seized on two occasions. In Hamburg, the senate has declared martial law. In all the working-class centers, the army and police are patrolling.

In Berlin, municipal employees, workers in gas and electricity supply, and the trams and underground, a substantial number of railway workers, some of the printers from the Reichsbank and at least three quarters of the workers in large scale industry are on strike. Technische Nothilfe[7] is running train services in the suburbs. The situation remains "grave"—that means the movement is strong—in Hamburg, Szczecin, Halle, Leipzig, Dresden, Hanover, Lübeck and Wroclaw.

The demands are as follows: immediate resignation of Cuno, confiscation of food stocks to ensure that the poor section of the population is fed, withdrawal of the decree forbidding the formation of workers' hundreds,[8] a minimum wage of 60 gold pfennigs[9] per hour, unemployment pay in proportion to the original rate, freeing of political prisoners. These are clearly political and economic demands. The first has already been won, and those about wages and food supplies have found an echo in the conditions put by the SPD to the bourgeois parties for the formation of the Stresemann government.

A battle won

The factory committees decided to end the strike on Wednesday, August 15. The government has instructed the press to play down

---

7 Technical emergency service: a strike-breaking body established by Noske in 1919.
8 Armed workers' defense groups, initiated by the KPD, but often containing substantial numbers of non-Communist workers.
9 There were a hundred pfennigs to a mark.

the importance of the strike movement. It is nonetheless the case that the factory committees, which have achieved a united front of SPD, USPD,[10] Communists and members of no party, and which in reality are standing on the platform of Communist demands, with unconditional support from the KPD, have just fought a major battle, though not yet the decisive one, and they have won it.

1. The general strike has removed Cuno from power.
2. It has mobilized masses despite the opposition of the SPD and the union leaders.
3. It has imposed material sacrifices and a new financial policy on the bourgeoisie.
4. It has driven the SPD into a corner and obliged it to become discredited through the Great Coalition.
5. It has extended and strengthened Communist influence.[11] In these solemn hours, the whole proletariat has seen that it could really rely on our party alone.

Even the mass of the SPD rank and file, as is shown by numerous local demonstrations and especially the social democratic conference at Brunswick, are clearly hostile to collaboration with the bourgeoisie. The Great Coalition is the work of the "Socialist" leaders. Now there will be a period of relative peace which should give it time to discredit itself more fully in the eyes of the petty bourgeoisie and backward workers in whom the name of a Hilferding still inspires some vague hope.

---

10 Most of the USPD had rejoined the SPD in 1922, but a small minority maintained the organization.
11 Just recently the increase in Communist influence made itself felt by elections in the metalworkers' union that were a great success for the KPD and by elections of delegates to the textile workers' congress, likewise a big Communist success. [Serge's note.]

Stresemann's finance minister was Rudolf Hilferding, a self-styled Marxist and former member of the USPD. But the new government was powerless in the face of hyperinflation, and its only strategy was to attack wages.

Reports from Germany

The Great Coalition at work

Correspondance internationale, September 8, 1923

The official campaign against wages

The new ministers of the Reich are turning out to be almost as wordy as M. Poincaré. While the French prime minister is making speeches on the tombs of his dead, these ministers are making speeches about the gaping hole into which their moribund Germany is going to fall. Stresemann of the upper bourgeoisie and the socialist Hilferding are at one in affirming that if their government fails, it will be "Germany's last constitutional government." "We are democracy's last resort." Probably they are right. But let's watch them at work. Or rather let's listen to them, for what they mainly do is talk.

They talk with particular emphasis of certain things they want us to remember. On August 22, Herr Stresemann told the party leaders that he would not hesitate to take dictatorial measures and that it was essential to increase exports and limit imports. Financiers and politicians assented. On August 23, to the Reichstag's budget committee, a major speech by citizen Hilferding. "Extreme gravity of situation, brink of the abyss, possible disappearance of Germany (sic)." The government, which itself is showing a deficit—and to some tune!—is obliged to subsidize private industry which is showing a deficit. "Without control of trading in the dollar, there cannot be any foreign or domestic policy." "Wages have reached and often exceed the peacetime level." The next day, Herr Stresemann, speaking to the association of manufacturers and traders, explained the allusion of his social democratic accomplice: industry will do its sums in gold. "As for wages, we must not dream of bringing them back to the level they reached in the flourishing Germany of yesteryear, they must be appropriate for the difficult situation we are facing at present…" At least he is speaking in a straightforward fashion. On August 28, interviewed by one of the staff of the *Münchener Neueste Nachrichten* (*Latest News from Munich*), Herr Stresemann, who is clearly obsessed with the point, came back to it once again. "Wages higher than before the war are becoming a great danger." On August 31, Herr Raumer, economics minister, insisted in a programmatic speech that wages had risen quicker than the mark had lost value; moreover, it was necessary to work harder, to export more… On Sunday, September 2, in Stuttgart, Stresemann joined in the chorus: the propertied classes must make sacrifices but the working classes must work harder.

So here we have a clear and consistent government campaign. The sacrifices which will be "imposed" on property owners have a place in it solely to serve as a counterbalance to the much more real sacrifices they want to impose on the workers. In all these speeches, three ideas recur time after time:

1. wages are too high
2. it is necessary to work harder (longer hours)
3. salvation lies in exports…

But from now on prices of coal, food, clothing, paper in Germany are above world prices, so German industry cannot attempt to regain its ability to compete except by gnawing away at wages... And this task has been enthusiastically taken up by the Great Coalition government which Kautsky calls the "last arrow in Germany's quiver" *(Arbeiterzeitung,* Vienna). The metaphor is well chosen. For this arrow is being fired by the social democrats into the back of the German workers.

At the same time Stinnes's paper, *Die Deutsche Allgemeine Zeitung,* is pursuing some significant campaigns:

1. against the payment of civil servants' salaries quarterly, in advance
2. against high wages (!)
3. against the overestimates it has noted in the official cost of living index
4. for the need to work harder

The paper of the big industrial employers expresses its satisfaction at the support given to the exploiters by the SPD in these charming terms: "When the train is running off the rails, you don't look at the color of the brakes." We shall see whether the socialist brakes can stop the Stinnes train from going off the rails...

In any case, one thing is sure: the social democrats in the Great Coalition are nothing but the accomplices and the tools—and consciously at that—of economic and political reaction.

By unemployment and by repression

The attack on the starvation wages of the German worker must in fact be pursued on the economic and political levels at the same time.

A large number of firms are closing down, either because they really are forced to by the crisis—which must be the case with small firms—or because it is in their interest to suspend work until the end of the war in the Ruhr and to subdue workers by unemployment. Nearly a thousand firms in Saxony are in process of being wound up. In Hamburg, the stopping of work in numerous factories is going to make over a 100,000 wage earners unemployed; the management of the textile factories in Neumünster has stopped production following a disagreement about wages. In Dresden, there are 17,000 jobless. In Bavaria and Silesia, the publishers of periodicals have ceased publication. German book publishers and booksellers say they are unable to publish any new books this year. In Berlin, only 30 tram routes will continue running, and the majority of the staff have been sacked. Workers are sacked and laid off, firms are wound up, closed down... For his part, the exploiter is quite sure of not going short of bread and butter; as for the workers, they must make do as best they can. That will teach them to be more conciliatory.

There is an obvious parallel here with the Russian Revolution. Our Russian comrades know that the sabotage of production by the employers (the closing of numerous firms, the lockouts disguised under the appearance of winding up, etc.) often, in 1917, obliged Russian workers to take over factories and workshops. On more than one occasion factory committees decided to resume work in firms where the bosses, who had not been expropriated, had deliberately stopped production. The German bosses should watch out: they think that by increasing unemployment, they are preparing a reserve army of labor which will be degraded and defeated: but it might, on the contrary, provide an army for the revolution.

Arrests will achieve nothing. Arresting the Russian Bolsheviks in July 1917[1] did not prevent October. In parallel to the verbal offensive of ministers and bourgeois hack writers, and to the very clear

---

1 After the "July Days" some Bolsheviks, including Trotsky and Kamenev, were arrested and imprisoned, while Lenin was forced to go into hiding.

economic offensive being waged by the employers, it is perhaps hoped that the police offensive against the factory committees and the KPD will stave off the danger. During the recent general strike, there were more than 200 random arrests in Berlin. The following day, more than 10,000 workers were sacked by way of reprisal, and the SPD minister Severing dissolved the Berlin organization of *Betriebsräte* (factory councils). The banned organization transferred to Jena (Thuringia), that is to say, it went underground. Searches and arrests followed. Almost the whole of the Berlin committee of the KPD is behind bars, as are almost all the Communist municipal councillors in Berlin. *Die Rote Fahne* has been confiscated several times this week, and has now been suspended for a week. The Communist newspapers in Wroclaw, Magdeburg and Hamburg have been confiscated or temporarily suspended; the conference of the KPD in Württemburg has been banned. It is said that the appropriate ministers are considering prosecuting the arrested militants for high treason. Providing the ministers in question aren't themselves locked up before the preliminary investigations are completed!

Hail the fifteenth zero!

The police are certainly very useful to a bankrupt bourgeoisie; but the eminent financial expert and socialist Hilferding, even with the assistance of all the republican and monarchist jailers in Germany, will have a hard job to get his masters out of the difficulties they have got themselves into...

On August 15, the money issued by the Reichsbank alone—for cities, large credit establishments, railway companies and states of the Reich are also issuing paper money for absolutely incalculable sums—came to 116,402,548,057,000 marks. Please note that this number has 15 figures. But since then it has been exceeded to some tune. From August 8 to 15, only 54,000 billion marks were issued; today, the floating debt of the Reich is more than a trillion, that is—imagine it if you can—a thousand million million... On August 15, on the other hand, the entire gold reserve of the Reichsbank did not exceed 516 million, whereas it was more than a billion on January 1 this year. Yet nobody is proposing to charge Herr Cuno with squandering state funds. And inflation continues, with all its consequences.

We'll remain with these consequences, since there has just been mention of excessively high wages. Wholesale prices of butcher's meat increased between tenfold and twentyfold during August; in many places, a comrade from *Die Rote Fahne* notes, in a whole month no more cattle have been sold for slaughter than on a single market day in 1913. As there are at least two markets per week, consumption of meat has fallen about sixteenfold.[2] In fact, meat has become a rare dish, reserved for the rich. Prices continue to rise madly. Since the advent of the Great Coalition, the shopkeepers who fought against Cuno have set all their prices in gold, according to the exchange rate for the dollar. A tram ticket costs 150,000 marks. A newspaper costs between 200,000 and 400,000 marks. A loaf of bread sold for ration coupons has risen to 520,000 marks, and bread coupons, a tiny but significant benefit for working class households, are going to be abolished. A pound of butter costs between three and four million, an egg has risen to 380,000 marks. All prices change from one hour to the next, making amazing leaps in the course of a single day, according to stock exchange rumors and the whim of traders. Postal rates and railway tickets are now calculated in gold, which for the first fortnight of September means a letter within Germany costs 75,000 marks. A meal in a cheap restaurant costs two to three million. And an employed comrade, a skilled worker, who has two children to feed, has just

---

2 Here, as in a number of places, Serge's arithmetic is hard to follow.

told me that in August she earned about 90 million. Doubtless citizen Hilferding thinks that is too much.

All the public baths in Berlin have closed; they were losing money. The phenomenal prices of food, electricity, gas, etc., are threatening to cause the closure of all the private hospitals and sanatoriums in the capital. Too bad for people who don't have a bath in their home and who can't go to the Black Forest to be cared for when they are ill!

The bourgeoisie won't let a halfpenny go

"The propertied classes must agree to make sacrifices." That is how the Stresemann-Hilferding government puts it, and we know that it is demanding the payment of various new taxes in foreign currency. An unavoidable necessity. According to the official budget report of August 20, state expenditure has increased 3,500,000 times—taking the pre-war level as one—and income 77,250 times. With a deficit of that size, the functioning of the machine will soon come to a halt. And then, if they want to make starving people work harder, they really must tell them that the rich are chipping in something...

Only there's a problem: the rich are idiots, the rich are stubborn, the rich don't want to pay. The Nation, the Republic, the *Vaterland*[3] can rot, I'm keeping my money! The association of Saxon industrialists has written to citizen Hilferding to state that the new taxes are too high; they can't pay. The landowning deputies in the Reichstag, appropriately harangued by Herr Helfferich—one of those morally responsible for Rathenau's murder—are demanding "dictatorship against the parties and against the mobs on the streets" and...lowering of taxes. Traders in Berlin are preparing to sack their staff and close their shops on October 1, if taxes remain at

---

3 Native land.

their present level. After all, they are fleecing the consumers as best they can, and they still can't make a living! A strike in the markets is being organized for the same reasons; the proprietors of cafés and restaurants are getting excited, protesting, talking of closing down... The Chambers of Commerce have declared that certain taxation measures cannot be applied. Small traders and manufacturers have ceased activity, killing two birds with one stone, hitting the proletariat and the tax collectors.

This spontaneous resistance by obstinate capitalists who won't yield a halfpenny, at a time when the very existence of bourgeois society is at stake, shows just how deep and insoluble are the internal contradictions which mark the doom of the capitalist system. As it is, they seem to be condemning the efforts of Stresemann and Hilferding to failure: these belated saviours of the bourgeoisie may make it scream, but will not succeed in making it pay even the maintenance expenses of the state; it will pay only when the working class has it by the throat. And they won't succeed in making the proletarians, who want to see things resolved, work harder than they can or will.

Phynances and stupidity

The day before yesterday, September 5, at Berlin, the dollar was quoted at 19,500,000 marks. The intervention by the Reichsbank on the stock exchange had no effect except to transfer a certain number of millions of gold marks into the pockets of the speculators. And yesterday, the dollar was worth 46,000,000; today it's worth 60,000,000. What will it be worth tomorrow? A hundred million? Now it is quite simply to be feared that in a few days the printed paper of the German state will no longer be accepted by foreign financiers. The most recent effort by the Reichsbank to stabilize the mark was of such an imbecile nature that the whole bourgeois press has made it public. The *Berliner Tageblatt* has told how the Reichsbank intervention lowered the price of the dollar and the pound sterling, for a few moments. The stock exchange pirates had merely to buy the foreign currency sold by the government agents cheap—so as to sell it again half an hour later at a higher price…

Herr Helfferich proposes

Alarmed by the fresh collapse of the mark, the Stresemann-Helfferich government is proposing to create a new German paper money for which the standard of value would be not gold but corn. Helfferich, the agent of the big landowners who want to restore the monarchy, the man involved in the Rathenau assassination, has clearly learned from the experience of Soviet Russia with its corn loans. The paper money he proposes to issue will be guaranteed by the private sector, in particular by agriculture, that is, by the big landowners. Henceforward all German finances will be in the hands of a landowning oligarchy. A fine plan that is! The only outcome of the present crisis would be to allow the landowners to rob the Reichsbank in a respectable fashion and to establish a sort of economic dictatorship.

Helfferich, a pompous scoundrel, is enough to make you laugh. Does he really imagine that, in the present stage of the class struggle, it is possible to capture power by a device appropriate to starvers and usurers?

The Great Coalition plots against the working class.

It is said that the government is preparing dictatorial measures. This is stated and reiterated every evening. But the financial and the overall situation have got so much worse in the last few days that there must be some truth in these rumors which are getting more and more detailed. A decree on the compulsory surrender of foreign currency is due to appear any day now. A strong man "commissar" will, it is said, have the responsibility for applying it. There is talk of establishing a sort of financial dictatorship of which citizen Helfferich will be the man in charge. There is talk of withdrawing the regulations which are an obstacle to exports. There is talk, finally, of government decrees on the intensification of labor, which in practice means extending the working day… All these measures will be enacted without consulting the Reichstag. Thanks to the support of the SPD, Herr Stresemann thinks he can quite openly disregard democratic and parliamentary practices. For action is necessary, and nothing can be asked of the masses without taking something from the propertied classes—or at least pretending to take it. The requisition of foreign currency will obviously run up against so many obstacles that it will inevitably fail to a very large extent. But its consequence will be to legitimize the legal, or rather the dictatorial, intensification of the exploitation of labor.

Note that the Great Coalition of bourgeois parties and the SPD is preparing this attack on the basic rights of the working class at the very moment when unemployment is spreading in all industrial centers and in all industries…

The continuing inflation was putting increasing strains on German national unity. The Ruhr occupation continued, and the right wing government in Bavaria was increasingly in conflict with the policies of Stresemann's "Great Coalition." Meanwhile in Thuringia the possibility emerged of a KPD-SPD coalition government.

The Ruhr profiteers

Correspondance internationale, September 15, 1923

"The inhabitants of the Ruhr themselves want to be rid of this abscess…" The abscess in question—the German expression can also be translated as "seat of gangrene"—is the Reich's financial assistance to the Ruhr. And the newspaper which is using these vigorous terms is none other than the bourgeois and very patriotic *Germania*. Recently, the German press has been almost unanimous in claiming that the expenses caused by passive resistance in the Ruhr are the main cause of the financial collapse of the Reich. Under the pretext, as fallacious as it was patriotic, of financing passive resistance, all the resources of the nation have been drained off and the coffers of the state have been emptied. Since the start of the occupation, 500 million gold marks have thus passed from the Reichsbank into the safes and pockets of rich speculators, hundreds of millions have been swallowed up by the safes of the big Ruhr industrialists— while the working population, whose passive resistance is the only genuine one, and which is bearing the whole burden of it, because it is consciously defending the future of the German proletariat, has been dying of hunger. Now the scandal is becoming public. It's a bit late, for now there is nothing left to give to the insatiable profiteers of the Ruhr. These, as the Russian paper in Berlin, *Nakanunie*, puts it very well, have won a battle, not against M. Poincaré, but against their own nation.

Here we have grasped in action one of the features of dying capitalism. The dominant class, pushing the logic of its instincts to the logical conclusion, becomes the enemy of the nations whose industrial and financial power it has helped to create. As soon as a leak is discovered that will sink the massive ship, all those on board think of nothing but looting. During the Russian Revolution, the émigrés looted, sold and resold the "homeland." The disaster of capitalist Germany has several comparable causes:

1. The flight of capital. The German capitalists moved thousands of millions of gold marks abroad.
2. Stock exchange gambling on a falling market; the en-

richment of the bandits of commerce and industry by
the fall in value of the mark (the process is well known:
low wages, cheap goods, victorious competition
abroad—and the ultimate ruin of the country).

3. The enormous swindle that was the economic war in
the Ruhr.

The capitalist is the enemy of the nation; from now on the true
interests of the nations are those of the workers' International.

The victims of the Ruhr

Will they be forgotten because Mussolini has opened fire on
Corfu,[1] because there is an earthquake in Japan, because Degoutte's
soldiers have been trampling on them for too long and because the
popular press needs some fresh, up-to-date dramas?

A hundred thousand people have been brutally driven out of
their homes. The whole working-class press has been gagged.
Dozens of working-class militants have been sentenced by court-
martials or are waiting to be sentenced. There is killing almost
every evening, at random, of those who pass along the dark streets,
a gaunt worker returning home without having found tomorrow's
bread... Towns are isolated as they were in medieval sieges. All
postal communications in various major districts have just been
suspended for three days.

In the hospitals of Frankfurt there is an old woman of 86,
eight pregnant women, a mother suffering from pleurisy accompanied by her sick child, the mother of newborn twins; all these

---

1 Following the killing of an Italian general, Mussolini had the Greek territory of
Corfu bombarded in August 1923. He could be seen as following the example of
the French in occupying the Ruhr.

women have been expelled from the "peacefully occupied" region by the French authorities.

There have been expulsions, and there still are expulsions, sometimes at a day's notice, sometimes at one hour's, of numerous workers' families, including old people, invalids and newborn children. Up to September 4, there had been 1,600 hundred expulsions in the Palatinate alone. Obviously the great majority of these were poor people.

And these impoverished people are at one and the same time making the fortune of the German profiteers in the Ruhr and the careers of General Degoutte's zealous underlings.

As far as we know, not a single voice has been raised in the advanced French press to stigmatize these disgraceful facts. The press of the French bourgeoisie in 1923 is as servile towards imperialism as the German press was in 1914. In 1914, 93 German intellectuals, the cream of the universities and the literary salons, spoke out in support of the invasion of Belgium. In 1923 the mandarins of the Sorbonne, the Collège de France and the Académie,[2] of all the professorial chairs and all the institutions of higher learning, are silent at the occupation of the Ruhr. All bourgeoisies, all imperialisms, all literary lackeys are the same...

A bluff: the confiscation of foreign currency

While notes for a 100 million marks are being hurriedly printed, Herr Stresemann, after a speech on the "age of revolutions" (to Berlin journalists on September 7), has again put on his dictator's mask. On September 8, an extraordinary decree appeared on the confiscation of foreign currency and securities. Its terms temporar-

---

2 Two of the most prestigious universities in Paris, and the five academies established to promote literature, science and art.

ily suspend articles 115, 117 and 153 of the constitution (inviolability of goods, residences and the mail). A high commissioner has been given the most extensive powers to confiscate foreign currency that has been held without permission. The confiscation of all property and long prison sentences will be imposed on those who resist the law. The rich must put the interests of the homeland first! Are you satisfied, proletarian? Just to please you, we have even struck a great knife-blow at the constitution...

Immune from confiscation are foreign currency and banknotes held for commercial and industrial purposes, those necessary for companies operating in Germany, those belonging to people normally resident abroad or to people who receive them "by virtue of moral obligations." Very good. But then which currency can be confiscated? What speculator is such an imbecile that he cannot invoke—with documents to back him up—commercial and industrial necessities in addition to the highest moral obligations?

At the very most this decree will enable the government to rob a few unfortunate holders of small amounts of currency, to assist some shady stock exchange vendettas, and to foster a demagogic agitation around some prosecutions which will be useful to citizen Hilferding.

A truth of Herr Stinnes

Under no obligation to cultivate the bluff of the taxation measures introduced by Stresemann and Hilferding, the journalists getting paid by Stinnes are continuing their direct campaign against the working class.

Under the headline "Truth," an "important figure writing anonymously" recently stated in the *Deutsche Allgemeine Zeitung* (leading article of September 8) that "to claim that Germany can be rescued from its current dangerous situation by taxing the propertied classes is a lie." For the truth is that "the German people must work at least two hours more, with at least the same intensity as before the war." In so many words.

This is the viewpoint of business circles who don't want to pay. Their resistance to taxes is growing, taking on varied aspects. On September 3 and 4, Berlin markets were completely out of butter and fats. The landowners in Herr Helfferich's party[3] don't want to sell them for paper money and are thus showing the government their disapproval of its taxation policy. The Bavarian industrialists are protesting against the new tax laws. The Saxon farmers too. In Bavaria, the whole of public opinion has been mobilized to this end. We should remember that the taxes on capital whose repeal they are demanding were voted for under Cuno on the eve of the last general strike in an atmosphere of growing anxiety. When the factory committees grabbed it by the scruff of the neck, the German bourgeoisie shouted out: "All right, I'll pay." But citizens Hilferding and Severing have soothed its fears. It is tightening its purse strings once more. It has lost sight of the fact that, despite being sometimes legally dissolved, the factory committees are nonetheless a little stronger every day.

Journeys

Herr Stresemann has gone to exchange compliments with Herr von Knilling, head of the pro-fascist Bavarian government. Herr Hitler, the Bavarian sub-Mussolini, the most competent person to organize the next fascist coup, has come unhindered to Berlin to confer with the nationalist orator Reinhold Wulle. Herr Stinnes and Herr Hindenburg[4] are visiting Ludendorff at his home in Ludwigshöhe (in Bavaria, of course). A reactionary plot is being hatched.

---

3 The DNVP.

4 Paul von Hindenburg commanded German forces in World War I. He was president from 1925 to 1933, when he appointed Hitler as chancellor.

However, Sedan Day (September 2)[5] has been a defeat for fascism. It didn't show itself on the streets anywhere, except at Nuremberg, where although there was an impressive mobilization—nearly a 100,000 demonstrators, one worker killed—the action was considered a failure for various reasons, notably because of internal disagreements that came into the open on this occasion.

All the severity of the Great Coalition is reserved for the revolutionaries—whose movements have been eventful in a different way. A local congress of factory committees was due to be held on Sunday (September 9) in Berlin. Severing banned it. Five hundred workers' delegates then took the train and met at Velten, where the political police came to move them on. The congress was concluded in the open air. The police from the social democratic ministry[6] arrived too late and attacked local militants, some of whom were arrested. It sounds like an account of a clandestine congress of Russian revolutionaries before 1917. The methods used against the labor movement by citizen Severing did not work for Tsarism. Will they bring good fortune to the party of Noske and Hilferding?

In the social democracy

While Stresemann and Hilferding are quietly capitulating to M. Poincaré and preparing to form, with the Comité des Forges,[7] a powerful Franco-German syndicate for the exploitation of the German proletariat from which they expect their salvation, the dollar has gloriously risen above a 100 million marks and social democratic workers, ever more anxious, ever more indignant, are wondering what their leaders are doing in the Great Coalition government.

---

5 The Battle of Sedan in the Franco-Prussian war in 1870 paved the way for the defeat of France and subsequently for the unification of Germany.

6 Severing, a veteran SPD member, was Prussian minister of the interior.

7 The French association of employers in heavy industry.

The internal crisis of the SPD is developing quite rapidly. On September 7, the leading militants in the social democratic organization in Berlin, after having heard reports from citizen minister Severing and the former USPD member Crispien, voted for a thoroughly subversive motion which noted the ineffectiveness of the Great Coalition, demanded a break with class collaboration politics, the exclusion of those leaders who advocated such a policy and the formation of a socialist government...

The Berlin "Mensheviks" are coming on well! M. Renaudel[8] will blush at belonging to the same international as these social democratic "office-holders" who have clearly come too much under the influence of Communist agitation. Their attitude should not surprise us. These militants are in contact with the masses, with people on the streets. And the movement which is taking the masses forward is irresistible. (And that is precisely why Stresemann and Hilferding don't want to delay the capitulation by a single hour.) Elsewhere, Saxon social democrats are demanding the expulsion from the party of citizen...Ebert. They're damn right. But who would have thought it?

In Thuringia...

In Thuringia, the social democratic Frölich[9] cabinet is on its way out, forced to resign by the Communists. It was a curious situation. The SPD had 22 seats in the Thuringian Landtag; the bourgeois parties had 26 and the Communists six. However, these six—representing the most conscious and energetic working-class element, and backed up for some time by the most advanced of the SPD workers—held

---

8 Pierre Renaudel, right winger in French Socialist Party (SFIO).
9 August Frölich—not to be confused with the Communist Paul Frölich, author of a biography of Rosa Luxemburg.

the balance. The Frölich government was not so much vicious as cowardly. By overthrowing it, the Communists have got the Thuringian SPD leaders cornered. Either they too will form a Great Coalition—which their own supporters don't want—or else they will have to resign themselves to carrying out a genuinely socialist policy, with the support of the masses and of the KPD. A terrible choice for the old reformists who are comfortably settled in—action or discredit!

...not a halfpenny!

The pro-fascist Bavarian government has decidedly not forgiven the Berlin rulers for having voted for the taxes of fear on the eve of the general strike, the first taxes aimed at the propertied classes voted through since the victory of the social democratic counter-revolution in 1918-19. The von Knilling government has announced that it will stand as the "defender of the true interests of the German economy," and demands moderations, reductions, special exceptions, delays, in short the cancellation of the new tax legislation without it even being very well disguised. Like Stinnes, it sees no salvation except in the intensification of labor. Fascist Bavaria has thus in no uncertain terms put itself at the head of the movement of protest by the bourgeoisie against the new taxes, and solemnly identifies the sabotage of these taxes with the "higher interest of the nation."

At least its policy has one advantage over that of Hilferding, namely honesty.

The *Kölnische Zeitung* and the *Berliner Tageblatt* have joined forces to denounce the "scandalous immorality" of the Ruhr profiteers, highly patriotic traders and industrialists who have used the millions (in gold) which Herr Cuno generously gave them to support passive resistance for buying foreign currency. The scandal, it is said, is only just beginning. We can bet that citizen Hilferding will hush it up.

The propertied classes—including the Ruhr profiteers—don't want to let go of a single halfpenny. Herr Stresemann had better hurry up and capitulate so they can shelter their safes behind the tanks of General Degoutte! Time is running out.

Continuing inflation was leading to outbreaks of popular violence, to which the authorities, local and national, responded with brutal repression. In Bavaria the extreme right was growing ever stronger.

The Sorau massacre

Correspondance internationale, September 22, 1923

Sorau, a small industrial town in Lausitz, has just (September 15) been the scene of a massacre. Workers there are on short time. Just recently they were receiving wages of nine to fifteen million marks a week, that is, a third, a quarter or a fifth of one dollar. The disturbances began in the market and ended (?) with a massacre. There are twelve dead, including two women, and several dozen injured. Noske's *Vorwärts* indignantly relates that the mayor of Sorau, urged by workers' representatives to withdraw the police stationed on the public square, replied: "I take full responsibility." The words are well chosen. German mayors today have got guts. But I like the way *Vorwärts* gets so indignant. Isn't this gentleman a social democrat?

The Sorau massacre has occurred at the very moment when we learn that the social democrats in Thuringia have decided to negotiate with the KPD about the formation of a workers' government. Red patches are growing across the map of Germany. But to make sure than they are genuinely red, the bourgeoisie is soaking them in blood. But when it does that to make it last, when each of its crimes produces the counterweight, if not the backlash, of a Communist victory, then the great settling of accounts is at hand...

Herr von Knilling threatens

Herr von Knilling is the Bavarian prime minister who has the job of filling in the gap until the restoration of King Rupprecht[1] or the advent of a Hitler. Herr von Knilling carries out his duties conscientiously, and not without a certain arrogance. Under his rule, the various Bavarian fascist organizations are able to infringe, openly and with impunity, the emergency legislation for the defense of the republic. Anti-Semitism is flourishing in Munich to such an extent that the newspapers recently reported the scandal of the expulsion from Bavaria of a foreign Jewish child adopted by Jews who had long been settled in Munich. Several large fascist mobilizations like those which took place in Nuremberg at the beginning of this month have gone ahead with the cooperation of the state railways. However, German citizens in the rest of the Reich cannot travel freely into this state which is part of the federation that makes up their own country.[2] Moreover, shady deals are being arranged between the leaders of Bavarian nationalism and the agents of the rival imperialisms in Britain and France, agents assigned to the most obscure tasks. Finally, to complete the main lines of this rapid sketch, let us remember that Bavaria has taken the lead in the protest movement of the propertied classes against the new taxes voted on the last day of the Cuno government.

---

1 Crown Prince Rupprecht was heir to the Bavarian monarchy, abolished in 1918.
2 The post-1918 Reich was a federation of states, each of which had its own government.

Herr Stresemann, having recently conferred in the most amicable fashion with Herr von Knilling, off the record notes he informed the German press of the complete agreement that had been reached between the leader of the Great Coalition and the official representative of the Bavarian reactionaries. This official optimism was exaggerated. The Stresemann-Hilferding government's indulgence failed to disarm counter-revolutionary Bavaria, which is confident in its strength and is systematically preparing for civil war.

On Sunday, September 16, Herr von Knilling made a speech in Munich to a mass meeting of a peasants' league, a speech which can be interpreted as a declaration of war against the Great Coalition couched in scarcely courteous terms, or else as a vigorous attempt at political extortion directed against it.

Herr von Knilling stated that the Stresemann-Hilferding government "should not expect to find in Bavaria the same kind of support that Herr Cuno received." South German fascism had much greater sympathy for the great squanderer of the Reich's gold reserves and the accomplice of the Ruhr profiteers! If necessary, Bavaria is determined to pursue "its own food supply policy." It will also have no fear of resorting to a tax strike. But it has no separatist intentions…of course not! However, "if the conflict in the Ruhr were resolved in a manner that was unacceptable to Bavaria, it would be prepared for all eventualities." The turn of phrase is deliberately vague and can be interpreted as one wishes. Even in the case of a left wing dictatorship, Bavaria would not secede from the Reich, but it would "strengthen its links with all the healthy elements in the other German states" in order to crush the enemy within. "Two irreconcilably hostile ways of thought are confronting each other in Germany: the national Christian and the international Marxist." The salvation of Germany lies in the triumph of the former. Not, perish the thought, through civil war, but "by such a strengthening of the patriotic movement than the anti-national tendencies can no longer show their face..." This is how Herr von Knilling understands the preservation of national unity and social peace!

Yet he is neither a contemptible joker nor a crude specious reasoner. He speaks on behalf of reactionary elements, the masters of Southern Germany, armed for the class war, ready to begin fighting, inspired by the most profound contempt for democratic hypocrisy, a contempt which they are willing to express aloud with only the strict minimum of rhetorical precautions.

On the streets of Berlin

You can't walk a hundred meters on the streets of Berlin without encountering the same sights of poverty. It grips the whole street. Every day, outside the shops there are gatherings for endless hours of women, children, old men, unemployed, penniless housewives, servants. They queue for milk (which is often totally unavailable), for potatoes (also in short supply), and for margarine (which traders have stopped selling for a day, while awaiting a profitable price rise). They are queuing as they did during the war, but with less resignation and in infinitely worse conditions.

Less resignation, for no egalitarian measures, no rationing obliges the rich to put up with the slightest fraction of the present deprivation. In infinitely worse conditions, because of the frantic stock exchange gambling which is one of the main causes of the famine. In the marketplaces, stallholders only start selling after 11am, when they have had the first news from the stock exchange. They get messages informing them hour by hour of the rate of the dollar, each increase in which immediately determines a general price rise...

The worker has received his wages on Saturday, say 100 million, when the dollar was worth 30 or 40. A good wage for a skilled worker. He thinks he has three dollars to spend for the week and it's scarcely half or a third of what he needs. On the Monday, his partner goes to the market: no milk, no eggs, no potatoes, no vegetables. The market gardeners are waiting, before selling, for Tuesday's stock exchange figures. By Tuesday the dollar has doubled, and prices have risen even more. Our housewife can scarcely buy a third of what she was hoping for. She has quite openly been robbed of two thirds of her week's money.

I'm passing close to a wretched queue outside a shop in a poor district. Thirty women. Threadbare shawls with holes and darns. Gnarled old hands. Faces marked by weariness and suffering. Their irritated voices make a low, continuous murmur. The shopkeeper has put his prices up three times in a single morning. There's one continuous shout: "Smash his face in."

But there are two green policemen, with polished peaked hats, chinstraps, and revolvers in their belts just three steps away from the starver's counter.

"Hilferding and Stresemann," a young worker calls, mockingly, as he passes. People laugh. You can laugh with hatred.

Further on, reading a poster, there is another bunch of people, discussing. The municipal authorities are increasing the price of gas with retrospective effect for the last 15 days, and calculating it in gold at the current rate of the dollar (150 million today).

An old gentleman, looking like a longserving office worker, takes off his pince-nez and says sententiously: "Rogues."

I get into conversation with another old gentleman. After a moment he declares: "It's clear. That's the way we'll have to go!"

"Which way?"

"The same way as the Russians, of course!"

It really is clear. Very clear indeed, if this reasonable gentleman, this worthy gawper on the Wilhelmstrasse can see it too.

The two little sentences he spoke to me are in the air. With minor variations, I heard them three times in the same morning.

Newspapers cost a million, a tram ticket two million. The trams—although the number of lines running has been cut to thirty—are more or less empty. In the third-class carriages of the suburban trains you hardly see anybody reading a newspaper. A newspaper is a luxury. You read it over the shoulder of a more fortunate neighbor. To pass the time on the journey you bring some old novel on paper yellowed by age…

Yes, sir, very probably that is "the way we'll have to go."

Murder of the hungry

From one end of this hungry country to the other, there is a wave of disturbances. Strikes, looting of shops, uproar in the streets, volleys of shots fired… In Upper Silesia, the landowners are refusing food supplies to the mining districts. They aren't happy with the new taxes. On Thursday (September 13), *when the workers get their wages, all the shops are shut.* At Beuthen, the poor people break down the grocers' doors. The police of Stresemann and the SPD opens fire: seven dead, 30 wounded.

Two days later, on September 15, brawls and volleys of shots at the Sorau marketplace: 12 killed, 46 injured.

In the Grand Duchy of Baden the strike which began at Lorrach has spread. The authorities have responded by martial law. Thus far there have been three dead, several dozen wounded and 200 arrests. Because it stated that "the government is shooting down hungry workers" the Mannheim *Arbeiterzeitung* has been suspended for three months, at the request of the Interallied Commission.

From Upper Silesia to the Rhine, this is a land of hunger, anger and despair. This is the land where they murder the starving.

Starvation wages

The inadequacy of wages is too blatant, the automatic theft from these derisory wages too flagrant, the impotence of the government too obvious. As obvious as its bad faith.

The great governmental coalition has been formed, let us remember, thanks to the acceptance by the bourgeois parties of a series of demands, one of which was the stabilization of wages.

As yet it has done nothing to achieve this, although the dollar has gone from eight million to around 230 million. But the head of the government, Herr Stresemann, supported by all the right wing press, has launched a massive campaign against high wages. He has finally got a categorical repudiation from the ADGB, even though it is led by old social democratic reformists. In their official reply to the chancellor, they compare the purchasing power of wages today to that of 1914; they conclude that a worker today has to work *seven hours* to buy what *one hour's* labor enabled him to buy before the war. According to these bureaucrats, who are counter-revolutionary but competent, German wages are now reduced to one seventh of what they used to be.

The trade union bosses of the ADGB have finally been forced to admit it publicly. For they are beginning to realize that *a final limit has been reached.*

And the libertarians?[3]

A comrade from South America asks me: "What role do you think the libertarians will play in the coming German revolution?"

---

3 It is interesting to contrast this dismissive account of German anarchism with the much more sympathetic account of Russian anarchism in Serge's pamphlet "The anarchists and the experience of the Russian revolution," published in *Revolution in*

What role? As far as I can see, none at all. None. They hardly exist. Only very rarely do you see a libertarian placard. Never, on any demonstration or in any circumstances, have I seen, in Berlin or elsewhere, a libertarian paper being sold or distributed...

However, two or three small libertarian publications (*Freie Arbeiter, Der Syndikalist*) do appear in Germany, very hard for anyone interested to find, completely unknown to the masses. The leaders of various "syndicalist" unions, scattered here and there, claim to have a 100,000 members who must be subdivided into half a dozen tendencies that are more or less vegetarian, nudist or attached to the ideas of Tolstoy... Germany has more than 20 million proletarians of whom about 13 million are organized.

Workers' Germany is on the verge of revolution. For those revolutionaries who have something more than superfluous old formulas to offer to the masses on the march towards decisive struggles, the time has come to confront their doctrines with life itself, that is, with the reality of class struggle. It is time for libertarians in Germany—if they exist as revolutionaries—to put forward their program for achieving results, their tactics, their teachings, to show the way. How can we make the revolution? How can we crush fascism? How can we provide bread for the industrial cities? How can we do otherwise than found tomorrow a proletarian state, than establish a red army already today?

They are silent. Or if they mutter, it is so low, so lamely that nobody can hear them. They do not exist.

Danger (London, 1997). But the fact that this item was included at all shows Serge's continuing concern to maintain a political dialogue with his former associates in the anarchist milieu.

Faced with the growing influence of the extreme right, the KPD adopted the tactic of holding public debates. These debates have sometimes been seized on by critics of the KPD as evidence of collaboration with the extreme right. The fact that Serge's articles appeared at the time in the open Communist press makes clear that the debates were conceived as a short term tactic with no further implications. As Serge shows in other articles, the debate was in any case taking place on the streets, as workers under Communist and fascist influence argued about the best way out of the crisis. It should also be remembered that at the time fascism was a very new phenomenon, and that the revolutionary left was still struggling to analyze it and to devise the best ways of fighting it. In late September, Stresemann called off the "passive resistance" in the Ruhr. The establishment of martial law by the Bavarian government led Stresemann and President Ebert to declare martial law throughout the Republic on September 26.

Fascists and Communists

Correspondance internationale, September 29, 1923

"The fascist cross and the Soviet star are joined together... Count Reventlow[1] and Radek are getting on together wonderfully well... The corrupters of Moscow, the Machiavellis of the Third International and the adventurers of German reaction have made a monstrous pact against democracy... Tartar Bolshevism, transformed into Germanic nationalism, is sharpening its knife—you know, the one they carry between their teeth!—to cut the throats of the innocent republics of Léon Blum and Ebert, of General Degoutte and citizen Noske..."

Communism is the living, flexible and logical thought of the vanguards of the working class, everywhere committed to the hilt to

---

1 Ernst Graf zu Reventlow (1869-1943): naval officer, then Pan-Germanist writer; joined the Nazis in 1927.

the revolutionary struggle. Principles of safety first, the wondrous professions of faith of inactive socialism, prestigious phrases—soft pillows for idle minds!—are not its style. Communism springs from the Russian Revolution, whose thought was always essentially action, the habit of plunging into the very heart of reality, of adapting to it, of ceaselessly forging there new weapons, tactics and strategies...

(Weapons, tactics, strategies...What horrible military vocabulary!—I agree, comrade. But it isn't my fault, or Moscow's. Should we, or should we not, in the class struggle today, have weapons, should we know, predict and calculate what we're doing, that is, should we have a tactic and a strategy?)

German social democrats and the French minority[2] think they can rest on the laurels of Versailles. The former think of nothing but rescuing the capitalist order which is under heavy threat to the east of the Rhine; the latter have nothing to fill their heads but the clever contrivances of the left wing bloc[3] and the next election campaign. The German Communists, however, are facing up to famine, fascist counter-revolution and Allied imperialism.—Every day, the pressing cries of the hungry rise up towards them; every week, striding over the bodies of poor wretches shot down by the municipal police in the marketplaces, people coming from all parties make their way towards them. Each week they are hit by repression. They have thousands of comrades in prison. They make up a party of revolution. In the face of fascism, they had to act.

"Our tactic towards fascism," I was told recently by a Berlin militant, "has already been crowned by success. Six months ago, fascism was making inroads into the working class here and

---

2 Those members of the French Socialist Party (SFIO) who refused to accept the majority decision of the party in 1920 to join the Comintern, and re-established the SFIO.
3 Electoral alliance of left parties—essentially SFIO and Radicals.

there. It was rising rapidly when the occupation of the Ruhr gave it the powerful additional boost of a legitimate awakening of national feeling. Now, though it is far from being defeated, its progress has been blocked. It is no longer the demagogy of anti-Semitic National Socialism, which has a grip on certain proletarian elements who have been demoralized by the squalid maneuvers of social democracy; instead our revolutionary arguments are beginning to bite on the middle classes who have been proletarianized and disoriented. Moreover, since German fascism is split internally into two tendencies, the Pan-Germanists and the separatists,[4] while working-class unity is being established more and more around the KPD—as is shown once again by the events in Thuringia—for the moment the Soviet star has the advantage over the swastika. And that's quite important, for things are no joke at present."

The fact is that "Sedan Day" (September 2) was a fiasco for fascism; that after two or three debates with Communist speakers, the National Socialist Workers Party published in its paper, the *Völkischer Beobachter* (*Popular Observer*) on August 14, a formal ban on its members debating with Communists; that the three public debates held between fascist speakers and our comrade Hermann Remmele—at Stuttgart on August 2 and 10 and at Göppingen on August 16—have, like Radek's articles,[5] made their way throughout the Germany of reaction, ready armed for civil war...

Let us look together through the little pamphlet which contains Remmele's speeches to the south German fascists, and we

---

4 Separatists sought Bavarian independence from the Reich, while Pan-Germanists wanted a single state for all German speakers.

5 The KPD published a pamphlet entitled *Schlageter. Eine Auseinandersetzung* (Schlageter: a Debate—Schlageter was a German nationalist killed by the French during the occupation of the Ruhr). This contained articles by Radek, Frölich, Reventlow and the neo-conservative Moeller van den Bruck.

shall be able to clarify our ideas on what imbeciles—or dishonest politicians—have called "National Bolshevism." "You are fighting Jewish finance," said Remmele to the fascists. "Good, but also fight the other finance, that of the likes of Thyssen, Krupp, Stinnes and Klöckner!" He thus got these anti-Semites to applaud the class struggle. "You are fighting against the workers because your masters, the big capitalists, want to divide and rule, to set members of the middle classes like you, who have been ruined and will be proletarianized tomorrow, against us workers!" Thus he got these reactionaries to applaud the united front of all the exploited. "Are you patriots?" he asked, and described how big German industry was associated in many profitable affairs with French capital, selling its manufacturing secrets, like the Baden Aniline trust,[6] preparing for Germany to be colonized and getting rich from the devaluation of the mark. "Which of you wants to get killed for this capitalist Germany?" And he had the whole hall shouting: "Nobody!"

The positive part of his argument is simple: "Hungry Germany can only liberate itself by first of all shaking the yoke of its national capitalism." "The Treaty of Versailles can only be canceled when there is no longer a capitalist Germany." "One people has already shown you how to liberate yourselves: look at the example of the internationalist Soviets!" "Together, we are 16 to 18 million proletarians whose wages have fallen by at least four fifths; and nine to 11 million people in humble circumstances who have been ruined. They used to tell you that communism would take everything away from you; now it's capitalism that has taken everything from you. The proletariat will liberate you as it liberates itself." "The national unity of Germany can have no other support than the international workers' movement."

---

6 The Badische Anilin- und Soda Fabrik, a major chemical company.

This Communist orator, speaking to fascists in Württemberg, made them cheer André Marty[7] and working-class France which would "produce thousands of mutineers like Marty, if the French armies marched against the German Revolution." By thus reminding Germans, deceived by the chauvinist incitement of Stinnes's press, filled with hate at the acts of Degoutte in the Ruhr, embittered by poverty, that there is a red France, the France of the Commune, a France which has made or attempted four revolutions in a century, and which will never be the executioner of a great movement of liberation, he is perhaps, for the people of *Le Populaire*,[8] engaging in base demagogic agitation.

The German Communists want to engage the fascists in discussion, with their full program, with all the powerful intransigence of revolutionary ideology. Examine Remmele's speeches in detail; you won't find a single concession, a single tactical omission. To arouse the virtuous indignation of the social democrats of France and Germany against this remarkable propaganda campaign, it was necessary to tear quotations out of context, to do violence to the facts, to deliberately ignore other facts—such as the huge labor of organizing armed resistance to fascism carried out by Communists throughout Germany—and to employ the most vulgar agitational devices. "Radek has shaken hands with Count Reventlow," wrote *Vorwärts*. (And Remmele replied: "We're offering you a united front, you who murdered Liebknecht and Rosa Luxemburg, you whose Noske has the blood of 15,000 revolutionaries on his conscience!")

The fascist movement is born of the wretched condition of middle classes pauperized by the struggles of the imperialist epoch

---

7 André Marty (1886-1956) led a mutiny of French sailors in the Black Sea during anti-Bolshevik action. A leading member of the French Communist Party until purged in 1952.
8 The paper of the French SFIO.

and disappointed by democracy, by pacifism, by reformism, by the milk and water socialism on which they were fed at a time when prosperity seemed to be their guaranteed destiny. It has raised up against the proletariat millions of men who are determined to risk everything because they have lost nearly everything, enemies of socialism which has deceived them, and for the same reason inclined to adopt the opposite of their beliefs of yesterday. In Germany, it constitutes the last resort of the capitalist order; and as it could count on social layers consisting of more than ten million people, it would be, when the time came, supported by high finance and heavy industry, officered by the police and the Reichswehr, led by the best strategists from among the Kaiser's officers, and hence a terrible instrument in the hands of reaction.

The German Communists approached it and hit it in the most vulnerable places; in its absurd ideology, in the conscious double-dealing of its leaders, in the anti-capitalist and anti-democratic feelings of its rank and file. The occupation of the Ruhr sent a wave of nationalism across the whole of Germany. The Communists sometimes neutralized it, sometimes transformed it into an additional revolutionary element. Instead of letting Ludendorff and Hitler mislead working-class forces into a repressive civil war, they have succeeded in neutralizing a section of the middle classes in favor of revolutionary internationalism which seeks—which is—peace between peoples.

Where they wanted people to cheer Hindenburg, we got them to cheer Marty.

Towards civil war

As Communists, we are far from failing to recognize the power, the creative capacities, the vitality which the capitalist system still displays. But it seems to me that it would be perfectly symbolized by a mad engineer. He would be a skillful builder of bridges, aqueducts and highly developed machines. He would produce admirable pieces of work—but not without exploiting his labor force pitilessly. But at certain moments, overcome by his madness, this technician, this logician, would commit enormous mistakes, condemning his entire work to ruin. European capitalism is indeed this mad engineer.

The German bourgeoisie has just lost a second war. The first, begun by opposing imperialisms when capitalist society was at its peak, led to ruin in Europe, caused the Russian Revolution and, in Germany, the revolution of November 1918. The second war, the economic war in the Ruhr, has confronted bourgeois France and Germany with the fact of an October revolution (though one which might well only happen in the springtime…). Why? Because the financial and industrial oligarchy to the east of the Rhine did not want to yield to its French rival any of the profits derived from the exploitation of "national" labor; because the Comité des Forges was determined to establish complete hegemony over German heavy industry, and imperialist France was determined to consolidate its prestige… What will happen to this prestige, which is certainly notorious, to this hegemony and to this wealth, if tomorrow red flags are unfurled over the cities of Germany? Herr Stresemann wonders with anguish. M. Poincaré isn't concerned. He is the master of the situation just as Napoleon was in 1812.[9] The mad engineer, I tell you! Even in his most lucid moments, he never ceases to carry within his brain the dementia that is dooming him.

Dilemma

Germany has capitulated. In order not to surrender a halfpenny of their wealth, the German capitalists are handing over to French

---

9 The year of his advance on, and disastrous retreat from, Moscow.

imperialism the Germany of labor, bound hand and foot and with an empty belly. But perhaps it is already too late. Passive resistance is ending in catastrophe. It has emptied the state's coffers, filled the pockets of the wreckers, and paid for arming the forces of reaction. As a result the wind of revolt has blown across the land and raised up the proletariat of the Ruhr against both French imperialism and "national" capitalism. The struggle is over. What is left is bankruptcy, the wreckers and reactionaries standing armed in front of their bags of stolen coins, the restless masses obeying the logic of facts, following the avalanche and rolling with it. Will Stresemann and Hilferding succeed in stopping the avalanche?

What would that mean?

Will they succeed, during the three to five months of cold and hunger which lie ahead, in producing out of nothing a paper money which is worth something? Can they give bread to 30 million poor people who no longer have any? Can they resist or channel to their advantage the civil war which is looming? Can they satisfy French imperialism without committing suicide?

If they can, then the mad engineer will carry on.

If they can't, then the revolution will begin.

In both cases, doubtless, M. Poincaré will have won: but capitalist Europe is running a serious risk of dying from its victory.

Between two dictatorships

The Great Coalition, "the last resort of German democracy," has become, as a result of its capitulation, almost as unpopular as the Cuno government was the day before the factory committees drove it out. The German People's Party, the German Democratic Party and the Catholic Center Party are, like the SPD, in the middle of internal crises. Herr Stresemann had announced—at the same time as the end of passive resistance in the Ruhr—in off the record statements that if necessary he will assume dictatorship. In this regard, the newspapers have spread the rumor that citizen Noske, the dictator whom commander Ehrhardt dreamed of some time ago,[10] had come to Berlin to confer with the head of state...

All very well, but...dictatorship against whom? You can't exercise a dictatorship in a vacuum. Against fascism and the large scale industry for which Stresemann is simply a rascally old lawyer? An absurd supposition. Against the proletariat? But citizen Noske could not repeat his achievements of 1919. Then he was able to arm against the workers all the reactionary scum, to use the likes of Ehrhardt, Lüttwitz and Hoffmann. If he tried the same thing now it would mean the immediate end of his party and shortly thereafter of his regime; for the working masses would not spare him, and Ludendorff would not show mercy to the "rogues who made the November revolution."

As far as the leftward evolution of the social democratic masses is concerned, there are a growing number of indications. The SPD regional congress in Berlin has just recognized (resolution published in *Vorwärts* on September 25) the bankruptcy of the coalition policy and demanded a return to class struggle. At the same time it voted for a resolution of support to the socialist prime minister of red Saxony, Zeigner, and congratulated him on his persistent campaign in favor of purging the Reichswehr.

The Great Coalition is no longer supported by either the majority of the bourgeoisie—who don't want its taxes and are more

---

10 Noske later claimed he had refused repeated requests from Ehrhardt to become dictator.

and more anxious to see a sharp turn to the right—or by the rank and file of the SPD who are understanding more and more clearly that the Communists are right. On one side white Bavaria is arming, on the other red Saxony is working. Between the two, Hilferding and Stresemann are printing more paper money.

Von Kahr and Gessler—imitation dictators

Now Germany has acquired two substitute dictators on the same day: von Kahr in Bavaria and Gessler in Berlin. On September 26 the Bavarian government suddenly took the decision to confer extraordinary dictatorial powers on Herr von Kahr, appointed General State Commissioner. For some days a Bavarian coup had been expected; the reactionary pro-fascist Munich government was making preparations. On the significance of these events, *Vorwärts*, which had a great deal at stake, said some very shrewd things. The difference between the Munich cabinet and the Bavarian ultra-fascists consists in one thing only: the latter believe the time is now ripe to resolve the situation by striking at "Bolshevism which is growing in Berlin"; the former think it is better to wait a little while yet. On the question of principle they agree.

So the establishment of reinforced martial law in Bavaria and the nomination of von Kahr had the effect of sounding the alarm throughout the Reich. Von Kahr is an old "fanatical anti-socialist" (*Vorwärts*). Whether he imposes his will on Hitler and Ludendorff or whether he comes to an agreement with them, in either case Bavaria forms a fortified camp of reaction from which we can expect daring raids to be launched any day.

The government of the Reich provided its reply the same evening by establishing in turn reinforced martial law throughout German territory. All constitutional liberties are suspended. Penalties for political crimes have been stepped up. Death penalty for high treason, insurrection, riot, resistance to lawful force, etc. Herr Gessler, the Reichswehr minister, has full powers to apply this decree immediately.

Herr Gessler! The measure is, it is said, in defense of the republic, and was made necessary by the Bavarian threat. And it is to Herr Gessler that the social democratic ministers and citizen Ebert have given the responsibility of applying it: Gessler, the official decoy for the fascist leaders of the Reichswehr, their friend, their accomplice, Gessler, whose chief collaborator is von Seeckt! So much naïvety must be suspect. The reactionary Reichswehr, organized in secret nationalist associations, commanded by the imitation dictator Gessler, will only march all out against the working class. All the provisions of the decree establishing martial law can moreover be applied much more easily to the Communists than to the Bavarian fascists. This final attempt by Stresemann and Hilferding to prevent civil war therefore seems in reality merely to increase the immediate possibilities for the reactionaries.

But only the immediate possibilities, for, in the present state of the working-class forces, it is certainly not reaction which will have the last word.

The fascist advance

The other Sunday Herr von Knilling, Bavarian prime minister, addressed a scarcely veiled ultimatum to the Reich government. On September 23 at the "German evening" in Augsburg, in the presence of Ludendorff, captain D. Heiss addressed his audience in these very words: "The time has come for rifles, machine-guns and our pair of cannon to go into action... And if we don't have the horses, then we shall harness ourselves to our guns!" "The Bavarian fist will resolve in Berlin the problem of German liberty." Ludendorff showed his approval.

That day's issue of the National Socialist *Völkischer Beobachter* carried the headline: "Let us arm ourselves for civil war."

These are not just words. Hitler is officially mobilizing his "shock troops." On September 22, the police proceeded to arrest a number of railway workers: to be precise, 25. The same day in Munich fascists from the Oberland fired on workers in the street, wounding one seriously.

Attacks on homes followed by disgraceful acts of brutality—in the Italian style—became widespread in Bavaria.

On September 22 again, at the other end of Germany, 16,000 fascists mobilized by the Olympia association gathered in Hohenburg (Mecklenburg).

On September 25, not far from Leipzig, on the frontier between Saxony and Prussia, there were clashes between fascists and Communists, leaving 11 wounded.

Elsewhere disturbances over food continued. Those in Dresden provided the bourgeois press with grounds for a continuing campaign for intervention by the Reich—and the Reichswehr in Saxony. In Upper Silesia—at Gleiwitz—the police opened fire.

The Reichswehr is "ready for any eventuality." Despite the revelations of Herr Zeigner and the efforts of the social democrats, the "democratic" minister Gessler is remaining at its head because he has "the confidence of the leaders" and the blessing of General von Seeckt. The green police have received supplies of grenades and, it is said, gas masks. The association of civil servants in the Bavarian state has issued a circular warning its members that they must obey the Bavarian government, even one born of a *coup d'état*. The Berlin government responds by instructing them only to obey its orders. One more scrap of paper for Herr von Knilling's wastepaper basket. Fascism is thus preparing to wring the neck of Ebert's republic and, after a sufficient number of summary executions, to impose its regeneration program: "eradication of Jewish Marxism, ten-hour working day."

The Great Coalition government is making its task easier by striking at the left. On September 24, it suspended *Die Rote Fahne* and all the Communist publications in Berlin for 15 days. However, *Vorwärts*, to create a diversion for social democrats, has discovered clandestine arms stocks in Berlin—truly not what we were short of—"supplied, if we take his word for it, by a military attaché at the Soviet embassy." Are these people more blind than dishonest, or more dishonest than blind? A cruel enigma!

Figures

From September 13 to 19, there was a normal rise of 165 percent in the cost of living. The minimum necessary for a week for a worker's family with two children was 1,400,563,440 marks. Nearly one and a half billion. The usual wage for a man working a full day is half that sum.

In August, 43 percent of industrial enterprises were in a precarious or bad state. At the end of August, the situation on the labor market was as follows: 7.06 percent of metal workers, 4.53 percent of textile workers, 12.9 percent of printers and 12.6 percent of clothing workers were unemployed. 16.58 percent of metal workers, 46.19 percent of textile workers, 32.09 percent of printers and 57.98 percent of clothing workers were working short time. Between July and August the number of unemployed had more than doubled, while the number of workers on short time had increased almost threefold.

From September 7 to 21, the sum of Reich banknotes in circulation rose from 518.8 billion to 1,182 billion, that is, more than a trillion. In the same period, the gold reserves fell by 20 million.

On September 22, citizen Hilferding managed to lower the rate of exchange of the dollar to less than a 100 million (it had previously reached 325 million, with an average of about 200 million, in the preceding days). But the retail prices based on a dollar standard of over 200 million did not go down. Between September 15 and 21 we can observe an increase of 148 percent in the wholesale prices index. Who is being robbed? The poor.

The extraordinary commissioner in charge of confiscating foreign currency, Herr Fellinger, is organizing police raids in the streets and in cafés. The first ones have brought in about 16,000 gold marks. Woe betide the passerby if he happens to have one solitary dollar in his wallet. But respect for the banks!

By the end of September the crisis was deepening. National unity was under serious threat with growing demands for separatism in the Rhineland and Bavaria. The conflict between Bavaria and the national government continued. The threat from the right was shown by the unsuccessful attempt of a right wing officer, Buchrucker, to seize the fortresses of Küstrin and Spandau near Berlin.

Red Sunday in Düsseldorf

Correspondance internationale, October 6, 1923

Sixteen killed, and about a 100 wounded. Such is the outcome of the "peaceful" separatist demonstrations in Düsseldorf, today, September 30. French soldiers intervened to restore order, siding exclusively with the demonstrators for the "Rhineland Republic" who had attacked the blue police. The tragic incidents in Düsseldorf have occurred at a time when the whole of Germany, disturbed by persistent rumors coming from the occupied territories, is expecting the proclamation of a Rhineland Republic as a signal for civil war and the carving up of Germany.

For some time French intrigues have been going on there. Many Rhineland industrialists think it is in their interests to unite with powerful French capitalism and make a clean break with a Germany where revolution is impending. There is a feverish agitation going on in the occupied regions calling for the creation of a buffer state to "ensure peace between France and Germany."

Make no mistake about it. Desired by French and Rhineland capitalists, whose only homeland is their safe full of money, the proclamation of a Rhineland Republic would create a double and terrible danger at the very heart of Western Europe. There would be the risk of war and indeed the certainty of war some time in the future: for just as Great Britain could not accept, 110 years ago, Napoleonic hegemony over the Confederation of the Rhine, so Great Britain today will not permit France to have hegemony over the continent, for that would bring her ruin and death. There would be the danger, nay the certainty, indeed the immediate certainty, of a growth of reactionary forces in Germany. Herr Wulle, one of the leaders of extremist nationalism, just recently told a journalist of our acquaintance in the lobby of the Reichstag: "The day after the Rhineland declares independence, we shall take those responsible by the throat throughout Germany." In any case, independence for the Rhineland would immediately give a powerful impulse to the nationalist movement. It would become the starting point for ceaseless agitation in favor of a war of revenge. Furthermore, it would have the consequence of separating the working-class masses of the rest of Germany from those in the Rhineland, thus weakening the workers' Germany of tomorrow. It is for these very serious reasons, for the peace of Europe and for the German revolution which is the only way of guaranteeing it, that the KPD opposes Rhineland separatism with all its strength.

Pseudo-dictatorship to the right

With a few days distance, it is beginning to be easier to see what was really behind the recent events in Munich and Berlin that led to the establishment of two dictatorships which are different but very similar, those of Herr Gessler and Herr von Kahr. Von Kahr, endowed with dictatorial powers, recently declared to the fascist paper *Völkischer Beobachter* that he considered himself as a temporary replacement for King Rupprecht and that he would rule against the left. His first measures confirm these statements and are consistent with his past as a committed separatist. They are as follows:

1. Cancellation, as far as Bavaria is concerned, of the law on the defense of the republic, which was issued by the Reich government just after the murder of Rathenau;
2. Dissolution of the social democratic defence organizations;
3. Dismissal of the liberal mayor of Nuremberg, Luppe, who some time ago asked for the support of the Reich police against the fascist gangs;
4. Search of the premises of the social democratic *Münchener Post*, with an impressive display of strength (armored cars and cars equipped with machine guns).

No action has as yet been taken against Hitler's gangs, which are continuing to mobilize. There is even better. Herr Gessler, dictator for the Reich, has suspended the *Völkischer Beobachter*, which nonetheless continues to appear under the protective guardianship of Herr von Kahr.

So what happened at Munich? What the Pan-German nationalists, with Hitler and Ludendorff, wanted to do outside the law was done within the law by the royalist nationalists. The coup was carried out in the name of the law.

And what happened in Berlin? Being powerless to affect this situation, the Stresemann-Hilferding government endorsed it by establishing military dictatorship throughout the whole Reich. At the personal request of President Ebert, the exercise of this power has been entrusted to Gessler, the Reichswehr minister, the member of the government who is closest to the Bavarians. At Munich, dictatorial authority has reverted to Herr Gessler's direct subordinate, General von Lossow, for whom von Kahr exercises the functions of general state commissioner. Pure diplomatic conjuring! General von Lossow is the friend and in effect subordinate of von Kahr. While the latter cancels the laws of the Reich—you really can't act more straightforwardly!—Crown Prince Rupprecht, prime minister von Knilling, and General von Lossow accompany him at a solemn military ceremony, the review of the traditional company of the Reichswehr at Munich on September 30, which ends with shouts of "Long live the king!"

In the face of monarchist, reactionary Bavaria, the dictatorship in the Reich is only an imitation dictatorship, a question of form and appearances and apparently, totally futile.

Genuine dictatorship to the left

The bourgeois and social democratic government in Berlin cannot and will not take any effective measures against Bavarian reaction. And it knows very well that the Reichswehr would not obey orders. But while it was officially established in response to von Kahr's appointment in Munich, Gessler's dictatorship is creating an intolerable situation in the red states of Saxony and Thuringia. It is well known that the left social democratic prime minister of Saxony, Zeigner, has long been contemptuously boycotted by the Reichswehr authorities, whose reactionary maneuvers he has obstinately denounced. President Ebert and all his fellow thinkers who are SPD ministers responded to him by placing workers' Saxony under the dictatorship of the Reichswehr lieutenant general Müller, who already on September 27 announced the dissolution of the legally constituted workers' hundreds. For the moment general Müller is hesitating to enforce this measure. But he is ruling Dresden after the fashion of the captain general of Barcelona.[1] His decree of September 27 sets out seven points (which I have abbreviated):

1. From today I exercise full powers [...]
2. Army officers and those ranking with officers have all the rights of police officials [...]
3. No new printed publication of any sort may be issued without my prior authorization [...]
4. All street demonstrations are banned; for meetings in closed premises prior permission must be obtained from myself.
5. It is forbidden to stop work in industries necessary for public life (water, gas, electricity, coal and potash mines, transport, food).
6. Public assemblies are banned.
7. All breaches of these decrees will be severely punished [...]

---

1 On September 13, 1923, Primo de Rivera, captain general of Catalonia, had declared martial law and taken over the administration of the province of Barcelona, dispossessing the governor. This initiated a period of military dictatorship in Spain.

Thus the workers of democratic Saxony, deprived of the right to strike and of all constitutional rights, no longer have any means of legal defense. The socialist government of Saxony—which is displaying a rather woeful caution—has been canceled at the stroke of a pen. The slightest sign of protest by Saxon workers can only be outside the law, and the Reichswehr is authorized by the Great Coalition to repress it with the greatest rigour!

The KPD has launched the call for a political general strike. To-morrow perhaps this general strike will spread to workers' Saxony, which will not easily accept the rule of the sabre and jackboot of the Reichswehr. What will happen then? The whole bourgeoisie, in-cluding that belonging to the Great Coalition, has for months been in full agreement on this point with the people in Munich: "The scandal of Saxony and Thuringia is crying out to high heaven and must be brought to an end." (Maretsky, a DVP deputy, supporter of the Great Coalition, in *Tag.*) Against a revolutionary movement, consciously provoked by General Müller, a united front would be immediately established including fascists of every shade, whether Bavarian, separatist, Pan-German or whatever, plus the Reichswehr and the democratic and social democratic government forces. So we can see the extent of the danger and the unscrupulous behavior of the citizen ministers Schmidt, Hilferding, Sollmann and Radbruch who are consciously preparing the repression of the workers' move-ment in Saxony and Thuringia using the methods of Noske, even if afterwards they get themselves hanged by Ludendorff.

Doubtless they believe they will have an even greater chance of being hanged if a socialist revolution triumphs in Central Germany.

Those who understand nothing

While the German Communists are confronting this complex and dangerous situation, while they are making great efforts to fortify the last proletarian bastion of central Europe against an imminent attack by the reactionaries, people who obviously understand nothing, either of Communist thought, or of what is happening in Germany (even though they belonged to the French Communist Party not long ago[2]) are writing things of precisely this sort:

"In the French context, the Radek-Rosmer[3] plan would be the equivalent of the advocacy of French national defense in *L'Humanité* by such names as Léon Daudet."[4] Poor wretches! You have to be very blind or very dishonest to confuse the national defense of an imperialist state with the "national" defense of an internationalist workers' revolution that is about to begin; or to fail to understand that in a country where the yoke of a foreign imperialism is added to that of national capitalism, the masses have as a result a double feeling of revolt which constitutes the most powerful revolutionary force; or not to understand that if the German Communists failed to recognize it, they would guarantee the victory of nationalist fascism, and the carve-up of Germany would establish, in a Balkanized central Europe, a lasting reinforcement of capitalist disorder.

But here let's pick out a cutting from *Germania* (of September 19), organ of the Catholic Center. In a "Political letter from Württemberg" the writer bitterly deplores the fact that Communist propaganda has penetrated among the Württemberg peasants who until recently only felt the influence of the Catholic Center and the National Socialists. *Germania*, whose competence we shall not

---

2 Serge is probably thinking of L-O Frossard and those associated with him, who left the French Communist Party at the beginning of 1923 and returned to the SFIO.

3 Karl Radek (1875-1939) of the Russian Communist Party and Alfred Rosmer (1877-1964) of the French Communist Party both held leading positions in the Comintern and were involved in giving support to the KPD in its response to the Ruhr invasion.

4 Léon Daudet (1867-1942), right wing anti-Semitic writer and one of the founders of the *Action française.*

challenge, is thus bearing witness to the value and success of the KPD's tactics towards the nationalist movement.

Well above the dollar

For some days we have been paying five million marks for a newspaper, 4.5 million for a suburban railway ticket (third class) or a local phone call, six million for a letter abroad and everything else in proportion. With a rate against the dollar which in the last few days has varied between 160 and 200 million, a newspaper at 40, 50 or 60 French centimes[5] a copy, the same for the tram and the rest in proportion. In this respect *Montag Morgen* has published a curious diagram of the rise in prices and the rise of the dollar. On August 6, the rise of prices was more or less proportional to that of the dollar. After August 20, the cost of living rose noticeably faster than the dollar. If both were rated at 100 on August 1, the difference between them was: dollar 509, cost of living 1,567. On September 17, the difference had increased further: dollar 1,210, cost of living 1,931. On September 24, the cost of living had increased more than twice as much as the rate of exchange: dollar 13,364, cost of living 39,200.

Life is more expensive in Berlin than in Paris or New York. And the German worker is still paid in paper marks! The dictatorship of the reactionary army was truly necessary, above all in the eyes of SPD ministers!

The great assault on the eight-hour day

The great assault on the eight-hour day has been launched all down the line. For the last three days the cabinet crisis has been in

---

5 That is, at least twice what a French newspaper would have cost at the same time.

the air. Chancellor Stresemann finally resigned yesterday evening (October 3) but was asked by President Ebert to form the new government. The crisis, announced 72 hours in advance by the nationalist organizations, became clear when Herr Scholz, leader of the parliamentary group of the German People's Party (Deutsche Volkspartei)—he replaced the present chancellor as its leader—presented the three demands of the majority of his group, demands which were quite unacceptable to the SPD:

1. Enlargement of the Great Coalition to include also the far right DNVP;
2. An end to the eight-hour day;
3. Resignation of the SPD ministers Hilferding and Radbruch.

Herr Scholz also demanded that a conflict between Bavaria and the Reich should be avoided.

Having thus been treated with contempt by the powerful party of the industrialists in the Great Coalition, the SPD showed itself as conciliatory as it could. Yesterday evening, Wednesday, a solution to the crisis was announced, with the SPD agreeing to dictatorial measures to increase production and to "minister Braun's flexible formula" on the eight-hour day.

In other words, in order to save themselves from being driven out of office, the SPD have agreed to vote for an enabling act giving exceptional powers to the government, which will give it the right to exercise a sort of dictatorship over labor; they have agreed to the suppression, scarcely concealed behind an ambiguous terminology, of the eight-hour day; to leave power in the hands of the counter-revolutionary Reichswehr and to stand back from any conflict with armed Bavaria, which is openly preparing its major military assault on proletarian Germany.

It wasn't enough. At the last moment, the bourgeois parties made a further effort to throw the SPD out of the government. And that is the point we have now reached.

The situation is clear. Herr Cuno fell, driven out by the general strike at a moment when a threatening wave of strikes and riots was spreading across the whole of Germany and making the bourgeoisie tremble with fear. The bourgeoisie had to call the SPD to its assistance: without them, its rescue would have been in doubt. In great haste, in a memorably anguished session of the Reichstag, it voted for taxes on the propertied classes, the taxes of fear. Since then, its internal situation has improved. With the complicity of the SPD, it has capitulated to M. Poincaré and established the dictatorship of the generals at home. So now it doesn't want to pay the taxes of fear. The SPD got it out of difficulties, but now is a nuisance. Armed with the dictatorial power of its generals, it would like to impose on labor the new efforts which are indispensable for the reconstruction of capitalist Germany. Kick out the socialists and a sharp turn to the right!

The social democrats in the government are pretty spineless, but they can't retreat too far without discrediting themselves in the eyes of their own party. Moreover, the treatment they are getting from the Gessler-von Kahr dictatorship in Bavaria is showing them what they can expect after a complete capitulation. For the law giving full economic and financial powers that the bourgeois parties need and that they want to use against the workers, with the support of the Reichswehr, and without even the formal control of SPD ministers, must be voted by a two-thirds majority in the Reichstag. This means that without the votes of the SPD it cannot be passed in any circumstances. So either the bourgeois parties will come to an understanding with the SPD, which is willing to be obliging to anybody, or else the Reichstag will be dissolved and the bourgeois parties, the military dictatorship and the fascist nationalist gangs will probably try to impose their will on the working class outside of legal channels.

Küstrin

The Küstrin incident shows the level of overexcitement now reached by certain counter-revolutionary elements. Commander Buchrucker, leader of the ex-servicemen in the Stahlhelm association—the strongest fascist organization in central Germany—attempted, on the night of October 1, to capture the fortress and the town of Küstrin. For what purpose, good God! The courageous commander doubtless imagined that he was giving the whole of Germany the signal of deliverance, in other words civil war against the proletariat. (They call it, in the words of Herr von Kahr and Hitler, war against Marxism and the Jews: they avoid the word socialism, which Hitler uses in the demagogic propaganda of the National Socialist Party.) He was followed by several hundred men. The Reichswehr had no difficulty in restoring order (one man was killed). Numerous arrests were carried out, but the men of the Stahlhelm, who had come armed from the area around Küstrin, were able to withdraw without any problems.

There is one remarkable detail. The first official communiqué in Berlin, now forgotten, about the brawl at Küstrin referred to a "national-Communist" riot. This official lie bore the trademark of *Vorwärts*. It appeared in the newspapers, alongside a decree from Herr Gessler, forbidding the publication of anything other than official information about such events. To prevent the spreading of false rumors…in future only official lies will be published.

The reactionaries benefit from martial law— a great deal

In Munich, von Kahr, merely imitating General Müller who is

running red Saxony, has banned strikes and threatened to apply the death penalty for acts of sabotage. In Saxony, General Müller has suppressed Communist newspapers, *Kämpfer* in Chemnitz and *Volksblatt* in Gotha. The Reichswehr is massing in the vicinity of Berlin. We are assured that 2,000 machine guns have arrived at Spandau—and that the counterrevolution can count on 50,000 armed men in Berlin and the surrounding area (figures according to *Klassenkampf*).

The cabinet crisis and the press campaign, spearheaded by *Kölnische Zeitung* and Stinnes's major paper, *Allgemeine Zeitung*, prove that the aims of the bourgeoisie's current offensive are, above all, economic. Its most urgent priority is the cancellation of the eight-hour day. It is interesting to note that on this point the German reactionaries are in absolute agreement with the French bourgeoisie. For months now *Le Temps*[6] has been pursuing a campaign for the lengthening of the working day in Germany—and also in France! While Herr Scholz was presenting his ultimatum to the SPD ministers, in Düsseldorf, general Degoutte was making known the conditions posed by the French for the resumption of work. And they are: repeal of the law on factory committees, the ten-hour day, etc. Stinnes, Scholz, Ludendorff, Degoutte and Primo de Rivera are all in complete agreement.

Social Democracy judged by its allies

It is curious to observe how social democracy is judged by the worthy German bourgeoisie, for whom, just a month ago, it performed such noteworthy service. A few days ago, under the signature "Ulysses," the *Deutsche Allgemeine Zeitung* published an intriguing

---

6 Influential conservative French newspaper (1861-1942); after 1929 it became the paper of the heavy industry employers' organization.

article entitled: "Germany and world revolution." Let us quote a few lines from it: "As long as Germany was one of the dominant nations in the world, the idea of revolution remained suspect to it and was repugnant to its bourgeoisie. The latter left the revolutionary principle to the social democracy, which, as the representative of the rising classes, was able to exploit it very successfully. But since the SPD has ceased to be a socialist party and is only a bunch of petty bourgeois full of fear and hope, it has lost the idea of salvation through revolution, and that idea, that invigorating element, no longer exists in Germany. When the author of these lines tried to present the World War as a worldwide revolutionary upheaval and to deduce from this fact some practical conclusions for German politics, he came up against a complete lack of understanding on the part of the social democrats. Social democracy had already turned away from the dialectical revolutionary conception of history and was dreaming only of pacifism. [...]

"Thus when this great party entered the government in 1918, it could no longer add anything precious or original to the political life of the mind for the German bourgeoisie. We must remember the bitter disillusion of the German bourgeoisie after 1918, when faced with the impotence of the social democracy in all spheres. They did not understand it. They expected it to contribute fresh forces...which Germany needed so much: a bold revolutionary conception of world history which concludes from the wretchedness of the present that there must be something better in the future."

When it had to be, the bourgeoisie was able to be revolutionary. Even today, to maintain its dominance, to subdue the proletariat, it does not hesitate to slough off the old, to cast its democratic clothing away, and to establish dictatorships, to set up as a principle the everyday use of class violence. It is quite right to despise the degenerate socialism, which first of all frightened it, in which it thought it had found its master, and which is now crawling on its belly before it.

When dealing with the Communists, its language is quite different: "Marxism is the mortal enemy of German culture," says Herr von Kahr.

For the last week rumors in Berlin have been promising a nation wide coup which was due to take place the day before yesterday, and which is now predicted for Friday... Apart from this expectation of a sudden action by right wing elements, martial law is hardly noticeable. General von Horn has not dared add to the normal persecution which the government dishes out to German workers. But isn't it significant that there has never been so much talk of a reactionary coup as since Herr Gessler has had all political power in his hands?

Small official posters prohibit the sale or distribution of the Communist papers *Der Rote Kämpfer, Die Arbeiterfaust* (The Red Fighter, The Worker's Fist). Yet this morning the citizen of Berlin can read *Klassenkampf* (Class Struggle). Thus every day, despite the suppression of *Die Rote Fahne*, the KPD publishes a new paper, either improvised illegally on the spot, or printed in the provinces. Proceedings have begun against those writing and distributing Communist leaflets that have been duplicated by hand and given out in the factories. Just like in Russia under tsarism!

Numerous Jewish families in Berlin have this week received threatening letters, signed by an "Anti-Semitic League," announcing an imminent massacre of Jews in the course of which "not even children will be spared." So there are people who think this is the way to save German capitalism!

Léon Daudet advocates the same methods to regenerate French capitalism.

Stresemann's cabinet collapsed on October 3, but was reconstituted on a similar basis on October 6, though without the "Marxist" Hilferding. One of Stresemann's main aims was to establish a ten-hour working day, thus destroying the basic gain of the 1918 revolution. Meanwhile "workers' governments" (SPD-KPD coalitions) were established in Saxony (October 10) and Thuringia (October 13).

Correspondance internationale, October 13, 1923

The cabinet crisis has been resolved, probably for a short time only, by the formation of a new Stresemann cabinet. It was merely the expression of an attempt by the big bourgeoisie to take dictatorial powers legally—more or less—while making no secret of the intention to use them exclusively against the working class.

In the *Vossische Zeitung*, Georg Bernhardt, who is by no stretch of the imagination a socialist, wrote quite explicitly: "Ultimately the question is who will pay the expenses of the last few months (the economic war in the Ruhr) and whether the stabilization of the German economy is to be accompanied by an extraordinary effort exclusively on the part of the working class." In fact, all the efforts of the Center Party and the German Democratic Party to revive the Great Coalition, all the indulgences of the SPD, which is willing to effectively sacrifice the eight-hour day, have failed in the face of the indomitable determination of Stinnes's party (the German People's Party), which wants a right wing coalition with the DNVP and no longer wants a government that is either parliamentary or constitutional.

In its opinion, the time has come for the dictatorship of the large employers. From today onwards, it is necessary to oblige the German people to work ten hours a day and to eat even less than they are eating now in order to pay the reparations, to pay the costs of passive resistance in the Ruhr—which has enriched the Rhineland industrialists and plenty of other swindlers—and to put German industry back on its feet so it can take its place in the international market. There is no way to impose such an effort on the working people of Germany—undernourished, overworked and embittered, while the best of them are conscious of their class interests—without a ruthless dictatorship whose immediate task would be to reduce all workers' organizations to impotence, decimate the KPD and enforce a thoroughly Prussian labor discipline.

This is what Herr Stinnes has long wanted. The great plutocrat, who during the war boasted of organizing the exploitation of occupied Belgium, and, after the war, came to an understanding with French capital (the Stinnes-de Lubersac agreement), has long been the promoter of a right wing, anti-working class, anti-democratic politics, which must begin by imposing the ten-hour day. During the cabinet crisis, of which he was one of the perpetrators, he was very visibly active in the Reichstag. On October 3 and 4, it was he who negotiated a resumption of relations between his German People's Party and the DNVP. His newspaper—*Die Deutsche Allgemeine Zeitung*—has been using a new language for the last few days. It speaks only of *"revolutionary methods"*—to be applied boldly by the employers—for the rebirth of Germany. It professes "joyous optimism and combativity that will irresistibly draw it towards the right and in which the sociologist will recognize evidence of the decomposition of the old parties." In its number of October 4 it declares that it is "dealing with a work (of regeneration) which is primarily the responsibility of the parties of the right and which obviously cannot be carried out democratically or through parliament." Do you recognize the language? Word for word it is the terminology of the fascist ideologists in Mussolini's press.

Die Zeit, inspired by Herr Stresemann himself, has envisaged the dissolution of the Reichstag and the exercise of extra-parliamentary power: bourgeois dictatorship without any mask.

A manifesto from the landowners demands a "fresh start," getting rid of social democratic influence, and the formation of a bourgeois government including the nationalists; it promises that if this is not done, "there will be torrents of blood." Meanwhile the Bavarian government has sent Berlin a telegram demanding the alleviation and revision of taxes on the propertied classes. The same day, in Saxony, General Müller banned until further notice the publication of all Communist papers.

Interregnum

The patching up has been arduous, but it has finally succeeded. The Great Coalition of the bourgeois parties and SPD has been reformed, without citizen Hilferding, who really was too incompetent. Right up to the last moment, the thing seemed impossible. There was talk of a "directory"[1] of six bourgeois, of a purely bourgeois coalition, of a dissolution of the Reichstag, of a right wing dictatorship... What new factor has come to modify the course of events? A mass of things are happening behind the scenes. We can simply note that:

♦   Herr Stinnes, according to the revelations of *Germania* (Catholic), decided on the crisis a few days before it broke out—the association of employers in the iron and steel industry—equivalent to the Comité des Forges— the *Verband Eisen-und Stahlindustriellen*—has, like

---

1 The term was deliberately reminiscent of the Directory established in France (1795-99) after the overthrow of Robespierre.

some landowners and Stinnes's newspaper, persistently
proclaimed the end of parliamentary politics and a right
wing dictatorship;

♦ The center parties (DDP and Catholic) did their utmost
to revive the Great Coalition;

♦ The social democrats sacrificed Hilferding and the
eight-hour day.

At the last moment the bourgeoisie backed off in the face of the
threat of civil war. The permanent class conciliators came out on top.

The impotence of the Stresemann-Robert Schmidt government remains total in the face of the victorious rise of the dollar,
the arrogance of the Bavarian reactionaries, the demands of the
kings of mine and ironworks, of bank and press.

It can do nothing but worship the dollar, capitulate to Munich,
and serve capital, a churlish master that is preparing to dismiss it
tomorrow. There is only one new claim in the programmatic statement of the chancellor, made on October 6 to the Reichstag:

"[…] To intensify production, we shall appeal to the goodwill
of the workers, and, if need be, to the law."

The compromise formula, accepted by the social democrats,
states in effect, after having discussed technical improvements, that
a "new set of regulations concerning working hours will be drawn
up, with the eight-hour day still being considered as normal in
principle." The Great Coalition, the last resort of German democracy, has been revived by virtue of this double-talk.

Meanwhile, the dollar has climbed the following heights: October 1, 242 million marks; October 3, 440; October 5, 600 million; October 6 (convertible currency at Berlin), 740 and 775
million, according to *Die Morgenpost*…

In the style of Nicholas II

On October 7, Herr von Kahr issued in Bavaria a new decree forbidding, on pain of imprisonment, the editing, printing or publication of any Communist publication whatsoever, in any form whatsoever. The style of Herr von Kahr's edicts is reminiscent of the *ukases* of the late Tsar Nicholas II—whose reign did not end happily despite the repeated use of such measures over many years...[2]

But in fact General Müller, the representative of Ebert and Gessler in Dresden, has effectively suppressed the Communist press just as comprehensively. (The *Sächsische Arbeiterzeitung*, imitating the example of the nationalist *Völkischer Beobachter* in Munich, has nonetheless continued to appear in Leipzig.)

In red Thuringia, General Reinhardt has taken on the job of disarming the working class and has ordered (Gotha, October 4) the handing over within nine hours of all weapons in the possession of individuals, under threat of death! Demonstrations and strikes are banned.

Red Germany

Under the combined pressure of the military dictatorship, of the offensive of large scale industry against the eight-hour day, of Bavarian fascism, of the sabotage of production ordered by the employers, and of deep poverty, working-class Germany is emerging from the profound lethargy into which it had been plunged by forty years of reformist socialism.

The red German bloc has been formed. For some days Saxony and Thuringia have had workers' governments composed of left social democrats and Communists. These two governments have

---

2 He was overthrown by the February Revolution in 1917.

made a pact of alliance similar to the one that unites, within the two states, the (left) SPD and the KPD. Their program of working-class defense includes the "republicanization of the Reichswehr."

"That's a nice mess!" will exclaim, in Pantin or Montsouris,[3] someone who understands nothing at all. "Communist ministers demanding the 'republicanization' of the German army!"

Let us explain to this intransigent revolutionary that the SPD ministers have established in Germany the dictatorship of the revolutionary army precisely in order to save both their own ministerial jobs and the investments of the big bourgeoisie: while our comrades in Saxony and Thuringia are entering the Zeigner and Frölich governments, under martial law and military dictatorship, in order, despite everything, to organize the arming of the proletariat. Let us also explain to him that the "republican" purging of a reactionary army, when the word "republic" merely means frustrating the will of the kings of iron and coal, may be a revolutionary action.

It may very well be that a historical proof of this will soon be given to us by red Germany. The situation there is, in fact, of such gravity that it cannot be overstated. All workers' freedoms have been suppressed, the right to strike has been suppressed, the Communist press has been suppressed, the workers' hundreds have been disarmed and effectively made unable to make their existence known: the Saxon police—headed by a social democrat—is actively infiltrated by fascist gangs; in Dresden, General Reinhardt, a former accomplice of Kapp,[4] is governor, and the whole of the German bourgeoisie is getting ready to put an end to red Saxony and Thuringia!

The workers in the two states can feel and see the ambush being

---

3 Suburbs of Paris. Serge is attacking ultra-lefts in or around the French Communist Party.
4 Wolfgang Kapp was the leader of an attempted right wing putsch in March 1920, blocked by workers' action.

organized all around them. One military provocation would suffice to leave them with no alternative but a general strike—the only weapon left to them—and hence insurrection, since strikes are banned and the rigours of martial law mean immediate armed repression...

Not to act, for these proletarians of red Germany, would mean agreeing to be treated as the losers in the social war without even having joined battle. But to act would mean rising in open revolt against the dictatorship of the generals and giving white Germany the go-ahead for an all-out attack.

The fate of the German revolution—and hence of the German proletariat in the next ten or 20 years—is being decided at this moment in a quadrilateral at the angles of which are Erfurt, Dresden, Leipzig and Vogtland. Remember those names, comrades!

A significant verdict

At this moment, there are a flood of indications of the determined will of the reactionaries to engage battle everywhere. In Prussia, public opinion has been closely following the trial of a small Prussian landowner from the outskirts of Potsdam, Karl von Kaehne. Everything in this case has general significance.

Von Kaehne was accused of having killed a young worker called Laase who had been gathering wood[5] on his grounds. Von Kaehne and his sons, whom he had raised as ferocious junkers,[6] had already been prosecuted several times for assault and battery against poor people who lacked respect for their property. One of the von Kaehnes, having once come across a peasant who was pick-

---

5 A long-standing class issue in Germany. One of Marx's earliest political articles (October 1842) was on the "Debate on the Law on Thefts of Wood" in the Rhine Province Assembly.
6 A Prussian aristocratic landowner.

ing mushrooms on his estate, had beaten him to the ground there and then. Against old von Kaehne there was the most serious circumstantial evidence to accuse him of murder. As for his character as a landowner and a tough Prussian junker, he proudly displayed it to the jury, with statements of the following kind:

"We are still armed and nobody has the right to criticize us for defending our property. I don't shoot at respectable people, but I am not afraid of shooting at scum." He admitted having stated, when told that the body of a prowler had been found on his land: "Let it stay there for the pigs to eat!"

The Potsdam jury found this quite acceptable and acquitted him (October 4). There are judges in Potsdam, good judges for the landowners, judges who know their jobs.

Potsdam is one of the citadels of reaction. Nonetheless, the police had to protect the acquitted man from an angry crowd who jeered the jurymen and wanted to lynch Herr von Kaehne with cries of, "Death to the bloody dog!"

The iron and coal chancellor

All capitalist countries have simultaneously two sorts of rulers: monarchs and ministers who pass away, and financiers and businessmen who endure. Thus Germany today has two chancellors. One, without money, without a press at his command, without any social influence other than that of his masters, who yesterday assumed powers that are much more apparent than real, and who will leave again tomorrow; meanwhile he bears all the formal responsibility. The other one owns mines, factories, estates, banks and newspapers; he is not accountable to anyone for anything; he is above the laws; he makes public opinion, cabinets, war and peace; he is irremovable. One is only the executor of the thankless governmental tasks of the bourgeoisie. The other is the brain of the bourgeoisie.

Stresemann and Hugo Stinnes

In the division of roles, the former—surrounded by his social democratic satellites—has as his main job to prepare the way for the latter.

Indeed, for the last few days Herr Stinnes has been behaving very publicly as the true master of Germany. Negotiations have not yet started between Messrs Stresemann and Poincaré. But Herr Stinnes is negotiating—in secret—with General Degoutte. Scarcely had he reprieved the cabinet of the Great Coalition when he addressed to it the ultimatum of October 9, summed up in the following ten points:

1. Compensation for the coal confiscated by the French during the Ruhr occupation
2. Compensation for the tax contributions imposed by the Reich on coal
3. Cancellation of this tax as far as the Ruhr is concerned
4. The right to dispose freely of coal supplies
5. Priority for the Ruhr in supplies of food and raw materials
6. Abolition of the coal commissariat
7. Recognition of the right of industrialists to negotiate with the French authorities and...
8. ...to resolve current questions with them
9. Possible participation of industrialists in a Franco-German state company of Rhineland railways
10. Working day of eight and a half hours in the mines and ten hours everywhere else

---

7 Bismarck was known as the "Iron Chancellor." Serge is also thinking of Stinnes's links with the employers in the iron and steel industry.

The government was summoned to respond to the iron chancellor[7] before Tuesday, October 9, at noon. Acting in advance of his reply, the Ruhr industrialists have required miners to extend the working day.

Never has the official government of a country been treated with such contemptuous arrogance by its true masters. Herr Stresemann and citizen Robert Schmidt have accepted without complaint the humiliation inflicted by Stinnes and have broken off all their current work in order to examine his "proposals."

The best part of all this is to see Herr Hugo Stinnes presenting himself as a victim—an all-powerful one!—of the economic war in the Ruhr, and (patriotically) demanding indemnities, compensation and privileges…

Herr Hugo Stinnes

Herr Hugo Stinnes developed his industrial and financial strength under the old imperial regime. The prosperity of the Empire was his prosperity. The Kaiser's armaments enriched him: he was the major supplier of coal to the manufacturers of cannons, his partners.

During the war Herr Hugo Stinnes continued to get richer: each shell manufactured in Germany brought him a profit; each corpse rotting on a battlefield brought him a profit… And on top of this he was plundering Belgian industry.

After the war Herr Stinnes joined up with the victors to exploit more or less all the nations of the earth, concluded a profitable reparations agreement with M. de Lubersac, and extended his empire over Vienna and Czechoslovakia.

The fall of the mark made him one of the profiteers who benefited from Germany's ability to sell at reduced prices. The war in the Ruhr meant that a substantial part of the Reich's gold reserves found their way into his safes.

Germany's capitulation will bring him large indemnities; the coming reparations agreement will be a goldmine to him; and the terrible poverty of the German nation will bring him to dictatorship...

Herr Hugo Stinnes is the magnate who owns the Rhineland coal syndicate, the German company for the coal trade and shipping, the Dortmund mining company, the German-Luxemburg mining and smelting company, the power stations of Aachen and Westphalia, the Gelsenkirchen mines, the Rhine and Elbe electricity company, that of Bochum, the Bohlen steel mills, the Siemens-Rheinelbe-Schuckert electrical and mining company, etc.

He owns several large daily papers: *Deutsche Allgemeine Zeitung* (General German News), *Rheinische Westfälische Zeitung* (Rhine and Westphalia News); he has an influence on the *Lokal Anzeiger* (Berlin), the *Tag*, the *Deutsche Zeitung* (German News), *Hamburger Nachrichten* (Hamburg Reports)... In each important city in Germany, there is at least one paper in his service. No precise evaluation of his wealth and power is possible.

He can negotiate on equal terms with the representatives of French imperialism; he has the habit of giving orders—and the right to give them—to Berlin governments. And he knows exactly what he wants.

What he wants

For the moment, in domestic politics, what he wants amounts to two things:

◆ To impose the ten-hour working day on the German people
◆ In order to do so, to take power, full power, dictatorship

His *Deutsche Allgemeine Zeitung* is carrying on consistent agitation for these aims. Let's take another look at the last few issues. The leading article on October 9 was devoted to a diatribe against those whose are sabotaging the intensification of labor and to a defense of the ten-hour day. The previous day the leading article proclaimed "The age of dictators"; Professor Richard Sternfeld referred to Sylla, Richelieu, Cesare Borgia, Cromwell and even Lenin.

If the German worker worked two hours a day more (without eating any more), then Herr Stinnes, Herr Klöckner, Herr Krupp and Herr Otto Wolff[8] think they could "pay the reparations" without losing anything—in fact the very reverse! In return for which, Senegalese bayonets would allow them to digest in peace…

In reality, the problem is much more complex. We doubt whether the harshest economic dictatorship, even exercised by the iron chancellor, could raise German production, the stagnation of which has profound causes which would only be cured by dictatorship if it were exercised by the proletariat. For the main causes are:

♦   exhaustion of a constantly undernourished labor force
♦   the poor condition of the plant of an industry which has experienced the fall in value of the mark
♦   the scandalously high profits of capital.

To kill *Die Rote Fahne*

After a fortnight's suspension, the Berlin Communist paper *Die Rote Fahne* (The Red Flag) had just reappeared. Four issues had appeared—it comes out twice a day—when Herr Gessler, minister cum dictator, saw fit, yesterday (October 10) to suspend it afresh, this time until further notice. In fact, after a fortnight's suspension, there could be no question of a suspension of less than three weeks or a month at the minimum. Till further notice is even better. The

---

8 A leading Ruhr industrialist.

measure applies to all the Communist journals of Berlin and the surrounding area which might attempt to take the place of Die Rote
Fahne. This paper has seen the number of subscribers rising constantly for some months. It is obvious that repeated suspensions—
we are up to the fourth or fifth in a short period of time—are
bound to completely disrupt its services, make it lose contact with
its audience, and deprive it of its subscribers. That's the result they
trying to achieve.

Thus throughout almost the whole of Germany, swarming
with fascist and nationalist newspapers, martial law has had the result of suppressing the Communist press and it alone. At Munich,
von Kahr has suppressed it permanently. In Berlin, Herr Gessler
and in Saxony, General Müller, have suppressed it until further notice. Elsewhere other generals...

We have also learned that numerous arrests of Communists
have just taken place in Wroclaw (October 10). Most of the leaders
of branches of the KPD in Silesia, and all the editorial staff of the
Silesische Arbeiter Zeitung (Silesian Workers' News) are said to be
behind bars. The semi-official Vossische Zeitung (Voss News) admits candidly that the aim of these arrests is to suppress "Communist propaganda for a workers' and peasants' government!"

Let's note this frank statement which is quite remarkable at a
time when propaganda for a fascist dictatorship is being developed
without the democratic and social democratic government ob-
structing it in the slightest way. Let's remember the Russian Revolution. Three months before the October Revolution, the eloquent
Kerensky suppressed and suspended *Pravda*, imprisoned the Bolsheviks, kept Trotsky in a cell, hunted down Lenin and Zinoviev,
while Kornilov, Savinkov and Denikin were allowed to conspire as

---

9 General Kornilov attempted a right wing coup against Kerensky in August 1917.

they pleased.[9] Herr Stresemann is wrong not to study recent history... History which might repeat itself!

46,844,781,444,537,903?

On September 30 the floating debt of Germany exceeded 46 trillion marks, to be precise, 46,844,781,444,537,903. But the dollar was only at 150–200 million. Today, October 12, it is quoted at five billion.

On September 30, Berlin had 160,000 unemployed.

The KPD and the Comintern were actively preparing for a bid for power in late October; Serge was obviously aware of these plans, although he could not discuss them in an open publication. The establishment of "workers' governments" in Saxony and Thuringia was part of the preparation for imminent insurrection; at the same time the situation was causing growing tensions within the SPD.

Constitutional dictatorship

Correspondance internationale, October 20, 1923

It's no longer the case that the situation is getting more tense every day. Now it's every single hour that brings us some grave news.

The Reichstag met on Saturday (October 13) and voted for the Enabling Act, giving exceptional powers which Herr Stresemann had demanded. We know that at the first session, two days before, in the course of which the lamentable spectacle of the impotence of

---

1 The opposition from both left and right.

the Great Coalition was displayed, the cabinet had been frustrated, mainly because the radical minority[1] abstained on the vote. I don't know in detail whether it voted and how. It isn't important. But it remained in the chamber to make up the quorum. Hence the dissolution of the Reichstag was avoided. So now we've got a "constitutional dictatorship" and a "strong man." The strong man is Herr Stresemann—since the Bavarian deputies and the SPD opposition remained on the floor of parliament.

To tell the truth, this comic performance, tinged with tragedy, doesn't fool anyone. The Great Coalition no longer has any authority. The most influential bourgeois elements belonging to it want a right wing dictatorship and are not very concerned with parliament, and even less with the SPD ministers. They are exercising dictatorship by making it more specific, by strengthening it every day. Herr Stinnes and Vögler[2] dictate the government's domestic policy. Herr von Kahr carries out his own policy and doesn't give a damn for the chancellor in Berlin. As for the social democrats, they fall into two categories: those who feel cheated, defeated by reaction, but without the slightest will to action, clutching on to an outdated dream of loyal opposition and the keeping up of republican appearances; and those who can see civil war coming and are turning towards the Communists.

Let's note the absolute uselessness, in parliamentary and all terms, of the parties of the middle and small bourgeoisie, the DDP and the Catholic Center, although they enjoy a strong parliamentary representation. The small and medium bourgeoisie, bankrupt or well on the way to it, no longer has any real prestige or influence. The time has now come for the plutocrats, for the mining

---

2 A steel magnate belonging to the DNVP.
3 That is, like the personal guard of a Roman emperor.

syndicate, for Stinnes and for the military adventurers who are promising to provide them with a praetorian guard[3]—Hitler, Ehrhardt and Rossbach.

Eve of battle in red Saxony

For the last few days Saxony has had three Communist ministers, Brandler, Böttcher and Heckert. Thuringia will have the same in the next few days. Nothing is more unusual, more preposterous than this event. In a country under martial law, where waves of riots are spreading from one frontier to the other, where the Communist press has been suppressed, where hundreds of Communists have been in prison for years, here are revolutionaries quite calmly entering governments solely in order—they make no secret of it!—to organize the resistance of the proletariat to the counterrevolution, that is, to prepare for civil war.

And what revolutionaries! Their very names speak volumes. Brandler is the most respected leader of the KPD. This former stonemason, stocky and broad-shouldered, about 40 years old, considered as one of the organizers of the March Action in 1921,[4] escaped the following year from a fortress and took refuge in Russia until an amnesty allowed him to return. Fritz Heckert, a mason too, five years younger, has also spent time in the prisons of the republic; indeed it was a Saxon minister who once had him locked up. Heckert has been politically active since he was 15, has always been a resolute opponent of social-patriotism, took part in the foundation of the KPD and is a member of its central committee. Böttcher is a

---

4 Brandler was KPD president at the time of the March Action, though he did not bear the main responsibility for it. He was sentenced to five years imprisonment.

5 The Halle Congress of the USPD in October 1920 voted to merge with the KPD.

printer. He was a member of the USPD and joined the KPD after the Halle Congress.[5] In 1920, general Maercker, one of Kapp's accomplices, had him imprisoned in the Königstadt fortress. The workers released him. A friend of General Maercker is exercising dictatorial power in Dresden, and Böttcher is finance minister!

General Müller quite clearly understands how outrageous the situation is. He has just responded to the formation of the workers' government by a very clear declaration of war. His decrees of October 13 dissolve the workers' hundreds—formed legally with the support of the Zeigner cabinet—require the handing over within three days of all the weapons in the possession of individuals, forbid the formation of action committees, and lay down penalties of imprisonment and fines for any infringements.

These two *ukases*,[6] which both begin with the words "I forbid…" are preceded by an explanatory commentary. The employers, according to this, are complaining of being molested, in various places in Saxony, by a "violent minority of workers." Older workers are complaining about the youth… Even *Vorwärts* is indignant. Take a quotation: "The proletarian hundreds have been dissolved in Saxony. In Bavaria, the reactionaries are still armed. *In such conditions martial law is unacceptable.*" (Emphasis in the original.) Do you understand, citizen?

Comrades belonging to the cadres of the proletarian hundreds have already been arrested.

The congress of the factory committees in Saxony and Thuringia, which was due to meet on October 18, has been banned.

Other measures of extreme gravity, which *Vorwärts* has no desire to tell its readers about, supplement these.

General Müller, who is thus attempting to disarm the prole-

---

6 A *ukase* was a Tsarist decree.

tariat, is arming reaction. In Dresden, Leipzig and elsewhere, the numbers of the Reichswehr have been swollen by the enrollment of volunteers who wish to contribute to the restoration of order. Joint companies have been formed for which the Reichswehr has contributed officers, arms, equipment and even uniforms. The Communist deputy Siewert has made it known that 2,500 fascists from the Stahlhelm have been armed in Dresden and the Erzgebirge. General Müller has agreed to it. His troops need reinforcements! By courtesy of martial law, a counterrevolutionary army is being formed in red Germany.

Even before the formation of the workers' government, the (left) social democratic cabinet in Saxony had announced measures against the industrialists who are sabotaging production. For the latter have stopped production in a number of firms in order to increase unemployment and worsen the situation of the workers. They will be forced—with the assistance of Heckert, Brandler and Böttcher—to reopen their workshops; they will be forbidden to close them. They are greatly "harassed" by this. This dormant war cannot last very long. Either the Reich government will back up General Müller and remove the workers' ministers in Dresden from office, whereupon the working class will have no alternative but a general strike, which would necessarily be insurrectional, or else the general strike will oblige General Müller to respect proletarian organization. Decisive actions, from which the signal for the German revolution may very well spring, seem imminent in red Saxony.

Why Social Democracy is changing

To grasp the effect of General Müller's decrees, one must try to imagine the feelings of an old social democratic worker whose newspaper brings him the following batch of news items:

In Baden, the general commanding the region has dissolved the workers' hundreds. The *Arbeiterzeitung* has been seized (October 11).

General Lossberg has banned the *Niedersächsische Arbeiterzeitung* (Workers' Newspaper of Lower Saxony) (October 11).

The *Dresdner Volkszeitung* (People's Newspaper of Dresden), which had reappeared after being suspended for a week, has been suspended for another 14 days.

The social democratic *Volksblatt* (People's Paper) of Göttingen has been suspended.

In Berlin, General von Horn has banned the formation of workers' committees to check prices and all comparable organizations. Foreseeing attacks on the property of farmers, he has declared that they will be punished severely. The troops are authorized to fire on anyone who ignores a challenge.

At Szczecin[7] General von Tschichwitz, military governor of Mecklenburg-Strelitz, has gone one better. Considering agricultural production to be of eminent public utility, he has banned strikes there on pain of imprisonment. But even better! Any healthy day-laborer is forbidden to be absent from work. In case of illness, a medical certificate must be produced within two hours.

The Berlin edition of *Die Rote Fahne* has been suspended. The authorities are looking for the publishers of the KPD illegal daily which is appearing regularly.

On the other hand:

The Berlin edition of *Die Deutsche Zeitung* (nationalist), suspended on the same day as *Die Rote Fahne,* has just been authorized to reappear; in the busiest thoroughfares of the capital Hitler's *Die Weisse Fahne* (The White Flag), published in Nuremberg, is on sale. Everywhere you can buy the fascist agitational

---

7 Formerly known as Stettin.

paper *Fridericus* which has never been interfered with...

Herr von Kahr has just declared Commander Ehrhardt—the man who escaped from Leipzig, who has been charged by the high court—immune from all prosecution on Bavarian territory. The high court didn't turn a hair. General von Lossow, whose job is to ensure that the laws of the Reich are respected in Munich, is reported to be about to resign.

Is it to ratify the decision of the Bavarian dictator? Is it because the reactionaries clearly need to have all their experienced murderers returned to them? The high court in Leipzig has just ordered the release of *oberleutnant* Rossbach, the organizer of the fascist cells in the Reichswehr, who was imprisoned some months ago charged with plotting against the republic.

On Friday and Saturday, there were food riots in Hamburg, Leipzig, Essen, Düsseldorf, Hanover, Frankfurt-am-Main, Gelsenkirchen and Wiesbaden. Some shops were looted. The blood of the poor was shed on the doorsteps of grocers' shops... The dollar is at five billion.

What the social democratic worker thinks, when he is informed of these things, has just been realized at Dresden, where innumerable workers' delegations, among whom social democrats were numerous, came from all points of the country to greet the first workers' government and to demand support and advice for organizing resistance.

Finally, *Vorwärts* has emerged from its lethargy. This evening it bears, this time as a headline, the little phrase that we read here for the first time yesterday: "Martial law is unacceptable." And it reveals to its readers that in Berlin General Horn has banned a manifesto by a social democratic temperance society which ended with these words: "Teetotallers, get organized!" Yes, it is unacceptable. But tell us, citizens, who wanted it, who established it?

Provoke in order to repress

It is an old tactic of all tottering reactionaries. Provoke a premature revolutionary action. Stifle the revolution before it has ripened. All the efforts of bourgeois Germany are tending in this direction with remarkable unanimity.

In Bavaria, the royalist dictator von Kahr has outlawed the Communists and the working-class movement, repealed the republican constitution and obliged the Reich government to accept the accomplished fact.

In the Ruhr and the Rhineland, the big industrialists—the very ones who, after getting rich out of the passive resistance, are still demanding that the Reich compensate them for the losses they claim to have suffered—have now declared that they are unable to pay their workers' wages. As they are negotiating and coming to an agreement with the French government, it is not a disguised continuation of the passive resistance, it's a lockout. The lockout of at least a million hungry, exhausted, desperate workers, who, like their French precursors of the last century, are willing to "die fighting" because they can no longer "live by working."

In Berlin, the Stresemann government is putting the finishing touches to its draft law on the working day: eight hours in the mines, ten hours everywhere else! And it proclaims itself, in an official statement of October 17, to be determined to have the constitution and the regulations of martial law respected...in red Saxony, not in Bavaria!

At any moment, in red Saxony, it may be the turn of grenades and machine guns to speak. Conflict is desired, sought and deliberately engineered by General Müller with the support of Berlin.

The press campaign by the papers of the extreme right against Stresemann has been toned down, as has that of the semi-official press against Stinnes. The patriotic alliance of the big industrialists, the fascists and the last democratic government has been sealed to save bourgeois order by shedding the blood of the workers of Dresden and the Ruhr.

Towards a German Commune

If this set of facts leaves no place for doubt, the events in Saxony have an even clearer meaning. The dissolution of the workers' hundreds (formed, let us remember, with the support of the Zeigner government) was decreed in conditions which were absolutely scandalous. General Müller had no right to take this decision without the consent of the state commissioner of the Saxon government, the Socialist deputy Meyer (from Zwickau), who came to present his objections to him. General Müller nonetheless issued his decree, arguing that he "had not yet been officially informed of Herr Meyer's appointment." This bureaucratic trick risks marking the beginning of civil war…

The workers' hundreds have announced that they will not be dissolved. Yesterday, October 17, General Müller's next move was a coup; he withdrew from the Saxon government command over all the local police force and put it under his own authority. The same morning he announced that the workers' hundreds would be dissolved, if necessary by force, with the assistance of the troops, that is, of that selfsame pro-fascist Reichswehr that he has just had reinforced by thousands of men from the Stahlhelm. The conflict is developing rapidly. The same evening, we learned two grave items of news. First of all, General Müller's ultimatum to the Socialist prime minister of Saxony, Zeigner. In an insolent letter, read out to the Landtag, the general asked him to formally disown, before 11am on October 18, the Communist finance minister, Böttcher, who has advocated the arming of the workers and a red dictatorship. To the applause of the workers' majority in the Saxon parliament, Zeigner replied that his government considered itself solely responsible to the Landtag, and he refused to be accountable to the military authority. What remains for the latter to do, except arrest the ministers and dissolve parliament? The second news item, quite unofficial, is a striking comment on the first: it is said the upper command of the Reichswehr has just sent large quantities of artillery to Saxony…

Throughout the whole affair, it is confirmed that General Müller has not acted without the agreement of the Reichswehr minister, Herr Gessler, and hence of the whole cabinet…

Von Kahr, for his part, is demanding from Herr Stresemann sanctions against red Saxony where, on October 14, the congress of the Bavarian factory committees was held at Plauen, attended by 500 delegates… Banned in Saxony itself by General Müller, the first congress of the Saxon workers' hundreds was nonetheless held on October 13, attended by 155 delegates. A workers' bloc has been established in Thuringia, where on October 13 was formed, under the aegis of the workers' government, an action committee of 20 members including representatives of the KPD, the SPD, the USPD, the ADGB, etc., and of joint organizations of proletarian defense.

On October 17, the central committee of the SPD adopted a resolution demanding—at last!—the immediate ending of martial law, and it sent Hermann Müller to negotiate with Ebert and Stresemann. There are many reasons to doubt whether this final effort to avoid a bloody battle in Saxony will succeed. However it may be, the workers' struggle in Dresden and the proletariat which supports it will not retreat. They will meet force with force, and the insurrection may take place tomorrow. For the whole German proletariat this categorical imperative is proclaimed to the rattle of machine-gun fire: revolution or death.

These things should be quite clear and deeply moving for all

8 Acting head of the French government at the time.

French workers, and above all for Parisians! For it is virtually a line by line reenactment of the Paris Commune. In 1871 imperialist Prussia had to be paid for the war that had been lost. Thiers[8] was determined to make the French proletariat pay just as Stinnes and Stresemann want to make the German proletariat pay French imperialism for their defeats in 1914-18 and in the Ruhr. On March 17, 1871, M. Thiers announced to the good citizens of Paris the "disarmament" of the working people who were in possession of a few cannon. This was while martial law was in force. The unfortunate attempt by the forces of order in Montmartre to seize the artillery belonging to the National Guard gave the signal for the proclamation of the Commune the following day. History repeats itself. Except that the German Commune will have no less than fifteen million fighters…

Social Democracy in a dead end

Nothing is more false, nothing more tragically lamentable at this turning point in history than the situation of the leaders of the SPD. It was they who, with Stresemann, established martial law in Germany—that is, gave the dictatorship to seven generals under the orders of von Seeckt—in order, they said, to make Bavarian reaction respect the republic. Yes, indeed!

Their aim was to avoid civil war at all costs. They still have three ministers, including the deputy chancellor, in the Great Coalition cabinet. And martial law is "Bavarianising" the whole of Germany, is directed exclusively against the working class, against a republican government headed by the social democrat Zeigner, and is leading the country directly, full speed ahead, towards civil war. And after some weeks the central committee of the SPD has gone so far as to request—without being able to enforce it—the ending of martial law. And *Vorwärts* is full of impotent and insipid protests…

If they had the slightest bit of political courage, the SPD ministers should give Stresemann a clear ultimatum and then go away. "They won't do it!" a social democrat assured me this morning. They know only too well that they would be told: "Fine: clear off!"

Almost all their party is abandoning them. Half the parliamentary group, which after all is not very revolutionary, wants a clean break with the bourgeois parties. A final chance to save whatever honor may remain to this wretched party. Whole regions are facing the facts, agreeing that the Communists are right, and forming a united front. After Saxony and Thuringia, it is being formed at Hamburg, Solingen and Frankfurt, and is the object of negotiations in Berlin. Trade union officials in Bonn are becoming the promoters of class struggle and the dictatorship of the proletariat. Twenty two associations of cooperatives—not normally a particularly unruly grouping!—are asking for a workers' food congress to be called, and posing the question of feeding the masses in revolutionary terms. The Berlin regional SPD congress is due to meet almost immediately; it is no secret that it will give the opposition a solid majority.

At this same time, the old theoretical review of German socialist thought, *Die Neue Zeit*, founded in 1885 and edited for 32 years, until 1917, by Kautsky, has closed down, for lack of resources, lack of readers, but also for lack of thinkers. The most authoritative voice of reformist socialism has gone silent... Could one imagine a more total bankruptcy?

Hunger riots

Hunger riots are becoming daily events. In the last few days, from October 12 to 18, there have been serious disturbances at Höchst-am-Main where French troops intervened, at Frankfurt, at Leipzig, at Bibrich—where the crowd disarmed the police before the French could restore order—at Gelsenkirchen, at Düsseldorf, at

Cologne, at Mannheim, at Halberstadt, at Ortelsburg, and in Berlin. In Berlin, bakeries and grocers' shops have been looted. It is noticeable that the green municipal police behaved much less brutally in these disturbances than previously. In many cases, they had a clearly sympathetic attitude to the starving crowd. On the other hand, at Meningen, in a clash of which we do not as yet have details, the Reichswehr opened fire and killed two civilians (October 14).

The people are hungry. Hunger is driving them onto the streets. Crowds of starving people, ready to become the terrible armies of revolution, are filling the cities of Germany. On July 1, there were 68,000 unemployed in Berlin. At the beginning of September, there were 110,000, on October 6, 160,000. Today there are over 200,000. It is estimated that in Germany as a whole (including the occupied regions) the number of unemployed is at least two million. And what poverty they are living in! The disguised lockout of industry in the Rhineland and the Ruhr must increase it considerably. Five to six million workers are working shortened days or shortened weeks. Our comrades from *Volkswacht*, at Lübeck, calculate that wages at present are not more than 15-20 percent of what they were before the war. But let's be more precise. From October 8 to 14, a metalworker earned for a week 6,500,000,000 (13 gold pfennigs per hour), that is two to three dollars at the very most. From October 11 to 18, a painter and decorator earned a little over six billion, and this was the week when the dollar reached seven billion. From October 8 to 15, a miner in Central Germany earned 4,075,000,000, or 12 centimes an hour at pre-war values, and two to three dollars... But on January 16 an egg cost 110 million; about one hour's work in the mine. Workboots cost between six and ten dollars. And these are only wages for workers doing full weeks.

Significant episodes

We will be forgiven for returning to them, for their importance is so great. Prosecuted in the Leipzig high court, on a count of plotting against the republic, accused of having laid the bases of some fascist organizations in the Reichswehr, on October 13, commander Rossbach received a conditional discharge. The grounds for the judgment made concerning him were that "there was no danger that he would evade justice." As soon as he learned of this, Zeigner, the Dresden prime minister, issued a new warrant for Rossbach's arrest. Too late; the man in question had already taken the train for Bavaria. A quite legal escape, laughingly justified on the grounds that there was…no danger of escape!

While preparations are being made for bloody repression in Dresden, the frontier incident between Thuringia and Bavaria has been settled by official statements emanating from Munich. On the night of October 9, Bavarian gangs on the frontier opened machine-gun fire against the Thuringian police. In Munich they have explained that the Bavarian police, reinforced by patriotic National Socialist organizations, thought it necessary to take measures against possible aggression by the reds… Thus Hitler's "anti-working class hundreds" are officially collaborating with von Kahr's police. But it is peaceful red Saxony which they intend to "disarm" tomorrow with cannon fire!

At the end of October the tide was beginning to turn. The proposed Rentenmark, despite Serge's legitimate skepticism, was soon to put an end to hyperinflation. There were still threats to national unity in Bavaria and the Rhineland. But the KPD's plans for insurrection were in crisis. At Chemnitz on October 21, the KPD failed to win support from the left social democrats for a general strike. Without that support a revolutionary offensive was impossible. An abortive rising in Hamburg was the result of a failure in communication.

Munich versus Berlin

Correspondance internationale, October 27, 1923

There is no longer any German unity. That established by Bismarck at Sadowa and Sedan[1] no longer exists. The Reich does have
a president, a government and an army. But these are just appearances, remnants of a past to which every passing day makes it more
difficult to return. To tell the truth, the Reich no longer has money,
army, reputation nor—consequently—power. M. Poincaré "recognizes" the Stresemann government less than he does that of the soviets, whose strength he knows in any case. Economically and
politically cut off from the rest of Germany, the Rhineland and
Ruhr are preparing to follow their own destiny. Bavaria is being
governed as an independent state. Saxony and Thuringia have
workers' governments. The state's coffers are empty. The fascist
army is refusing to obey. The semi-official press is in reality at the
service of a secret government of financiers who are absorbed in
preparations for civil war.

The end of German unity is the great historical fact which the
events of the last few days have suddenly thrown into relief. Let us
try to give a brief and clear overall view, before recalling the conclusion they lead to.

Since Monday October 15 there has been a ripening conflict
between red Saxony and Berlin. It turned out that General Müller,

---

1 Prussian victories over Austria at Sadowa (1866) and France at Sedan (1870)
led to the establishment of a united Germany (1871) of which Bismarck was the
first chancellor.
2 At the time of writing Serge may have been aware the KPD had decided to
retreat from its plan for a general strike leading to insurrection, but obviously he
could not yet discuss this in public.

dictator at Dresden, was being so provocative (threat to dissolve the workers' hundreds by force, ultimatum to Herr Zeigner) only because he had the support of the bourgeois majority of the Great Coalition government. The Reichswehr was being strengthened in Saxony. We could expect from one hour to the next—we can and must still expect![2]—a final provocation which would leave the central German proletariat no alternative but to embark on a general strike which would inevitably become an insurrection.

But then from Friday October 19 to Saturday October 20, the situation changed completely. Democratic opinion, the Reich government, and social democracy all suddenly found themselves faced with a new factor: the open revolt of reactionary Bavaria. It all sprang from a trivial incident. General von Lossow, representing in Munich the military dictator of the Reich, Gessler, in reality a friend and underling of Herr von Kahr—as we pointed out the very day martial law was declared—had neither the courage nor the will to enforce in Bavaria the suspension of the fascist organ *Völkischer Beobachter*, as decreed by his superior in the hierarchy. Called upon to act, he replied in a telegram which was not in code (hence open to public curiosity) that he could not apply measures which had been rendered inapplicable by the mood in the state. Called on to resign, he refused, and put himself under the protection of the Bavarian dictator. At the beginning, Herr Gessler did not want to broaden the conflict, and treated it merely as an act of indiscipline by an individual general. But von Kahr, so that all Germany should be under no misapprehension, broke off relations with the Reichswehr minister. Herr Gessler and von Seeckt had no alternative but to dismiss General von Lossow from his duties. Which they proceeded to do. Von Kahr responded by ordering the Reichswehr troops quartered in Bavaria to take orders only from the Bavarian authorities, and by appointing von Lossow, their commander, as from now on officially his subordinate.

Bavaria no longer recognizes the government in Berlin and has now stripped it of part of its army just as it has already robbed it of the Nuremberg gold reserve.

A situation which workers' Germany had already recognized as existing in practice has now been formally confirmed. The Bavarian region is serenely continuing on its way towards civil war. It will not allow the democratic, republican and social democratic circles any loophole. It is treating them with contempt.

It sees its interest as being identical with that of "the whole of Germany" (statement by Herr von Kahr, October 20). National unity matters little unless it is reactionary unity.

From these events we see the following ideological and practical conclusions emerging:

♦ It is the German big bourgeoisie, aspiring to impose a class dictatorship, which has struck the first decisive blow against German national unity.

♦ This bourgeoisie feels strong enough to refuse any compromise with the democratic middle classes and with social democracy. It wants a military decision within a short space of time: the crushing by force of arms of the working class of central Germany. It has revolted against the Berlin government only because it is still striving to delay the advent of social war.

In Saxony: Russian intervention and "Tartar News"

The break between Munich and Berlin is a victory for red Saxony: it would not have happened if successive Berlin governments had

---

3 The DVP.

told General Müller "to act with the utmost severity," which was what was demanded by Bavaria, Stinnes' party,[3] the nationalist press and even the papers controlled by Herr Stresemann. Faced with the determination to resist on the part of the Saxon workers, the ministers in Berlin hesitated. Perhaps not for long. Perhaps long enough to cause their downfall.

For red Saxony is defending itself well. On October 18, in the Dresden Landtag, Herr Zeigner made quite a peremptory response to General Müller's ultimatum: he made his revelations about the "black Reichswehr."[4]

The trial of the German National People's Party in the Leipzig High Court has revealed the existence of this clandestine army commanded by Generals Ludendorff, Lettow-Vorbeck and Maercker (the Maercker of the Kapp putsch). For months, students have been receiving military instruction in the Königsbrück camp. The same thing has been going on at Küstrin where, moreover, seven political assassinations have taken place within a short time. Stralsund, Döberitz and Lubben are other centers for "black" military detachments. The same thing in Pomerania, Silesia, Mecklenburg. In Leipzig, fifteen hundred young men from the "black" Reichswehr have just been incorporated into the official army… "There would be no point in revealing more," Herr Zeigner has said. "France has been fully informed about this," he added.

Poincaré's France certainly sees no disadvantage in arming the German bourgeoisie against the proletariat.

For his part, the Communist finance minister in Saxony, our comrade Böttcher, has taken measures against food shortage. He had undertaken a survey which showed that seven hundred thousand inhabitants of Saxony—manual and white-collar workers,

---

4 This was set up secretly by von Seeckt and Severing in 1923 to bolster the official armed forces which were restricted in size by the Versailles Treaty.

peasants, people on small unearned incomes, pensioners, war wounded—amounting to one seventh of the total population, were in such difficulties that it was the urgent duty of the community to give them assistance. The banks and industrial circles refused any assistance to the state with a view to the organization of substantial assistance to the poor, so Böttcher turned to the International Workers' Aid, which immediately made available to him two thousand tons of corn; then he was in contact with the Soviet government from which he hopes to receive within the next month, in exchange for manufactured goods, twenty thousand tons of cereals. This will be, we believe, the first Soviet intervention in Germany. The intervention of Russian corn against hunger and fascism.

Alarmed by the determination and skill of the workers' government, the German bourgeoisie is concentrating all its forces against it. Some major newspapers, *Deutsche Allgemeine Zeitung, Tag, Zeit, Lokal-Anzeiger,* are preparing public opinion for military intervention in Saxony by publishing more and more highly fanciful news about "Communist terror in the industrial regions." The radical (bourgeois) press has found a witty name for these false reports: "*Tataren Nachrichten*"—Tartar news. Nonetheless they provide justification for the official reinforcement of the Reichswehr in the south of Saxony (October 18, 19). Herr von Kahr, for his part, has broken off diplomatic relations with Dresden and banned the export of milk and butter from Bavaria to Saxony. The Wroclaw military command has likewise banned the export of potatoes from the Silesian region... General Müller, in a manifesto dated October 20, an arrogant document insulting the workers if ever there was one, says he is called on to defend "the free state of Saxony" against "the economic chaos desired by the Communists." According to persistent rumors, it is said that Saxon industrialists will soon be demanding the protection of the Munich government against "red terror."

A visit to Hitler

Last week a German journalist, belonging to avant-garde circles, was able, by claiming to have an introduction from Mussolini, to penetrate inside Hitler's premises. His reports, published by various German and Russian papers unsigned, or under the prudent initials "LH," are very interesting.

Hitler aspires to play in Germany the role of a Mussolini. His headquarters occupy various premises in the Schellingstrasse in Munich. At number 39 of that street are the editorial offices of the *Völkischer Beobachter* (Popular Observer), his official organ; alongside are the actual headquarters. His cars occupy a neighboring garage.

A certain Herr Stolzing, editor of the *Völkischer Beobachter*, fulfils the role of political adviser to the valiant "colonel." This Herr Stolzing, a Bavarian, was until recently Czech, called Czerny and organized the Sokol[5] "sporting associations" in Bohemia.

This Herr Stolzing made the following statements about the intentions of the National Socialist gangs to the interviewer:

"In the Ruhr, we wanted active resistance, by acts of systematic sabotage and by guerrilla warfare. By so doing we should have equipped an army prepared for real war."

"Without weapons?"

Herr Stolzing replied with a laugh:

"We must not undermine the myth current abroad that Germany is disarmed. I can tell you we are not short of weapons. All we would need in addition for all-out war is about a thousand cannon."

In foreign policy:

"Annexation of Austria and the Czech Germans. Concessions to Italy in the Tyrol, since (fascist) Italy is our natural ally... Nothing in common with Soviet Russia."

In domestic policy:

---

5 The *Sokol* (Czech for falcon) was a Czech nationalist gymnastic organisation.

"We demand action. One morning soon we shall go into Saxony and Thuringia, which have been sovietized, in order to root out Marxism with the methods which have been successful for Mussolini."

"What are your predictions for the immediate future?"

"In three weeks time, the peasants will no longer deliver food to the towns. Stresemann will be finished; von Kahr will have finished his role (he isn't a dictator, he is an excellent civil servant). All the active forces are with Hitler. The day we march on Saxony, our friends in Pomerania, Mecklenburg and Prussia will rise up immediately."

Just bluster? In international politics, yes; and everyone recognizes it. In domestic politics, no. The Küstrin incident, Zeigner's revelations about the "black" Reichswehr, von Kaehne's trial at Potsdam, and finally and above all Bavarian policy, confirm these statements. They were made in the headquarters of a political party, under military guard, where everyone is in uniform (old Austrian uniform, admittedly), where the sentries present arms to Hitler when he enters! During a recent burglary, weapons were stolen. The numerous telephone conversations which took place in the presence of the fake representative of Mussolini were always about orders for arms and ammunition.

The Great Coalition government wants to disarm the workers' hundreds in Saxony and Thuringia. It has done nothing against Hitler's gangs, which are a much more direct threat to the republic—because it can do nothing, not having any forces in Bavaria and because its class mentality, its reactionary mentality, makes it see danger among workers and not among fascists. Off-the-record reports of this week's cabinet meetings put it precisely: "It appears to the majority of the government that the workers' hundreds constitute a greater danger than the nationalist organizations..."

Hunger on the streets

The street in the grey light of morning. Outside the dairies, there are neverending, pitiful crowds of poor women. They settle down, they bring folding stools, chairs and their needlework with them. They bring their children. One woman, not fully hidden by the mist, in the corner of a doorway, is breast-feeding. It is cold and the damp pierces through the old clothes of the poverty-stricken. They have been there for whole days waiting to buy a bit of margarine. Facing them, the inevitable green-uniformed policeman, miserable and bad-tempered because he is ashamed of his job. Perhaps his wife is there, with the others…

A truck passes, loaded with potatoes. A clamoring crowd converges on it from both pavements. Kids clutch onto the back of the heavy vehicle, and throw armfuls of the precious vegetables down into the road, to be picked up immediately. The driver speeds up. A policeman shouts himself hoarse, all in vain. I see quite a well-dressed gentleman, doubtless an office worker, calmly pick up a few spuds and stuff them into his pocket. I see a greying, bent old woman running, breathless, to get a bigger share…

The street is hungry. The street has faces of despair, of anger and of hatred.

All day until midnight, at busy crossroads, groups of men are talking. The unemployed. I've often listened to their discussions: the Communist, the Social Democrat and the National Socialist are usually all there and the Communist has the best of the argument.

Sometimes, suddenly, these groups gather, form an angry procession, shove the trembling police out of the way, and attack the shops. This happened in the last few days in various districts of Berlin, and in a number of cities of Germany. An eyewitness told me about one of these instances of looting. He was astonished at the sense of order of the starving people. Methodical looting, no unnecessary violence against property or people. They didn't take luxury items. They took bread, fat, shoes. Suddenly achieving a primitive awareness of their right to life, men condemned to die of hunger took what they needed to live. It was only when the police intervened that the expropriation degenerated into a riot.

But the police are hesitant, they don't shoot as readily as they did six months ago. They feel submerged in a mass movement—and they are hungry too. In the brawls at Schöneberg[6] and near the Stock Exchange the changed attitude was very visible. Near the Stock Exchange the other day unemployed workers stopped some bosses' cars and set about pushing them towards the River Spree. A policeman harangued these hungry paupers, appealed to their reason and their human feeling and—since they have more of these qualities than Stinnes and Poincaré—resolved the incident when it was about to become tragic.

The big department stores have their iron grilles half closed; the grocers don't pull them back at all. The hungry street makes them afraid. They can feel it becoming a formidable revolutionary force.

Two days ago, bread cost 620 million marks; today, October 21, it costs 2800 million.

In the fray

Now, to complete the overall picture of the situation in the last few days, here is a bunch of facts.

Herr von Kahr has refused to renew the residence permits for Bavaria of a number of official Russian figures, carrying Soviet diplomatic passports, notably Krestinsky, Steklov and Tsyurupa.

---

6 A district in Southern Berlin.
7 That is, the "red battle standard" rather than the "red flag."

Die Rote Fahne has been allowed to reappear for two days before being banned again (October 21). During its suspension, the illegal *Die Rote Sturmfahne*[7] appeared regularly.

The police has occupied the printshop of the Communist *Hamburger Volksstimme*. The Communist paper in Bremen has just been suspended. At Heide, Bremen, Altona and Dresden there are reports of workers being arrested. At Altona, the unemployed committee has been rounded up (October 17).

At Mannheim, there have been food riots and a 24-hour general strike (October 16-17). The police opened fire on the demonstrators, leaving seven dead and 150 wounded.

The reformist general trade union federation—the ADGB—in Halle has demanded the requisition of foodstuffs (October 17).

The Berlin functionaries of the ADGB have voted by 1500 to 50 against general strike in the event of a Reichswehr attack on red Saxony (October 17).

At Aachen, today, Sunday October 21, a Rhineland Republic has been proclaimed. The separatists have without difficulty seized the city which is occupied by Belgian troops. The latter are observing a neutrality which is certainly sympathetic...

At Berlin, the same day, the local congress of the SPD gave a majority to the "left" opposition.

An immense danger is emerging in the Ruhr and Rhineland. Financial aid from the Reich to industry in the occupied territory stopped on October 20. The big industrialists have declared that they are unable to pay wages. Six hundred thousand workers, weary after six months suffering, will find themselves without bread. What will they do tomorrow?

At Chemnitz (Saxony), a congress of all the workers' organizations in Germany, including the organizations banned and dissolved by General Müller, met on Sunday (October 21) and decided to respond immediately to any Reichswehr action against red Saxony by a general strike. As I am finishing writing these reports, I am told that troops have opened fire in Dresden. If it is true, battle may be joined within a few hours. "Everything is at stake!" wrote Brandler on Saturday. It is certain that if the Bavarian reactionaries carry out a coup, the proletariat of central Germany will not be able to tolerate for another hour the unspeakable provocations of a general who is in a hurry to play the part of a Galliffet.

Double standards

Herr von Kahr has made the Seventh Division of the Reichswehr, quartered in Bavaria, take an oath of loyalty to Bavaria. He has forbidden the publication of appeals by the Reichswehr minister, Herr Gessler, and by General von Seeckt. He has suspended until further notice the Munich *Allgemeine Zeitung* (the bourgeois "General News"), which was guilty of having printed these official statements of the Berlin government. The Federal Council (Reichsrat)[8] has been asked to "arbitrate" the conflict between Munich and Berlin. The impotence of the Reich could not be more complete.

Herr von Kahr claims he wants to "defend German unity" against the "Marxist influences" affecting the Stresemann cabinet.

Meanwhile impressive troop movements are taking place in Saxony. The Reichswehr from the most reactionary regions in Germany is concentrating its forces, fully equipped for war, in the industrial districts of red Saxony. General Felsch is operating in the Königsbrück-Bischofswerda-Dresden region; General von Ledebur around Leipzig; Colonel Faehrenbach in the Hof area. At Meissen (on October 22) troops, retaliating against a revolver

---

8 The upper house of parliament, with representatives from the various states of the Reich.

shot fired from a house window, wounded several people. At Pirna, General Felsch ordered soldiers to open fire on demonstrators (one killed).

Speaking in the Dresden Landtag, Herr Zeigner exposed the duplicity of the Great Coalition (October 23). The Berlin government had sent him a letter assuring him that the reinforcement of the Reichswehr in Saxony had as its primary object the protection of the state's frontiers against possible aggression by the Bavarian fascists. But General Müller, the commander-in-chief of the troops, said he was authorized to "restore constitutional order in Saxony." One provocation after another. After his anti-Communist manifesto last week and his second threatening letter to Herr Zeigner, he ordered a march past in front of the Dresden town hall by Mecklenburg infantry, a squadron of hussars, armoured vehicles, artillery, cyclists and sappers. These purely strategic maneuvers are harmonized with economic maneuvers which are perhaps even more worrying. The blockade of red Saxony is a fact. Industrialists are boycotting the workers' government. The military command of East Prussia and Silesia had banned the export of potatoes to Saxony. This ban was lifted on October 20, but traders asked such a high price—in gold—for their potatoes that Saxony, with its low wages, could not afford them. Bavaria put a ban on sending dairy products to Saxony. Its ministry of food is carrying out a particularistic[9] policy. According to Heckert, Saxony today has 900,000 destitute out of 4,800,000 inhabitants. In the textile industry they are working two days a week. In the coalmines, they work between 24 and 32 hours in six days. At Brona (Leipzig) for the second week of September, miners got a wage of 700 million, while a season ticket

---

9 The principle whereby each state in a federation governs itself without regard to the interests of the rest of the federation.

on the regional railways cost them 500 million. Many have had to give up claiming their coal ration, because they can't pay transport costs. The millers have no corn left. The management of the Reich granaries is asking a price for its cereals that is 41 percent higher than the stock exchange's—a price nobody can pay... But for Russian corn, catastrophe would be imminent. So the situation in Saxony is more serious than ever.

City without bread

Berlin has no bread. Mobs, police, scuffles outside bakeries. On October 22 and 23 the police had to intervene four times to prevent looting. It didn't always succeed. Groups of unemployed made their way without warning into a shop and said calmly: "Give us bread—or so much the worse for you!" They were allowed to take what they wanted. Elsewhere poor people turn up with their billions of marks, and, finding the shops empty, become enraged.

It is said that there is no shortage of corn: this famine is simply the result of inflation and speculation. For the last six or seven days the dollar has doubled in value almost every day. On October 15 it was quoted at 3,600 million; on October 23 it was sold in Berlin for 70,000 million. The price of bread has risen in proportion. All those in the population who had the money hastened to stock up with bread before the increases of the coming days. The poor are left high and dry with no bread...

The Great Coalition abolished ration cards for bread: that was one of citizen Hilferding's reforms; the result was so visibly that the rich would grab all the bread that it constituted a major danger; hence the coupon has just been reintroduced (as from October 24).

To resolve this situation, Herr Stresemann has given responsibility in the cabinet for food to Count Kanitz, an agrarian, a big landowner, who has just resigned from the DNVP. The SPD ministers have agreed to collaborate with this gentleman: but he has no intention of collaborating with them: as soon as he was appointed, he issued a manifesto (October 22) to farmers and patriots declaring that he was determined: "never to agree to measures which interfere with the interests of production." These are the very words used by industrialists and landowners who refuse to pay taxes on property because they "interfere with the interests of production."

Berlin has no bread. The bourgeois parties and the SPD in power have appointed one of the great starvers of the people to look after food supplies for the country!

Hunger and rioting everywhere

The separatist movement in the Rhineland region seems to have collapsed pathetically. At Aachen, the great majority of the population showed themselves so hostile to the two thousand armed bourgeois who put up the green, white and red flag on the town hall, that the Belgian military command didn't dare take them under its protection. The Rhineland Republic only lived for a few hours (October 22). By the way, where did the weapons come from to arm the shock battalions of the separatists?

At Hamburg, on October 23,[10] street fighting and intervention by the navy. The blood of the poor on the streets. Lead instead of bread. Court-martials. Tomorrow, perhaps, executions. Order. For the moment there are four killed and 108 wounded on the side of the rioters. The police have seven dead and about thirty wounded. Hamburg is governed by a coalition of bourgeois and socialists. The

---

10 In fact the Hamburg rising was planned by the KPD as part of a national movement; orders cancelling the action failed to reach Hamburg. Serge was doubtless aware of this, but could not say so in the public press in a near civil war situation.

SPD have urged the workers not to follow the Communist call for a general strike. "Communist riot," says the press. Of course this is a lie: our party rejects isolated, partial actions, easy to put down, which weaken and undermine revolutionary preparations. But doubtless the Hamburg Communists did fight on the barricades put up by unemployed, strikers and starving people who couldn't wait any longer... These disturbances in Hamburg had a major significance. A whole section of the German proletariat is running out of patience. About six million men can no longer go on living—and they don't want to let themselves die of hunger. We know what price is paid by militants of the workers' parties who urge them not to fling themselves into premature actions. This active army of the German revolution wants to go into the firing line.

Strikes in the port of Bremen (October 23), where the workers' hundreds are occupying various public buildings. Food riots at Szczecin. The landowners in the area around this town are refusing paper money, and demanding that their potatoes be paid for in gold-based currency. Riot at Erfurt. The police open fire—one dead. Attempts at looting at Brunswick and Munich. Munich also is without bread (the same day).

On the single day of October 24: disturbances at Brunswick, Frankfurt-am-Main, Cologne, Kiel, Essen, Gelsenkirchen, Oppeln, while bloody battles continue in the streets of Hamburg.

The Ruhr industrialists (Stinnes, Klöckner, Vögler) in their negotiations with the Franco-Belgian engineers' commission are refusing to pay the arrears of the tax on coal. "It's beyond their means." They cannot even guarantee the payment of wages! There is a conflict: since the Franco-Belgian commission will not yield, work cannot resume in the mines and factories. German industrialists and French engineers are accusing each other "of full responsibility for possible complications..." Sickening hypocrisy. This clash of interests between German and Allied capitalists is causing unemployment for half a million workers whose hunger, despair, anger and blood ready to flow have become arguments for bargaining across the table of a boardroom...

Inflation to cure inflation

The value of the dollar doubles almost every day; all prices likewise. What is left for a worker, three days later, of the wages he collected on Saturday? His paper billions have automatically undergone three consecutive reductions by half. I know workers who, on October 19, got five billion for their week's wages. Four days later it would no longer buy a loaf. All the groups who stay arguing in the streets until midnight come to the same conclusion: "It's time to put an end to it!"

The ADGB, the cumbersome machine of the reformist unions, has begun to move. It has demanded of the Great Coalition government—which the SPD entered months ago on condition that wages be stabilized—that wages be paid immediately in paper with a real value. Herr Stresemann "satisfied their demand" straightaway. An official statement to the press has announced that as of this week small denomination notes from the gold loan will be put in circulation. Eight million a day will be printed... moreover, the Rentenmark[11] will be launched... What a lot of new paper in prospect. "Let us expect," shrewdly writes the *Berliner Börsenzeitung* (the paper of the Berlin Stock Exchange), "a new inflation..." But where will its true value be?

This is so true that even before its use as current money has been generalized, the gold loan haZs already fallen in value. This false German dollar was quoted in Berlin, on the evening of October 24, at sixty-three billion while the dollar—pure and simple!—

---

11 Temporary currency (November 1923 to August 1924) replacing marks made worthless by inflation.

was worth ninety-five billion! The gold loan has already lost nearly 30 percent of its face value.

The gold loan has not produced results. Its failure is quite clear. Can you create real value by marking on a bit of colored paper that this is "the real one, the true one," that it is worth gold?

The bonds issued by the big firms will enable them to engage in profitable financial schemes; but their value will correspond to traders' prices, which in turn are determined by the general level of inflation...

There remains the Rentenmark, resulting from the combined plans of Herr Hilferding, a social democrat, and the monarchist landowner Helfferich. The Rentenmark has been issued by a new bank to be managed by a board of directors comprising representatives of finance, commerce, industry, agriculture, in short of the oligarchy which is battening on Germany and exploiting it. The value of the Rentenmark is guaranteed by a 4 percent mortgage on the goods of the said oligarchy; a mortgage, that is a convention, a piece of paper; the goods remain in their possession. As from April 1, 1924, property owners commit themselves to pay to the state 6 percent on the part of their goods that is not mortgaged; and this 6 percent must be reimbursed to them out of the bank's profits. Quite a complex scheme from which it emerges that the oligarchy of property owners:

♦   acquires control over the Reich's finances;
♦   issues paper money which, to put it bluntly, is guaranteed only by its word;
♦   will lend nothing tangible to the state before April 1, 1924.

There is no example of currency being issued in this way since

---

12 The post-Robespierre government in France, 1795-99.

the memorable and sad experience of the territorial warrants of the Directory.[12]

The creation of real values depends on two conditions—real backing, really at the disposal of the state; and the confidence of the community. The Reich's treasury is empty. The wealthy classes do not give and do not want to give to the state. They have no confidence in it and they are afraid of the proletariat which may, soon, find itself the master of the state. The middle and lower classes no longer have any confidence in the word of the rich... No resources, no reserves, and no confidence. The government of capitalist Germany cannot relieve bankruptcy except by schemes which all more or less come down to reckless speculation on public credulity.

The legal exchange rate has been re-established; in Berlin there is a ban on publishing rates of exchange from foreign stock exchanges...

By the last week in October the revolutionary opportunity had gone by. On October 29 the Reichswehr overthrew the workers' government in Saxony. Serge, writing in the public press of the Comintern, put the blame, with considerable justification, on the right and left of the SPD; the KPD's self-criticism would come later.

The failure of the left Social Democrats

Correspondance internationale, November 2, 1923

For a second time since the August general strike, the SPD has just saved the stakes of the German bourgeoisie. At the beginning of last week, a major proletarian offensive was possible, seemed on the point of being launched, indeed, I'm prepared to say it was inevitable. General von Lossow and Bavaria had gone into open rebellion against the Reich. A whole current of radical opinion was emerging in favor of a bloc of republican parties around red Saxony: the journalists Georg Bernhardt and von Gerlach supported this position. The Rhineland separatists acted; their initiative brought out the full extent of the danger to German unity posed by reactionary intrigues. Meanwhile the Reichswehr moved into red Saxony. There, anger and indignation were expressed energetically at the workers' conference in Chemnitz.[1] The left social democrats, in Berlin and Dresden, had committed themselves to refusing to accept any armed attack on Saxony. Food riots were stirring up crowds of unemployed outside every town hall in Germany.

At this point, a general strike, coming up head-on against the bans of the military dictatorship, would have drawn in all the working masses and won the sympathy of all republican elements. It could have had clear slogans, fitting the aspirations of the majority of workers and of the middle classes:

"Bread!" "An end to martial law!" "Peace for workers' republican Saxony!" "Unity of the Reich!" "Disarm the Bavarian reactionaries!" "Workers' government!"

This mass movement did not take place.

The KPD was ready. A large and vigorous minority of hungry workers were ready to fight if necessary. Rather than attacking bakeries, the unemployed of Germany would have very happily fought for a workers' government. Democratic opinion, that of the middle classes, would have understood workers' action at that moment. What element of inertia prevented it?

Two things. The determination of the social democrats in the government to persevere with their treachery at all costs. And the

---

1 The conference had been called by KPD and SPD ministers to discuss the economic situation, and was attended by delegates from unions and factory councils as well as the KPD and SPD.

indecisiveness of the left social democrats.

The former, to tell the truth, is a counter-revolutionary factor. As for the latter, many of us do not as yet know the full extent of it. The left social democrats are only reluctant revolutionaries; they still all too often treat the likes of Ebert, Wels, Robert Schmidt and Sollmann, not as deserters who are infinitely dangerous to the working class, but simply as party comrades who happen to belong to a different tendency. But it's not a question of tendencies! In disintegration, social democracy has preserved, within the framework of its formal unity, two hostile parties condemned to fight to the death every day. This party once again includes, side by side, Spartacists and Noske's soldiers. But to become conscious of themselves, to become genuine revolutionaries, the former still have to shake off the influence of the traditions of the old social democracy, the fetishism of unity, some remaining republican illusions. As for the latter, they have long been genuine counter-revolutionaries.

The lost opportunity may recur, perhaps even very soon. But we should observe that the failure of the left social democrats, in the third week of October, has done the German bourgeoisie a service that is more or less equivalent to that rendered by the official SPD in August, when it joined the Great Coalition.

In the last week, the positions of the German capitalists in the social war have in fact been significantly strengthened. Fifty thousand men of the Reichswehr have entered red Saxony. Though it is bluff and fraud at the beginning of a new financial tactic, the appearance of "real value" paper money will give some relief to the middle classes and to small traders. The conflict with Bavaria has become chronic and is returning to normal. The negotiations with the Reparations Commission finally seem about to begin... The time now seems right for a bourgeois offensive: we have just learned that it has taken place against red Saxony.

Never yet have the power of class consciousness and the effective value of the revolutionary spirit been so clearly visible in Germany as today, where the rule of the bourgeoisie endures only thanks to the treachery of the leaders of the social democracy and thanks to the failure of the advanced masses in their party.

The ultimatum to Zeigner

The underhand comedy between Munich and Berlin is still going on. Von Kahr seemed to be reverting to a more favorable attitude towards Herr Stresemann; the Reichsrat, arbitrating the difference, gave its approval to Stresemann; von Kahr thanked Stresemann for his loyalty during the Palatinate incident; then suddenly, on October 25, von Kahr declared that he no longer wished to discuss with a Berlin government "under Marxist influence." He called on Stresemann to resign. Berlin replied with a sharp note, holding over the head of the Munich dictator the "censure of the German people." And...

And Berlin sent an ultimatum to the workers' government in Dresden (October 28). Berlin demanded the withdrawal of the Communist ministers whose attitude was "anti-constitutional." The ultimatum expired the next day, Sunday, at noon. If Herr Zeigner resisted, "serious measures will be taken."

While this ultimatum was being drawn up in Berlin, the Reichswehr was shooting on a threatening but unarmed crowd at Freiberg (Saxony), killing twelve workers and wounding a hundred! The third murder of workers in red Germany in less than five days. With reference to the previous incident (October 24, Pirna, one dead!) the commander of the Reichswehr has had notices

---

2 Allgemeiner freier Angestelltenbund, the union federation organizing office workers.

posted proclaiming that "the troops will not discuss nor hesitate to make their orders respected; they are not the police, they must act in all circumstances, they will act, with pitiless rigor..." As in wartime; as in enemy territory.

Red Saxony is enemy territory. All the social democratic and trade union organizations in Saxony (SPD, ADGB, AfA[2], League of Civil Servants' Unions) have appealed to working-class Germany for assistance. "Saxony has been handed over to sixty thousand Reichswehr troops. At Pirna the brutality of the soldiers has been so repugnant that National German municipal councillors have associated themselves with the general protest. At Dresden they have arrested the police chiefs—social democrats—in the exercise of their functions..." For his part, Herr Gessler has officially denied that the Reichswehr entered Saxony to defend the country against a possible Bavarian aggression; it was simply a question of restoring order.

The most outrageous part of all this is the attitude of the SPD ministers in the Reich government—Robert Schmidt, Sollmann, Radbruch. In the cabinet meeting, they voted for the ultimatum sent to Zeigner!—In the opinion of even moderate social democrats, this means suicide for the Great Coalition. "After that, they have to leave!" From all parts of the country indignant protests are reaching the SPD central leadership, which claims not to know what has being going on. It was traveling. It will discuss it... *Vorwärts* says Herr Stresemann and citizen Robert Schmidt were right; all the faults are on the side of the Saxon Communists who "weren't able to take on the role of a governmental party" (!!!) *Vorwärts* can say what it will; its whole party understands that the social democratic ministers—so subservient in the face of von Kahr—have made themselves impossible: useless to the bourgeoisie, detestable to the proletariat and even to the republican element in central Germany.

This is their second major squalid trick within a week: on October 24 the printers in Berlin threatened to suspend the printing of all bourgeois newspapers and banknotes if the Communist paper *Die Rote Fahne* was not given permission to reappear. For the newsagents' windows are overrun with Hitler's *Völkischer Beobachter, Fridericus, Die Weisse Fahne* (The White Flag) and the *Deutsche Zeitung*. But the whole Communist press has been stifled. In the face of this strike threat, presented by a trade union majority, despite all the urgings of the reformist officials, the government and the military command in Berlin have responded (October 26) by banning strikes in the capital!

Whatever path we have taken, we are now at a turning point. The bourgeoisie is going onto the offensive. The Great Coalition has probably had its day. What next? After this there can only be a dictatorship, not a constitutional one this time, not constitutional at all. But which?

It's a trial of strength.

Buchrucker and Thorell

The trial of the fascists who, a few weeks ago, tried a surprise attack on the Küstrin fortress, began on October 22 at the Cottbus court, behind closed doors. The chief accused, retired commander Ernst Buchrucker (a former participant in the Kapp putsch, who distinguished himself at the time by shooting Cottbus workers) was sentenced to ten years in a fortress on a charge of high treason. With one exception, his twelve fellow accused were all sentenced to periods of less than two years imprisonment (October 26). The preliminary investigation had lasted several weeks.

For the insurgent workers of Hamburg three days investigation was enough. As early as October 28 the court-martial at Hamburg pronounced its first death sentence. The condemned man is a young Communist worker age twenty-two, called Thorell, who fired at a policeman (without killing him), which earned him first of all six years in prison, then death on a charge of high treason. Thorell was so badly treated after his arrest that he lost an eye...

The same court sentenced an unemployed man with no means of support whatsoever to ten months in jail for stealing a loaf.

High treason for the worker Thorell: a firing squad, unless citizen Ebert exercises his presidential right of pardon (which is doubtful). And even if he is pardoned, the revolver shot of the classic "while trying to escape" still remains possible...

Ministerial Marxism

Herr Stresemann does not have the slightest concern about lightening the burden of his colleagues and collaborators, the SPD ministers. Tired of being reproached, by Herr von Kahr, for concessions to Marxism which he has never made, on October 24 he got the *National-Liberale Korrespondenz*, the official organ of his party, to publish a detailed response to the Bavarian dictator. Herr von Kahr will certainly not be convinced by it. But I'd give a lot to see the faces that the SPD ministers must have made while sampling this off-the-record prose.

Is it Marxism, enquires Herr Stresemann's paper, to repeal the last economic constraints, imposed by the state? As for the repeal of decrees dating from the time of demobilization at the end of the war concerning the protection of labor; the repeal of the tax on coal; the renunciation of parliamentary formalities and the enabling act giving exceptional powers; the founding of the new bank to issue Rentenmarks; the temporary suspension of the eight-hour day; the ending of export controls—is all that Marxism? Do not all these measures have as their aim the reconstruction of the capitalist economy?

From our side we can add:

And martial law directed exclusively against the working class?

And the never-ending indulgence of Berlin towards the arrogant fascism of Munich? And the military occupation of Saxony? And finally the ultimatum of October 27 to the workers' government in Dresden?—in a word the dictatorship of the generals? Is that Marxism? But why bother?

More and more the social democrats in government seem, to the bourgeois parties for whom they are dishonoring themselves, to be inferior and contemptible allies, in dealing with whom anything is permissible...

Besides, I think they are about to leave, driven out by an outburst of anger and disgust on the part of their own party...

"Real value" paper and wages

For some days everyone has been talking about paper money with "real value." On Saturday, October 27, the first small denomination notes of the Reich gold loan have been put into circulation, while we await the Rentenmark. Municipalities, and even large industrial firms, are authorized to issue paper money with real value guaranteed by a deposit of securities from the gold loan... The problem is solved.

Oh yes. Inflation, bankruptcy, the billion mark—it was all nothing, and now it's all over; recently the most optimistic estimates set the total real value of all German paper money in circulation at 120, 150 million gold marks. We think this estimate is greatly exaggerated. And they've just put into circulation, on the very first day, ten million dollars worth of small denomination notes for the gold loan—a hundred million in paper money at real value. Be patient; in a few weeks we shall have a billion worth. That's how easy it is to stave off national bankruptcy.

Think about it for a moment. First of all, if it was that easy, why not do it earlier? Secondly, if the gold loan is covered, if it has been a success, why didn't they say so? And finally, is a stable currency the main thing when you're in the position that capitalist Germany has reached?

It's possible to find an answer to the last two questions. The gold loan has not been a success; it hasn't given the state much; the individuals who contributed to it mainly got more worries: their complaints have filled the economic pages of the main newspapers. It is far from having adequate backing; whenever its price has not been artificially supported, it fell below the dollar: by 15 percent on October 1 and 3, by 25 percent on October 10. The issuing and putting into circulation of the small denomination notes of the gold loan constitute both a return to inflation and a speculation on the confidence—which in any case is non-existent!—of the public. The gold loan is quoted at a rate noticeably lower that the true rate of the dollar (today, October 26: dollar at New York, 80 billion marks; gold loan at Berlin, 65 billion) which stock exchange stratagems have diminished by 30 to 40 percent on the Berlin Exchange (today, October 26: New York 80, Berlin 52.6) and already the big stores will accept it only at a rate which is 10 to 15 percent lower than the official rate.

The Rentenmark will have no real value unless industry, commerce, agriculture and the banks want it to; and they will not want it unless it is in their interests, that is, if their economic and political plans triumph, which for the moment is very dubious. But even if we admit the possibility that tomorrow Germany will have paper money with real value, does it follow that the two million unemployed will get enough dole to live on? That the five million workers on short time will get enough to live on? That in general wages will meet the needs of workers? For it isn't enough for a worker to get something other than counterfeit money every Saturday; his pay has to guarantee bread for every day of the week. The most real values, if they only permit him to live three days out of six, are not much use to him.

A dole payment of two gold marks per day, to 1,500,000 un-employed, would cost Germany ninety million gold marks a month. No financial scheme can procure such a phenomenal sum. The unemployed will therefore carry on dying of hunger.

Without sacrificing all its profits, which it will never agree to do, German industry cannot proceed to any increase in wages. Al-ready the prices of its goods are higher than world market prices; its competitiveness has been abolished, and no longer being able to re-duce salaries, it thinks only of lengthening the working day. Wages paid in "real values" are possible, if not probable (and hasn't a start already been made?) The printing of paper marks continues. In any case, the payment of benefits and wages in banknotes that may pos-sibly be worth something will not bring any significant improve-ment to the condition of German workers. Perhaps a little less at the mercy of daily speculation, they will nonetheless remain hungry!

They are complementary

To judge by appearances, the conflict between Berlin and Munich, Stresemann and von Kahr, seems irreconcilable. In reality, the con-flict scarcely exists. Two years ago Herr Stresemann professed the opinions which today Herr von Kahr is vigorously proclaiming. As "republicans" they are birds of a feather, in the service of the same social class and are carrying out two different aspects of what is es-sentially the same policy, in two different contexts. They are not in conflict; they are complementary.

For the last three months we have seen in Germany, every day more marked and more daring, the general offensive of reaction, that is to say, of large-scale industry and the big property owners, against the working classes. Initially reaction attempted to take dic-tatorial power by a coup; faced with the dangers of civil war, it hesitated, withdrew, allowed the re-establishment of a Great Coalition cabinet; then another road to power presented itself; it took that route and persevered methodically; the job is to achieve dictatorship without too sudden a shock, by making important gains each day in a form which could be described as legal.

This is Stresemann's aim in Berlin and von Kahr's in Munich. Behind both of them there are the same sources of money. Each advance by Bavarian fascism allows the federal chancellor to display simultaneously his powerlessness to impose respect for democracy, the weakness of democracy and the political insignificance of the SPD. Each retreat by Stresemann encourages, stimulates and strengthens the reactionaries in Munich. The rulers in Berlin have as their obvious task to discredit the republican regime, to delude the proletariat for a little longer—just long enough to disarm it—in short, to prepare the way for a right wing dictatorship, for which the rulers in Munich are preparing an army and setting up a center of organization and influence, and to which they are giving great prestige.

Is this game conscious or not? In the minds of the majority of right wing politicians, there can be no doubt that it is envisaged with the greatest lucidity. Only the SPD and the center parties are doing their best not to recognize it. And even for them it has become difficult.

Fascist Bavaria has given the dictatorship to an anti-Semitic monarchist, has suppressed Communist organizations and press, bullied the social democrats, openly armed hundreds of thousands of reactionaries, confiscated part of the Reich's gold reserves, repealed various Reich laws, broken with the "legal dictator" in Berlin, Herr Gessler, stripped the Reich of part of its army, and taken under its protection a general in revolt against his superiors and placed him at the head of its army. But, "in the differences which have emerged between Berlin and Munich, it would be very wrong to see any attack on the constitutional order of the Republic"; these are the very words of an off-the-record statement a few days ago.

As for Saxony, it set up a workers' government and formed workers hundreds for the defense of the republic... An impermissible attack on the constitution!

And *Germania* (Catholic Center) remarks naïvely: "The Saxon government, which has responded to all the formal demands of the constitution, has been dismissed by the Reich government, which is not entitled to act thus by any paragraph of the constitution."

One more betrayal

Let's remember the facts. A press campaign—which was so dishonest that the (bourgeois) DDP denounced its odious nature in a telegram to Herr Stresemann—informed Germany that "Communist terror" was being established in Saxon. These were the "new Tartars." General Müller clashed with Herr Zeigner. There were rumors that General Müller would be dismissed (Bavaria rebels against Berlin, the von Lossow incident). "Easing of the situation in Saxony." Meanwhile, over fifty thousand Reichswehr troops invaded Saxony. The first murders of proletarians went unpunished. Left social democracy showed itself to be much less determined, less combative than had been believed on either side of the barricade. "Relaxation of tension with Bavaria": Berlin accepted the accomplished fact. On Saturday, October 28,[3] an ultimatum from Stresemann to Zeigner: the workers' government must resign or the Communists must leave it within twenty-four hours. On October 29, the Zeigner cabinet refused to back down. On October 30, Dr. Heinze, the Reich commissioner for the "free state of Saxony" went to Dresden. Troops, led by a mil-

---

3 October 28 was in fact a Sunday.

itary band, occupied the ministries. Squads of infantrymen, with bayonets fixed to their guns, drove the workers' ministers out of their offices. Zeigner left his office surrounded by loaded guns ready for firing. General Müller banned the Landtag from meeting. The workers' government declared itself to be the only legal government; the ADGB and the unions of civil servants and white-collar workers, the SPD and the KPD issued calls for a three-day general strike in protest. The publication of these calls was banned.

Was this the great class battle we have all been waiting for for months? October 30...

The next day, Germany learned that a right wing socialist government (Fellisch) had been formed at Dresden. Social democrats had accepted, from the hands of Herr Heinze, the ministerial portfolios which had been brutally snatched from their party comrades. Bowing and scraping to the Man of Order, they entered the ministries, which were still occupied by troops. Smirking officers saluted them. The general strike no longer had any meaning. A strike for what? For whom? Socialists had regained power. Virtually nothing had happened, after all! *Vorwärts* explained that you really couldn't leave the Communists in power in Saxony... Herr Stresemann was right. All the blame lay with the Communists.

The right wing press exclaimed along with the *Deutsche Allgemeine Zeitung:* "At last!" The whole democratic press condemned the chancellor's coup against red Saxony. For having criticized "Herr Stresemann's putsch" too severely, the *Berliner Volkszeitung* (DDP) has been suspended.

Only *Vorwärts* considered that there was no doubt as to the legality of the decisions of citizen Ebert and Herr Stresemann.

4 Vereinigte Sozialdemokratische Partei Deutschlands: the official name of the SPD after the merger with the USPD in 1922.

Not that it approved them completely; on the contrary, it was very grieved. The SPD ministers explained that it was only under protest that they endorsed the measures against Saxony; moreover, if they didn't walk out, they didn't actually vote for them either... There is nothing so ambiguous, so disloyal, so pathetic, so confused as the explanations of the central leadership of the United Social Democratic Party.[4] "Do not be so quick to judge us... We are going to consider... We shall explain to you... We shall act..." These men feel that reaction is playing with them, is dishonoring them. They have just stuck a dagger in the back of the German revolution, but the deed was done very clumsily: their whole party saw the criminal act and can see the depth of the wound...

The bourgeoisie has just given this debased and apathetic social democracy the humiliation it deserves. The Berlin *Deutsche Zeitung* of October 30 declares: "Social democracy has been overpowered. It has bowed down right to the ground in the hope of avoiding the blow. According to all the rules of tactics, this is the moment for its enemies to strike. Now or never!" The more it degrades itself, the more its masters despise it. The more it retreats, the more it is in danger. It's an object lesson.

The threat against Thuringia

There is a precise, material danger, unfortunately worse than that which is facing the SPD, confronting the betrayed proletariat. Red Saxony is a demolished citadel. There remains Thuringia, on the road to Berlin, between Bavaria and the red capital of Germany. The

---

5 The Bund Bayern und Reich, a monarchist, Christian, anti-Semitic organization with 30,000 armed men.

Sozialistische Parlementarische Korrespondenz (Socialist Parliamentary Correspondence) has revealed what sort of a plot is being hatched against Thuringia, where there is still a workers' government.

The fascist organization Bavaria and Reich[5] is watching the Thuringian frontier. At Coburg, Kronach and Bamberg illegal detachments were already gathering their forces on October 22. Hitler and Ehrhardt had their headquarters at Coburg. The following illegal units were there: nine companies of Ehrhardt's naval brigade, three companies of shock troops from the National Socialist party, three from the Oberland, a battery of four cannon, a train equipped with two radio transmitters and various groups from the Young German Order.

The infantrymen wore helmets. The former Duke of Coburg-Gotha was present at the maneuvers. Cannon were seen at Fechheim (three), at Weissenturm (two) and at Burg (also two). A division similar to that occupying Coburg was concentrated at Kronach. At Bamberg, the Reichsflagge organization was deploying its forces; an area was reserved for artillery and machine guns. Aeroplanes could be seen bearing the fascist swastika. "These troops are paid in Austrian crowns and French francs." (*Vorwärts*).

They are threatening the industrial regions of central Germany. When General Müller and the SPD ministers in the Fellisch government have sufficiently demoralized and disarmed red Saxony, when Herr Stresemann has extracted from citizens Robert Schmidt, Sollmann and Radbruch all the possible low tricks that will benefit the bourgeoisie, then the gangs of Hitler and Ehrhardt, duly backed up by the Reichswehr, will take their turn on the stage.

In the Social Democracy: The wave of nausea

The Socialist President Ebert has had the workers' government of Dresden dissolved. The Socialist leaders Wels and Dittmann have formed the Fellisch government at Dresden. The masses of the party, represented by their officials—who represent them badly!—are disgusted.

In this respect the meeting of SPD office-holders in Berlin of October 31 was significant. A woman militant, Wurm, declared to applause from the entire hall that "if the Communists are wrong, they still want to serve the proletariat," while others pretend to be mistaken in order to serve reaction. A delegate from Freiberg (Saxony) described the appalling massacre of October 27. The Reichswehr attacked unarmed crowds. It sent artillery into action against the unemployed. Armoured cars, patrolling through quiet streets, responded to the throwing of a stone by machine-gun fire that left sixteen people dead. Fire was opened on workers' stretcher-bearers who were picking up the dead and wounded; their Red Cross flag was riddled with bullet holes. In total, twenty-seven dead, twenty-two seriously wounded and fifty others injured. For the first time voices were heard calling so clearly and strongly for civil war. By an overwhelming majority the meeting associated itself with the decision by the SPD office-holders in Leipzig to demand the expulsion of citizen Ebert from the party… The brief resolution ended with the words: "This meeting finds it unnecessary to give reasons for this demand."

The SPD leadership and its parliamentary fraction have nonetheless attempted (today, November 1) a final effort to remain in power after long discussions in the course of which it was observed that "the SPD is far from exercising within the government the influence which it has a right to"(!)… The social democratic ministers of the German bourgeoisie will only keep their portfolios:

♦   if a civil state of emergency replaces martial law

(Gessler, von Seeckt, Müller, Reinhardt, etc. remain at
the head of the Reichswehr)

♦   if there is energetic action with regard to Bavaria (has
there ever been anything else?!)

♦   if the police alone has the responsibility for maintaining order in Saxony... (at last...)

A hundred SPD deputies out of 130 have voted for this moderate and belated "ultimatum" to Herr Stresemann.

The avalanche

While these sad comedies are being enacted on the political stages
of Munich, Berlin and Dresden, the revolution is advancing like a
slow but sure and powerful avalanche. The extent of the financial
bankruptcy—and the indescribable suffering it involves—is sufficient proof.

From October 11 to 20, Reich expenses rose to
324,117,027,000,000,000 marks: 324 quadrillion. Income, on the
other hand, reached the total of 2.5 quadrillion (to be precise,
2,456,918,405 million), that is less than one percent of expenditure. On October 20, the floating debt of the Reich reached 407
quadrillion... But then the dollar was worth only about twenty billion; today it is worth 200—and I am a trillionaire just like everyone else, which I assure you isn't much fun... Banknotes for a
trillion marks have appeared. It seems that every day paper money
worth over 500 trillion marks is being issued. It is regretted that it
is not yet possible to issue a quadrillion per day, for want of paper.
They are also printing, night and day, the new "real value" paper,
the gold loan: 3,000,000 in paper gold dollars have already been
put into circulation! and have already lost between 30 percent and
50 percent on the black market...

According to the official cost of living index, the general increase in prices between October 22 and 29, has reached a peak of 349 percent. In the last few days, with an official exchange rate of about 65 million marks to the dollar, the prices of foodstuffs and other essential articles correspond to a rate for the dollar of between 200 and 300 billion. And this difference was mainly paid by poor people who have no dollars...

By early November the Stresemann cabinet was in disarray; the SPD ministers withdrew on November 2, 1923. Meanwhile the right wing threat from Bavaria was growing ever stronger.

Two anniversaries: November 7 and 9

Correspondance internationale, November 10, 1923

This year, the proximity of these two revolutionary anniversaries will force itself on all minds in Germany with pitiless rigor.

November 7, 1917 (October 25 in the Julian calendar): led by the Bolsheviks the proletarians of Petrograd seized the Winter Palace; the proletarians of Moscow entered the Kremlin... An era of unspeakable suffering opened for the Russian people: but it was also an era of heroism, of victory, of resurrection. Russia, reduced during some dark days to a territory no bigger than the Grand Duchy of Muscovy in 1500, went on to extend once more from the Baltic to the Pacific Ocean, from the Arctic to the Black Sea. In four years of bitter warfare, the great capitalist powers would not succeed in defeating it. It finally imposed on them respect, peace and trade. It was to remain an invincible revolutionary stronghold, the place of asylum and refuge for all defeated revolutionaries: it would give itself new laws, boldly reform its ways of life and persevere—by the harshest paths, doubtless, but freely—on the road to socialism.

November 9, 1918: the efforts of the sailors at Kiel and Cuxhafen brought down the façade of the German Empire. For a year, until the tragic days of January 1919, when Liebknecht and Rosa Luxemburg died, the German social democracy, allied to the volunteer corps of the bourgeoisie, Noske allied to Ehrhardt, was to build on the corpses of proletarians the edifice of a democratic republic. It constantly threatened the crowds inspired by the Russian example with famine, with foreign intervention, with an outburst of reaction… At the end of five years of social democratic democracy, Germany, powerless, is observing French intervention in the Rhineland and the Ruhr; its twenty million proletarians and its ten million people in humble circumstances are hungry; armed reaction is striding towards power… Because it postponed the final struggle for five years, the German proletariat merely has greater difficulties to overcome. Today, as in 1919, when the Spartacists showed it to them, there is only one road to salvation: the one where the revolutionaries have gone before them

Two anniversaries; one great confrontation in the eyes of history between reformist and revolutionary methods.

For a right wing dictatorship

"They are complementary," I wrote recently about Stresemann and von Kahr. Just take a look. Remember that about a week before the social democrats left the Great Coalition (November 2) Herr von Kahr had made known his intention to have no further dealings with a Reich government "under Marxist influence," that is, containing social democrats. On this point too Herr Stresemann satisfied the Bavarian reactionaries—enough to encourage them, not enough to disarm them: that is his role.

So citizens Robert Schmidt, Radbruch and Sollmann are unceremoniously sacked from the Reich government. It would be the right time for the SPD to draw up a balance sheet of its collaboration with the bourgeois parties, which has cost working-class Germany the incredible poverty of recent days, the dollar at one and a half trillion marks, the dictatorship of the generals, the daily murder of workers, some two to three hundred corpses of those who have died of hunger piled up at the feet of Ebert's presidential chair. But in the drab manifesto published in *Vorwärts* on November 4, the SPD blames the Communists for the bloodshed—in Hamburg—in order once more to reject their proposal for a united front... And without containing a single robust word, this document ends with an appeal to the unity and steadfastness of the party, powerful guarantees of the security of the German republic, the only ground on which the struggle for socialism is possible.

The same issue of *Vorwärts* comments on strange rumors emanating from Munich. On Saturday, November 3, a fresh coup was reported in Bavaria, the removal of the Knilling government by von Kahr—though it had caused so little trouble—and the sending of an ultimatum to Berlin demanding the immediate establishment of a right wing dictatorship. If this did not happen, Bavarian troops would march on the capital. This news is now denied, but in a confused manner, accepted as half or two-thirds true.

The DNVP and the Bavarian minister of justice, Doctor Gürtner, have in fact voted a resolution in this sense, and have, moreover, demanded Ebert's resignation. On the borders of Thuringia, fascist troops continue to mass, not without incidents; several times in the last few days the Thuringian police have been shot at... Hitler, in hysterical speeches, is telling his people to be ready to march on Berlin (Munich, October 31) in order to "raise the old black, white and red flag over the imperial palace." Ludendorff, who writes leading articles for the *Völkischer Beobachter*, is currently named as one of the leaders called on to direct the coming military operations.

For a long time there has been the greatest confusion as far as information is concerned: there is no serious news item which is not successively announced off the record, then denied, re-stated, modified and finally confirmed. Lies, false information, the official denial of true facts, and false "off the record state-ments" are the means used daily and methodically by the main-stream press and by the state to prepare public opinion, to deceive it, mislead it, or surprise it, as the situation requires. The military offensive against Saxony was announced by Stinnes' newspaper eight days before it officially began. General von Los-sow's revolt was kept silent for three days before being made public. Bavaria's categorical refusal to dismiss von Lossow and put the Reichswehr back under the command of Herr Gessler was almost completely ignored. The "denials" made today do not explain why, on Saturday, November 3, Herr Stresemann, after a discussion with the Bavarian ambassador von Preger, hurriedly left the cabinet during a meeting in order to confer with the pres-ident of the Republic and the Reichswehr minister.

Fascist Bavaria is strong and armed. The Reich government is weak and disarmed. In Berlin, even von Kahr has the uncondi-tional support of the landowners' German National People's Party and of heavy industry. Either he will dictate his will or he will try to impose it by force. Besides, German fascism is in a dilemma: the fact that it is now fully armed, its political successes, the weakness of the social democracy, repeated promises of a prompt liquidation of the regime born on November 9, 1918, and finally the interests of the capitalist groups which are financing it—but don't intend to finance it indefinitely without visible results—everything is push-ing it to take action in order not to be discredited.

In the last days of October, when the attack on the workers' government in Dresden was beginning, other significant rumors were circulating in "informed circles." There was talk of a reconcili-ation between von Kahr, Ludendorff and Hitler: it was announced that a Reich government would be proclaimed in Munich… Let's remember this idea at a time when a nationalist campaign is being launched against Ebert "under whose presidency one cannot imagine a national government" according to the *Deutsche Zeitung,* whose sentiments are endorsed by the *Kreuzzeitung* (Gazette of the Cross) and by the landowners' *Deutsche Tageszeitung.*

We should take satisfaction in this vigorous clarity of the reactionary offensive. We need even more to shake social democracy from its unbelievable inertia. On the day when a man like von Kahr finally decides go beyond threats and to take action, it may well be that all the working masses and a good half of the ruined middle classes will stand up against him, led by the party of the revolutionary proletariat.

(A detail, indicative of the impotence of Herr Stresemann and Herr Gessler towards the Bavarians. A decree issued by Herr Gessler, dated October 30 and published after five days delay, has just banned until further notice the *Völkischer Beobachter* on all the territory of the Reich, except Bavaria…)

The financial muddle

I would say that the "financial chaos has reached its peak," but the old cliché would be inaccurate: every day, in the endless realm of bankruptcy, new records are set in order to be broken the following day.

We have, or are on the point of having, in circulation ten different sorts of paper money, of which four apparently have no real value, since the other six are called "real value."

1: The paper mark, of which the billion is now the smallest unit.
2, 3, 4: The paper marks issued by towns (the states of the Reich, the directors of the railways).

5: The gold loan *(Goldanleihe)* or German dollar.

6: The Rentenmark with "real value."

7: Vouchers with real value, issued by banks and commercial firms.

8, 9, 10: Paper with real value issued by towns, states and railways. I'm not sure this is all.

Who profits from this variety of paper money? It serves only the speculation of financiers, who have all become very questionable. And at whose expense does this profitable speculation take place? At that of the state and the mass of workers.

The gold loan is the object of scandalous gambling made even easier by the official—and artificial—rate of the dollar on the Berlin Stock Exchange and by the conspicuous ineptitude of the Reichsbank. On the one hand, they have striven to give the gold loan a rate higher than that of the dollar; on the other hand, they haven't been able to satisfy the demands of the public to whom the possession of any foreign currency remains forbidden. The result is a further fall in value of the paper mark—which we suggest should be called the *wages-mark*—scandalous losses for the Reichsbank, scandalous gains for a few profiteers. Here are the details, according to *Vorwärts*:

A shrewd banker has bought 2,000 "German dollars" at the rate of 65 billion marks, that is, for 130 trillion. The Reichsbank delivers the notes to him only after a long delay; it remains understood that the banker should pay the *Goldanleihe* on the day of delivery at the rate of the day when he subscribed. The Reichsbank, in exchange for its 2,000 German dollars, receives in paper marks only the value of 200 dollars. The banker has gained 1,800 dollars; the Reichsbank has lost them. These abuses have been widespread for weeks. There is now talk of remedying the situation by making people pay for the gold loan at the rate of the delivery date... "This scandal," says the social democratic paper, "goes far beyond that of credits in paper marks…" Worse and worse, isn't it?

But since the gold loan has no real backing, it will be subsequently exchanged for Rentenmarks. The new bank issuing Rentenmarks opens a credit of 900 million for the Reich this year, well below the real needs of the nation. If the 500 million of the gold loan have to be deducted from this credit, what will remain for the state? The gold loan will have brought it nothing but losses; the Rentenmark will just slip through its fingers. The state will have submitted itself to the financial control of big capitalism without deriving the slightest profit.

Another disastrous aspect of things. The rates quoted on the New York Stock Exchange in some sense regularize those of the black market in Berlin itself. At New York, on November 2, the dollar was quoted at 1,428 billion marks. The same day, in Berlin, the dollar and the gold loan were officially worth 625 billion. On November 3, the dollar was worth 1,219 billion at New York and only 418 billion at Berlin. The unconvertible rate of the paper mark is decreed at the rate of a billion for a gold pfennig. Germany has become the country where the dollar can be bought most cheaply. Will not international speculators take substantial advantage of this in order to siphon off what real values are left in the country?

Prices in Germany are fixed by the rates on the New York Stock Exchange, so that the artificial fall in the dollar, solely profitable to international gamblers, is achieved at the expense of the masses of consumers.

The purchasing power of the gold pfennig has fallen in staggering proportions. In 1914 a rye loaf cost 14 gold pfennigs; on October 31, 1923 it cost 18; likewise, rice has gone from 25 to 32 pfennigs; sauerkraut from 8 to 13; beans, from 20 to 38; beef, from

85 to 142; pork, from 75 to 330; bacon, from 95 to 464; butter, from 125 to 181; sugar, from 25 to 40; fish, from 30 to 90; an egg, from 7 to 19; coal (a hundred bricks of compressed coal) from 100 to 178.5. These figures give us a simplified measure of the cost of living. We should recall these facts, while the representatives of workers and employers are discussing (since October 31), in meetings chaired by the labor minister Brauns, the fixing of wages to gold values. The invariable argument of the employers is that there can be no question of a return to peace-time wages; "current wages must be in proportion to general impoverishment." Herr Brauns adds that they could not be paid in real values except "to some extent" and "after some time."

Effects and causes

Last week, on October 31, Berliners paid 64 billion for a pound of smoked sausage, with the dollar at a rate of 65 billion. Meanwhile, at a meeting held in the town hall, the mayor of Berlin said that "more than 300,000 Berlin workers are unemployed." A report by Frau Weil made known the destitution of twelve thousand orphans sheltered and nourished by the city, which has accommodation equipped to take only 4,000 children. Often up to three abandoned children have to sleep in the same bed...

I met a doctor from a poor area, one of those who, a few months ago, had to go on strike to obtain a very modest salary from the sickness insurance fund. "Since the onset of autumn," he told me, "we are all seeing a sudden development of illnesses caused by hunger. Scrofula is normal among infants in working-

---

1 A railway station in the eastern part of Berlin.

class districts. Dropsy occurs frequently. There has been a reappearance of the 'hunger sickness' which we saw at the worst times during the war: the flesh swells, goes dull and offers no resistance to the touch. Bone decay, forms of enteritis and all the varieties of tuberculosis in the long run gnaw away the organism which has been enfeebled by starvation. Have you noticed the complexion of faces you see, for example, near the Silesia station?[1] This greyish, yellowish, discolored hue puts the brand of hunger on people's foreheads. A diet which is inadequate in fat, sugar and meat exhausts all the reserves of the organism whose capacity for work rapidly diminishes. Are you surprised that these people are slow to awaken to revolutionary consciousness? Remember that their vital energies have been undermined by famine..."

"Do you know what is going on in the schools? A rapid survey, carried out on October 27 in nine school districts of Berlin has recorded the presence in class of 470 children who had not eaten anything all day! The parents warn the teachers: if the child faints, don't be surprised! And then, 'don't be too hard on her: she's hungry.'"

We arrived at the Alexanderplatz—one of the busiest squares in Berlin; comparable to the Place de la République in Paris—to find a long queue of old men and women, of people of no discernible age, of children with poor little wizened faces. "Look! They're waiting for the soup kitchen."

I bought a paper for 10 billion and found the new prices: milk, 20 billion for a litre; gas and water, 21 billion for a cubic meter, tram ticket 10 billion; loaf (four pounds), 25 billion... My paper also told me that on the other hand: "Before the war Herr Hugo Stinnes' fortune was already estimated at 100 million gold marks, and like all the big industrialists he was able to multiply it several times during the war. The Montan factories and the electricity works, in which Herr Stinnes possesses the majority of shares, his shipping companies, his coal marketing company at Mülheim and his transatlantic shipping firm in Hamburg are each worth about a hundred million gold marks. To this must be added his involvement in business abroad, in the mining industry, oil shares, banking, shipping, his various possessions in Germany itself: newspapers, printing presses, paper-works, forestry—the whole constituting a fortune which doubtless rises to billions in gold marks and could be expressed in paper marks only by using astronomical figures... Only posterity will know the truth about a financial power which, exceeding that of the likes of Morgan, Rockefeller, Cecil Rhodes, Harriman, Carnegie, Rothschild, Vanderbilt, has reached legendary proportions and given birth to a sort of myth..."[2]

The death of a people, the end of a culture; what an inexhaustible source of wealth!

The suicide of the German republic

Will the suicide of the German republic be consummated for its fifth anniversary? Fearful gatherings of people are arguing passionately outside newsagents' shops. Papers are too dear; people come to read the headlines and what can be seen of the front pages in the shop windows. Then they discuss with their neighbors, creating curious little open-air meetings.

The most recent news, extremely alarming, has made the republican papers take on a panic-stricken tone. In Bavaria, on the borders of Thuringia, in Pomerania, in Mecklenburg, in East Prussia, in Silesia, fascist forces are mobilizing for a military march on Berlin, announced for November 7. The mass of the fascist army is concen-

---

2 Almanac of the Oderberg District, Dortmund, quoted by the *Vossische Zeitung* (Voss Gazette) of November 4). [Serge's note.]

trated on the borders of Thuringia under the orders of captain Ehrhardt who is seen as the "dictator of tomorrow." Erhardt is said to have called on the Stresemann government to resign... The Young German Order from central Germany has been mobilized on the night of November 3. The Stahlhelm association has mobilized its five thousand local groups. At Coburg, the fascist headquarters, the streets are full of young men in full uniform, with white armbands, helmets and rifles. Captain CL Faber, correspondent for the *Montag Morgen* (Radical) in this "theatre of war," notes the presence of concentrations of artillery at Burggrub and four thousand Austrian fascists at Kronach. "The fascists," he writes, "seem to be intending to make a sudden attack towards Eisenach-Erfurt-Weimar and thus cut the Stuttgart line, that is the line to north Germany; at the same time they would take over some important arms factories." Meanwhile they are carrying out requisitions, expulsions of Jews from Coburg, maneuvers and troop reviews under the inspection of the escapee from the Leipzig High Court, whom another journalist calls Ehrhardt, "for whom all doors are opened."

The government knows what is going on. Is it counting on the Reichswehr? "The Reichswehr will never fire on the Reichswehr," claim the nationalists. Moreover, the Bavarian fascists seem not to be irregulars and to be acting with the approval of Herr von Kahr. The radical press wants a call for republican volunteers. A meeting of republican youth (November 4) has decided in principle to answer the call. Herr Sollmann, recently a SPD minister, spoke some memorable words there, doubly memorable for a Socialist and an ex-minister of Stresemann: "If the Republic dies," he said, "it will be because of the cowardice of its leaders." How right he is, and how well he knows himself!

---

3 The *Zentrale* was a committee smaller than the Central Committee, which looked after the day-to-day running of the KPD.

Is there not a lot of deceit mingled with this cowardice? No measures have been taken against the fascists in recent days. But *Vorwärts* has made "sensational revelations" about the Communist danger. Brandler, for whose arrest there is a warrant, has gone into hiding. It is said that they are looking for the whole *Zentrale*³ of the KPD. In Berlin there have been numerous arrests of militants accused of taking part in the formation of workers' hundreds. A ministerial edict has banned the congress of factory councils from being held anywhere in Germany...

The fruits of Social Democratic treachery

It seems that we are in a state of complete political confusion, but that is only an illusion; reaction is at work. The departing SPD ministers have not yet been replaced. The act giving exceptional powers, which was to be valid only as long as the Great Coalition cabinet was in power, and which was therefore automatically can-celed by the resignations of citizens Schmidt, Sollmann and Rad-bruch, remains in force. There was talk of making up the cabinet with non-party figures. Then it was admitted that, yielding to de-mands from Bavaria and heavy industry, Herr Stresemann was ne-gotiating the entry of the DNVP into his government. That would amount to the establishment of a right wing dictatorship with the appearances of legality. The DNVP are imposing as a condition the removal of the SPD from the Prussian government and the granting of the most important portfolios to their party. Some cu-rious feelers have been put out. There has been talk of a directory to be headed by Herr Minoux, who has just resigned from his job as general manager of Herr Hugo Stinnes' companies in order to devote himself to politics. Count Reventlow has published an ac-count of a recent interview between Herr Hergt, one of the DNVP leaders, and General von Seeckt, commander-in-chief of the Reichswehr, at which perfect agreement is said to have been reached. It seems that everything is combining to establishing a Stinnes dictatorship, perhaps soon a Stinnes-Ludendorff dictatorship.

Let's dwell on the numerous indications of a coup in the course of preparation, or more precisely already being carried out. Herr von Preger, Bavarian representative in Berlin, has given a member of the staff of the *Münchener-Augsburger Abendzeitung* (Munich and Augsburg Evening News) precise statements as to what his government wants: "We remain German with all our soul. We have no intention of splitting off from the Reich. But we want an end to what are called the gains of the revolution and to restore order…" This political program can be expressed in three words: Bavarianization of Germany.

Herr von Kahr, continuing to apply this program, has banned the sale in Bavaria of the main Berlin liberal papers: *Berliner Tageblatt, Vossische Zeitung, Mittag Zeitung* (Midday News), *Vorwärts*, and also the *Frankfurter Zeitung* (Frankfurt News), (November 5). That's enough to tell us what he means by the freedom of the press. In Saxony, General Müller means exactly the same; he has just banned the publication of any information other than official communiqués about incidents in which the Reichswehr has used its weapons—that is, the murder of workers. At Zwickau, the same general has banned a conference of SPD office-holders.

General Reinhardt is operating in red Thuringia. And what he is doing would be quite unbelievable if recent events in Germany had not accustomed us to every kind of duplicity on the part of the official government, to every kind of cowardice on the part of the social democrats who tolerate this duplicity and cover up for it, and every kind of effrontery on the part of the armed reactionaries. Twenty to thirty thousand Bavarian nationalist volunteers, paid by the Munich government and the tycoon Hugenberg, have gathered on the frontier of workers' Thuringia. The castle of the Duke of

Coburg is serving as Hitler's official headquarters. Interviewed by a staff reporter of the *Berliner Tageblatt*, the head of the Coburg police said that "nothing now can prevent the explosion of a national movement." The central committee of the Stahlhelm association sent a formal appeal to Herr Stresemann on November 5, urging him to establish a national dictatorship. The statement concluded with the words: "Act so that others are not forced to act!" In bourgeois democratic circles and even in Catholic circles there is great alarm. The government has announced that it will deal with any situation that may arise by sending Reichswehr troops to the frontier between Thuringia and Bavaria. But General Reinhardt, who is required by Herr Gessler's instructions (according to *Vorwärts* and according to a letter from the Reichswehr minister himself, made public on November 8) to defend Thuringia against any possible attack by nationalist gangs, has had posters put up in all the towns of a state where, in the opinion of the bourgeois press "there is exemplary order," declaring that he "has come to restore order, to put an end to red terror and to disarm the workers' hundreds." The defense of Thuringia has become military occupation and the disarmament of this proletarian state! By a decree of November 5, however, Herr Gessler has taken upon himself to protect the Reichswehr and to suppress any offense against the army.

In effect, we are already living in a regime of reactionary dictatorship; it lacks formal authority, something which is quite a problem since the working class, in a situation of being defeated without having fought, remains formidable to the ruling parties whose aim is a brutal intensification of the exploitation of labor. Now we can see the terrible consequences of the betrayals of social democracy, repeated and obstinately continued (entry of the SPD into the Great Coalition, subsequent reconstitution of the Stresemann cabinet, proclamation of martial law, vote for the act giving exceptional powers) and also the unforgivable failure of the left social democrats who let slip the opportunity for a workers' offensive when the troops entered Saxony. Now the enemy class has taken the initiative. In the class war, battles which were not joined—retreats—can be counted as defeats and cost as dear as defeats.

Pogroms in Berlin

Today, November 5, we have seen in the center of Berlin some authentic pogroms in the old Russian style. This terrifying display of human bestiality, which everywhere the Soviet regime has effortlessly made impossible, occurred in the capital of Germany and was able to continue with impunity for almost an entire day. In a street close to the Alexanderplatz[4], a young Jew was grabbed in the street, stripped of his clothes and beaten; he escaped naked from a jeering mob and got away with his life only thanks to the courage of a master butcher who hid him in his shop and then stood at the door with an axe keeping everyone out. In another nearby street, just like at Zhitomir under Tsar Nicholas II, the bedding and crockery of Jewish families were thrown out of the windows. That happened right in front of the windows of the *Polizeipräsidium*[5] and a barracks of green police. The police intervened only belatedly, gently and apparently with reluctance. A Jewish doctor (a patriotic bourgeois with a war medal) says that police officers drove past a group which was knocking him about and refused him any effective protection. Wouldn't you imagine you were reading a report from Odessa, dated 1905?

During and after the disturbances I went through the districts where the anti-Semitic riot took place. I got a very clear impression of an organized action. I saw groups of young "unemployed" anti-Semites going up the Friedrichstrasse, clearly led by the inevitable cy-

4 A square in central Berlin.
5 Police headquarters.

clists who in Germany have the job of stewarding all political demonstrations. Moreover, for months the nationalist press, led by the *Völkischer Beobachter*, has been advocating the "liberation of Germany from the Jewish yoke." And events even more abominable than those in Berlin took place near Coburg, in the region occupied by the Bavarians. In the village of Altenhausen on November 5, uniformed nationalists surrounded the homes of several Jewish families and made them appear before a sort of court martial where the majority of the adults were sentenced to be hanged on the spot. The victims of this atrocious hoax escaped only after a bad dream lasting a whole night in which they were robbed of everything and ill-treated.

We should stress that these pogroms are not the work of the unemployed as such, but of a very particular minority recruited among the unemployed by the nationalist agitators. In the main districts of Berlin, large spontaneous demonstrations of the unemployed have taken place without any sort of outrages occurring. It's true that bakeries and pork-butchers' shops were looted all over the place. But these actions should not be confused with those of the anti-Semites, although the police have persisted in lumping them together and have announced, to the great pleasure of the shopkeepers, that five hundred and thirty looters have been arrested (November 7).

In Germany, just as in Tsarist Russia, anti-Semitism is the necessary diversion provided by nationalism for the anger of the unthinking crowds and the brutality of the hired rabble which it needs to control the streets and create the illusion of a popular movement. The police did not act severely against the Berlin pogroms, probably because they were part of the theatrical staging intended to prepare opinion for the advent of a right wing dictatorship.

Via bankruptcy to capitalist dictatorship

On the day when the hunger riots and pogroms in Berlin began, the dollar was worth, at the official rate, 420 billion, and a three-pound wholemeal loaf cost 140 billion. A ruinously expensive measure, disastrous like all those taken in the financial sphere. The five hundred million from the gold loan which was supposed to provide the general public with a stable means of exchange have disappeared without trace in circulation, which is monopolized by wealthy speculators. These are making huge profits according to a plan which can be sketched out as follows:

♦ The financial speculator buys from the state, at a nominal rate, "German dollars" which he pays for in paper marks (and which he often arranges to pay in arrears at one fifth or one tenth of their official value).

♦ He deposits in the state loan bank his real-value notes and receives a credit in paper marks which can be reimbursed in paper marks, and with these he recommences operations.

♦ Alternatively, he sells his "German dollars" in private dealings at five or six times their face value (about two trillion with an official rate of 420 or 625 billion).

♦ With the paper marks he has now got back, he buys, at the face value of 420 or 625 billion, genuine American dollars, which in reality, on all the world's exchanges, are worth seven to ten times more, and which he rapidly smuggles abroad.

The result of these various operations multiplied infinitely is the bankruptcy of people on small fixed incomes, the exploitation of the mass of consumers and the systematic theft of state wealth.

Since the five hundred million from the gold loan is already exhausted, the Stresemann cabinet has just decreed the issuing of a new gold loan of three hundred million at six percent. A fictitious value, established without any sort of backing, destined to be stolen like the first issue. These eight hundred million in "real value" paper, which speculation has managed to swallow up in a fortnight, can be reimbursed in Rentenmarks still to come. So, before even having been collected, the first credit annuity in Rentenmarks granted to the Reich by the capitalist corporations' and which was to the sum of nine hundred million in gold, is about to be exhausted.

This fact should be brought to light, as well as the deliberate delays to the issuing of Rentenmarks, for they explain this mad financial policy. The bankruptcy of the Reich remains an incomparable source of profits for capitalist and financial circles, at whose mercy it moreover places the state. By means of the bankrupting of the democratic republic, which they don't even want to hear tell of any more (in official government documents there is no longer any reference to "defense of the republic" but only to the "safeguarding of German unity"), these circles have achieved financial, economic and political dictatorship.

Nearly ninety different sorts of paper money with "real value" are in circulation, issued by states, cities, chambers of commerce, public bodies and large industrial companies. But wages are still paid in paper marks. The ultimatum of the ADGB to Herr Stresemann—an ultimatum which led to the launching of the small denomination notes of the gold loan, which you can't find anywhere—was stillborn. But it seems that nothing can now disturb the unimaginable passivity, the vast cowardice of the great social democratic organizations.

Though the tide had turned, Germany remained profoundly unstable. The KPD was ousted from the Thuringian government. On November 8, Hitler attempted a putsch in Bavaria, but he was abandoned by his allies and ended up in jail.

Hitler: A fascist ideology

Correspondance internationale, November 17, 1923

Even in the opinion of some of his political admirers, Adolf Hitler
has just come to a miserable end. A few months ago, at Nuremberg,
the leader of the National Socialist Party reviewed nearly a hundred
thousand well-armed troops. He had just assembled nearly thirty
thousand men on the frontier with Thuringia. He thought the time
had come to move from threats to actions, and intoxicated with the
popularity he had achieved with a glib talent as an orator, the support of the authorities, the persistent advertising of the bourgeois
press and the secret funds of Herr Hugenberg, he thought he could
become, by firing a few revolver shots into the ceiling of a public
meeting hall in Munich, something like a new Emperor of Germany. "I am assuming the leadership of the affairs of the Reich," he
calmly announced on the evening of the putsch. Where does this
failed Mussolini come from? He is about thirty-five. Before the war
he was a sign-painter and not German! He is Austrian or rather
Czech German.[1] He only recently became a citizen of the Reich.
During the war, as an NCO then, it is said, as an officer, he didn't
distinguish himself in any way. There has been some difficulty in
creating retrospectively a certain reputation for brave deeds.

His successes as an organizer are indisputable but are not particularly surprising. A political adventurer, given suitable support
by the reactionary forces in power and financed by big capitalists,
can always, in periods of poverty and upheaval, recruit gangs who
are ready for anything. This is the only way to explain the spread of

---

1 Hitler was born in Austria, and his paintings were mainly postcard-sized copies
which were hawked around pubs. Serge's account shows just how little known
Hitler still was in 1923.

what has oddly been called the "national socialist movement." Curious to understand its ideology, I sometimes read the *Völkischer Beobachter* (The Popular Observer), its major daily paper based in Munich, made famous by the incident it provoked between the Reich and Bavaria. I also have before me the report given by this paper of a meeting held on the parade ground at Munich, on October 30 this year, with the leaders of the party and attended by several thousand. The honorary president of the National Socialist Party, Anton Drexler, is just as unknown to the general public in Germany as the other main speakers, Max Weber,[2] Hermann Esser and Dietrich Eckart. The great man, the party tribune, is "our Adolf Hitler," and constantly every effort is made to stress his mission of saving Germany and his inestimable personal merits. The very mention of his name unleashes "enthusiastic applause." His speech takes up three columns and is a curious document as to the demoralization, intelligence and ideological poverty of the crowd he is addressing...

Hitler's main argument is that parliamentarism has ruined Germany. All ills spring from the parliamentary regime. "The very day the Reichstag was created, the German people were condemned to death... A people required to submit to the majority is a doomed people." The remedy lies in the end of parliamentarism, the end of the rule of parties, the uprooting of Marxism. "Marxism is the great undertaking of the Jews for the conquest of the world." The Jews are said to be starving the poor, undermining national unity and supporting parliamentarism. The German people must be pulled out of the abyss by the affirmation of a new purely national ideal and by dictatorship. "German people, the hour of de-

2 Disappointingly, this is not the sociologist Max Weber, who died in 1920, but probably Dr Friedrich Weber, head of the Bund Oberland, who worked closely with Hitler at this time.

liverance has struck... To Berlin!"

I am not distorting or overstating, even if I have abbreviated.
Between these ideas, these summary, vulgar and sometimes outrageous affirmations there is no logical connection. A lot of exclama-
tions, a familiar tone, a constant appeal to primitive feelings
through terms like "my children" and "our people," and then a fren-
zied conclusion, that's all. At bottom it is a naïve demagogy exploiting national feeling, the discredit of reformist socialism and
parliamentarism, poverty and the old hatred for the usurer and the
financier who too often happen to be Jewish. This is the whole ideology of national socialism. That of Italian fascism, if it is not much
more logical or better constructed, nonetheless has more cohesion
and is also more high-flown. This German movement is indeed
fascist, but already it is a degenerated, vulgarized, stupefied fascism.
Terrible symptoms of the decadence of a capitalist regime which
can no longer even provide the masses with an ideology worthy of
the name!

The Munich tragicomedy

Must we come back to the Munich tragicomedy? Some details of
it are scarcely known as yet. The coup was announced for November 7, the anniversary of the Bavarian revolution. It began
with an anti-Marxist diatribe, in the Hitler style, by the dictator
von Kahr. Hitler and his men broke into the hall. A rifle was fired
into the ceiling, there was panic followed by the first splendid
words of Hitler, perched on a table, to the hall which was to applaud him: "If calm is not restored instantly, for God's sake, I
shall install machine guns in the gallery." Calm was restored and
von Kahr was led away politely, "white as a sheet," together with
General von Lossow and several others. An hour later von Kahr
returned, "just as pale," and announced that he was taking on "in

my capacity as representative of the monarchy," the functions of chancellor. Hitler took the dictatorship, Ludendorff the army which was to march on Berlin. The next day, a dramatic twist. Von Kahr and von Lossow dropped their accomplice Hitler and got an excellent bargain, although a rather risky one. They got rid of a burdensome rival, imposed themselves on the bourgeoisie as saviours of social peace, the unity of the Reich and order, and acquired the right to recognition from Stresemann and Ebert. What Hitler had clumsily tried to impose by force at the risk of provoking some vigorous responses from the proletariat, von Kahr, being cleverer, obtained legally without effort: the first after-effect of the putsch in Munich was the dictatorship of General von Seeckt in Berlin... But here are some further details. "King" Rupprecht who counts a great deal on the benevolence of the French general staff, with whom it is claimed that his supporters have frequently held talks, would be alarmed to see old Ludendorff, dear to the Hohenzollern and not well thought of in Paris, leading a restoration of the monarchy.

During the few hours that the putsch lasted, the gangs of Ludendorff and Hitler went to the editorial offices of the *Münchener Post*, the SPD's Munich paper, which they ransacked from top to bottom; they likewise ransacked the home of the SPD leader, Auer, arrested Socialist and Communist municipal councillors during a committee meeting and had them taken to a wood to be shot. *Vorwärts* claims that only the sudden change in the situation in Munich prevented them from being executed. Posters displayed in Munich ordered all German citizens to lay hands on socialist and republican figures, Ebert, Scheidemann, Oscar Cohn, Theodor-Paul Lévy, Theodor Wolff, and Georg Bernhardt and to hand them over to the authorities "dead or alive."

Why did the attempt fail? Why did Herr von Kahr at the last moment drop his "loyal opponents" with whom he was so often in agreement? The answer seems simple to me. Heavy industry, high finance and the military caste were afraid of civil war and they considered that after the events of the last few days, the disarming of red Saxony and the complete collapse of social democracy, they no longer needed a coup to establish a dictatorship. The demagogues and impatient elements like Hitler have now become rather an embarrassment to them.

Hitler has fled, like Rossbach, who was active alongside him, the Rossbach who was just recently released by the special court established at Leipzig under the law for the protection of the Republic. Contrary to what is being said, I don't think their political role is over. One day we shall see them again amid civil war, at the head of gangs of murderers. Ludendorff has been arrested and set free again after giving his word of honor to abandon political activity. A day or two before the putsch he had already given his word of honor to von Kahr not to act without first canceling the agreement between them. But all that is make-believe.

The SPD senators of Hamburg for their part are showing much less indulgence for the Communist prisoners taken after the recent uprising. They have no intention of releasing their imprisoned Communist colleagues, without a shadow of proof of their guilt.

The first week of the new inflation

The first week of the new inflation has gone by. And we can draw up a balance sheet. I mean the inflation "in gold," that is, of paper said to be of "real value." These pieces of paper, monopolized by the arbitrage[3] which sells and resells them at four or five times their

---

3 Trade in bills or stocks on different markets to take advantage of different prices.

value, remain unseen and impossible to find. But their appearance
and the fixing of an official rate for the dollar and the gold mark
(respectively 630 and 150 billion) has within six days, from November 3 to 9, had the result of a very steep increase in all prices
calculated in gold. In paper marks, the increase for this week has
reached the record figure of 502 percent. In gold, the index for the
average standard of living has suddenly gone to 76.2 percent (the
figure 100 corresponds to the average standard of living in 1913).
The prices of foodstuffs, also calculated in gold, have increased
more, going from 93.5 percent to 152.6 percent. We can deduce
that even before being known to the mass of the population, paper
money with "real value" has lost a third of its purchasing power.
Inflation, a monstrous attempt to swindle the masses of workers
and consumers, is beginning again on new base...

The Berlin printers' strike

No newspapers today, Monday, November 12, and a crisis of paper
money. The presses which print the paper money have ceased to
work. Defying all the bans on strikes decreed by the military authorities, the printers of newspapers and of the Reichsbank have
been on strike for three days. This movement, in response to the
indefinite suspension of *Die Rote Fahne*, has been on the point of
breaking out for several weeks, and has been persistently sabotaged
by the union leaders; it could not be delayed any longer, but it has
taken on a primarily economic character. For the week November
3 to 9 the printers earned three and a half trillion paper marks (a
little more than a dollar at black market rates) or at face value 22.5
gold marks. Before the war they earned 35 gold marks a week, and
since the war prices have more than doubled. Negotiations with
the minister of labor have informed them of the good will of the
government and of the employers.

This is an important strike. We must stress that it is taking place despite the severe measures of martial law and reformist sabotage. It bears witness to a will to resist on behalf of a section of the working class which is far from being revolutionary. The government may well not be in a hurry to put an end to it. It is an excellent opportunity to blame the workers for the serious consequences of the shortage of paper money. For their part the printers are taking advantage of the situation; they have cut off Herr Stresemann's subsistence and have suppressed the whole bourgeois press at a time when public opinion was following events anxiously. Only two papers are appearing: *Vorwärts*, where the type was set with permission of the unions, and the nationalist *Deutsche Zeitung*, (German News), typeset by scabs.

The disarming of red Thuringia

The disarming of red Thuringia is being carried out—or rather has been completed—thanks to the disinterested support given to the military dictatorship by the social democrats. The workers' government of Thuringia no longer exists since November 10–12. Presided over by the social democrat Frölich—who is far from being of the same caliber as a Zeigner, whatever reservations we may have about the latter, it included three Communists, Tenner, Korsch[4] and Neubauer. It is now clear that the experience of our comrades in Thuringia was a difficult one. At no time did they succeed in drawing the social democratic majority out of its passivity. The workers' government was formed in order to achieve, together with red Saxony, a workers' bloc in central Germany. For their part, the social democrats very much hoped not to have to do

---

4 Karl Korsch (1886-1961), now best known for his philosophical writings.

anything about it. When Herr Stresemann undertook his offensive against the workers' government in Dresden, they refused, despite the efforts of the Communists, to show solidarity with red Saxony. Even better, prime minister Frölich promised Herr Stresemann to liquidate the workers' coalition without any intervention by the Reichswehr. Nonetheless the Reichswehr entered Thuringia without encountering the slightest resistance. Social democratic police chiefs were seen complying with the disarmament of the workers' hundreds. Comrades who know the state well say that the masses' will for action was great, unanimous and enthusiastic... The dishonest sabotage by the SPD ministers broke the workers' resistance, at least for a time. Our comrades left this false workers' government, slamming the door behind them. For their part, the Thuringian social democrats published on November 12 a long anti-communist manifesto accusing our comrades of shirking their responsibilities and "pretending to form a united front in order to foment riots" (sic). The Thuringian social democrats published this sad document while, throughout central Germany, Communist workers were being arrested, while they were often persecuted in prison, while all their press was being suppressed, while in Bavaria von Kahr was dissolving the KPD and confiscating its property!

The abandonment of the Rhine and the Ruhr

We have often written before: the German nation, considered as a unit of labor and culture, has no more dangerous enemy than its own "national" big bourgeoisie. Now the coming end of the drama of the Ruhr is giving us a truly tragic confirmation of this fact. For long months, suffering the rule of the German occupation made worse by continual military sanctions, dying of hunger, the Ruhr proletariat has resisted French imperialism; meanwhile the funds intended by the Reich to support passive resistance were swallowed up by arms for the black Reichswehr and by the strongboxes of the big industrialists of the occupied region. Those who profited from the passive resistance are now negotiating with the French victors. In the debate going on at present between French and German capitalists, the labor, hunger, revolt and blood of the miners and iron and steel workers of the Ruhr are the object of the most Machiavellian schemes. The Ruhr industrialists have already stated that they cannot guarantee, under the conditions imposed on them by their powerful rivals, the payment of wages: they are shutting the factories and the mines. As of December 1, if not earlier, there will be a complete lock-out throughout the Ruhr.

The new minister of the interior in Stresemann's government, Dr. Jarres, former lord mayor of Duisburg, a man of the right and a known supporter of Rhineland separatism, has begun his ministerial activity by cutting off food supplies to millions of unemployed, locked out by their employers, in the Rhineland and the Ruhr. Two million workers, who have borne the full burden of the passive resistance, now have no other means of subsistence.

No means of subsistence!

What do the tycoons of mines and ironworks, of whom Stresemann and Jarres are only the agents, want to achieve? The crime they are committing against all "their people" by condemning the workers of the Ruhr to hunger and unsuccessful food riots could have only the following aims:

- to create an untenable situation in the Ruhr that would make the French capitalists more accommodating;
- to oblige the French capitalists to provide for the needs of the Ruhr in one way or another, which would

have the double advantage of costing them a lot of money and confirming the political separation of the occupied region of the Reich (German heavy industry seems to have decided in favor of such a separation);

♦ to provoke a workers' uprising which could easily be repressed with the support of French troops, an uprising from which the proletariat would emerge demoralized and beaten, to resume work on the conditions that Degoutte, Stinnes, Krupp, Vögler and the experts of the Comité des Forges would like to impose on them: ten-hour day, suppression of the factory councils, repeal of the Reich's social legislation...

To break the Berlin printers' strike

General von Seeckt, "in possession of full military powers through the territory of the Reich" is issuing Tsarist-style edicts everywhere... On November 12, he had posters put up formally forbidding all the printers in the Reichsbank to stop work. The decree instructed strikers to return to work without delay, threatening that if they did not they would suffer all the rigors of martial law. The edict didn't impress anyone. A few weeks ago General von Horn banned strikes in Berlin. Nonetheless, not a single bourgeois daily appeared, apart from one miserable nationalist rag set by non-union labor. Having observed that his threats were useless, dictator von Seeckt has just decided to break the strike by repressive measures. On November 15 there were numerous arrests of trade union

5 Sealed orders whereby the pre-Revolutionary French king could order imprisonment without trial.

officials, mainly social democrats, from the striking organizations. Let us mention those of the president of the union of Berlin printing workers, Robert Brauns, of the president of the printers' assistants, Gloth, and of the delegate from the bookbinders, Gäbel. Six other well-known trade union officials are victims of the military authority's *lettres de cachet*.[5] Various members of factory committees and less well-known militant strikers have just been imprisoned. Since all these arrests were carried out by virtue of the military dictatorship, they had no need of any legal justification; the victims have no right to any legal defense...

We think that these means, imitated from Tsarist Russia, will not succeed in breaking a strike originally caused by hunger. Admittedly they are planning to use other measures against it which are outrageous even in the Germany of the generals. Unemployed printers from the Brandenburg province and from Berlin—there are several thousand of them—will be required to replace the strikers on pain of having their unemployment pay withdrawn. Required to become scabs or to lose their last piece of bread! The *Oberpräsident* of Brandenburg has signed this decree. The leaders of disintegrating bourgeois Germany think they can do anything they like. Which should cause us greater surprise: their lack of psychology or their class cynicism?

(In the last few moments I have heard that the strike has been broken: "Faced with the threats of the military authorities, taking account of the negotiations in progress and the promise to release the arrested militants," the officials of the print unions have decided to resume work.

It's a defeat. Worse: it's a capitulation.

When the KPD proposed a general strike, the social democrats replied that the Berlin working class "was too hungry to fight" but that they were going to prepare a workers' offensive throughout the

Reich territory. But throughout the Reich territory, are workers not likewise "too hungry to fight?")

Arrests, arrests, arrests...

Arrests of striking printers... Arrests of striking millers (Berlin, November 15)... Arrests of Communists (on any pretext)... Arrests of journalists... There is talk of nothing but arrests. (In Berlin—not in Munich!) According to the most recent news several dozen Communist militants were arrested yesterday and the day before (November 13-14) at Cottbus, and in Berlin and its surrounding area, on the traditional charge of "plotting against the security of the state." The journalist Walter Oehme, who has made revelations about the reactionary forces, has been put behind bars thanks to General von Horn. A Jewish social democratic journalist, correspondent of a New York publication, has been arrested for having sent his paper too graphic an account of the recent pogroms.[6] Journalists with credentials from major foreign newspapers are prudently taking care not to sleep at home... The prisons are crammed. Arrests at Chemnitz, at Leipzig, at Dresden. At Hamburg, a trial of four-hundred workers is being prepared...

But Ludendorff is at liberty—didn't he give his word of honor to...carry on?—and is making speeches over the graves of the victims of his failed coup on November 7. Ehrhardt, the escaped prisoner from Leipzig, for whose capture there are still posters in the stations promising "a substantial reward," is showing himself at parades in Munich and demanding that he be amnestied. Rossbach, freed by the Leipzig High Court, is reorganizing Hitler's gangs. In

---

6 The charges were later dropped. [*Serge's note.*]

short, nobody has been troubled after the abortion of the grotesque plot in Munich. But, the day after the ransacking of the editorial offices of the SPD paper in Munich, Herr von Kahr finally closed down all the socialist press in Bavaria. To regain some influence with the National Socialists, who were very angry at his about-turn, he has announced that the KPD is dissolved...

A final detail of this overall picture: Crown Prince Wilhelm has returned to his estate in Silesia. On this point, it is not generally known that he was given permission to return by the Stresemann cabinet at a time when it still included the social democrats. Perhaps our great Socialist politicians wanted to stir up discord between the monarchist clans of Wittelsbach and Hohenzollern[7] by facilitating the Crown Prince's return. They have achieved this result, but at the price of a new outbreak of reactionary intrigues.

A comic paper

Uncurbed repression against the left. Arbitrary actions by the generals. Non-stop reactionary and monarchist plots. The instigators of reactionary civil war go unpunished. Outrages by the nationalist gangs. Arms for the nationalists. Open preparation of a coup on a massive scale. That is the balance sheet of the present period. The United Social Democratic Party has finally begun to seek remedies to all these ills, remedies that are worthy of the Second International. To seek? What am I saying? It has found them. Listen carefully. Don't dare laugh. The SPD is demanding a meeting of the Reichstag. It... ah! But this time it will be serious! It is preparing to ask parliamentary questions! It is going to ask seven questions, perhaps even eight, of Herr Stresemann! Even if it means provok-

---

7 The Wittelsbach were the Bavarian royal family; the Hohenzollern, formerly the Prussian royal family, had been emperors of united Germany from 1871 to 1918.

ing a new cabinet crisis, it will no longer give him a vote of confidence! You must believe me!

Vorwärts sets all this out with imperturbable gravity, foresees a dissolution of the Reichstag and prepares its readers for intense struggle...through the ballot box. For, you see, if the Reichstag is dissolved according to the terms of the constitution, elections must take place within a period of sixty days. The fact that gentlemen like Stinnes, von Kahr, Stresemann, von Seeckt and Ludendorff don't give a damn for the constitution doesn't seem to have occurred to the editorial staff of *Vorwärts* as yet. *Vorwärts* is a comic paper.

By mid-November Stresemann's government was drawing to its close. However, it succeeded in carrying through two important measures. The establishment of the Rentenmark on November 15 meant that hyperinflation was at last being checked. And on November 17 the legally protected eight-hour day was finally abolished.

The fate of the eight-hour day

Correspondance internationale, November 20, 1923

The fate of the eight-hour day is being decided at this very moment. The "demobilization decrees" of 1918, which provisionally established the eight-hour day, expired on November 17. They have remained in force for five years, without the SPD—which for the first two years was a leading party in the German Republic—ever thinking of bringing in a law to guarantee the gain of the eight-hour day, despite its temporary character. The eight-hour day has now been legally canceled, a few days ago. Herr Stresemann never concealed his intention not to extend the demobilization decrees. Doubtless the reformist unions asked for them to be extended; but the bourgeoisie would be very stupid and very soft-hearted to yield to the timid, hesitant and formal demands of the unions. In Berlin and various other cities the authorities have clearly stated that there can now be no question of maintaining the eight-hour day. On this subject, the opinion of the German bourgeoisie is unanimous. In the Ruhr in particular, the lock-out in the mines and the iron and steel industry had the object of imposing the ten-hour day on workers. "The Ruhr employers state that they are not in a position to continue production if expenses are not considerably reduced. The only way to reduce them, they believe, is by extending the working day and dismissing about one third of the labor force…" I take this precise accusation from *Vorwärts* which thus explains the complete cessation of work in the Ruhr mines that has been announced for November 30.

In a country where there are, at the lowest estimate, a million and a half unemployed, where several million workers are already working short time, where it is impossible for the state to give assistance to the unemployed, where the unemployed are condemned to the most wretched poverty and death by starvation, the heads of industry see no salvation—for their profits and for the social order they represent—except in increasing unemployment and extending the working day. They are thus, quite deliberately, creating an intolerable situation: for the masses of unemployed cannot consent to die slowly and peacefully of hunger, and nor can the masses of workers still employed in the mines and factories accept complete enslavement, which, moreover, would mean the unemployed were condemned without hope of appeal…

But the bourgeoisie is calculating shrewdly. It believes it will be safe against an insurrection, thanks to the dictatorship of General von Seeckt and even more thanks to the incredible cowardice of the social democracy; it no longer fears the ADGB (Federation of German Trade Unions), which is demoralized and penniless, and whose leaders, like those of the SPD, are willing to put up with anything...

In the coming days the eight hours will be discussed in the Reichstag. Already it is being said in Berlin that the social democrats, who were supposed, this Tuesday, to overthrow the Stresemann cabinet with a great barrage of questions, will do nothing of the sort. So the man at the center of the intrigues against the working class will probably remain in power. Unless the reactionaries want to replace him with somebody more energetic. The social democrats will abstain from voting and the eight-hour day will have had its time...

Rentenmark and wage-mark

Berliners facetiously ask each other; "Have you seen the Rentenmark?" As people might say at Tarascon: "Have you seen the Tarasque?"[1] But this is no joking matter. We must take note of the total scandalous failure of the first "real value" currency created by the Reich government...to satisfy a demand from the trade unions concerning the payment of wages in paper that is worth something. The 800 million of the gold loan has been entirely swallowed up by financial speculators who have achieved enormous profits from it. Not one worker in Germany has seen a single banknote even of the lowest value.

So now we have beginning, in identical conditions, the experience of the Rentenmark...

The Rentenmark has been in circulation since November 15. Nobody has seen it. Apparently you can get it clandestinely at

---

1 A legendary monster associated with the small French town of Tarascon (Bouches-du-Rhône). A model of the monster is brought out for local festivals.

crazy prices. Wages continue to be paid, without any hope of a change, in paper marks which we have now definitely decided to call wage-marks. Of the appearance of the Rentenmark, the general public knew nothing except for some indirect but very suggestive information.

A statement to the press tells us that, on November 15, the chancellor met the directors of the Rentenbank. The president of this bank made him a speech about the appropriate way of stabilizing the financial situation in Germany. The directors of the new bank have all been selected from among the most influential figures in industry, trade, agriculture and banking. All, in short, are big capitalists. And here is the obligatory advice they came to impose on the head of government:

German foreign policy must take account of the economic weakening of the country (translation: accept all capitulations that suit capitalist interests). The state budget must be balanced by measures of strict economy; administrative staff must be limited in numbers (translation: sacking of civil servants, ten-hour day, abandoning nationalized enterprises to private capital...) Taxes "harmful to production and trade" must be removed (obviously taxes on property, capital and profits)... The financial autonomy of the states must be extended (as Bavaria wishes, and to ensure that the Rhineland state of tomorrow belongs to the plutocrats alone)... Production expenses must be cut by lengthening the working day (final agreement!).

The directors of the Rentenbank stressed to the chancellor that the creation of the Rentenmark was a sacrifice agreed by the pos-

---

2 Later Hitler's economics minister (1934-37), but then interned by the Nazis; acquitted at Nuremberg.

sessing classes who are fully entitled to compensation. In reality these gentlemen already constitute a "Directory" which has the government of the Reich by the throat, since they can cut off its resources whenever they please; and it has been widely noted that they have, for obviously political reasons, delayed the appearance of the new paper money by several weeks.

It's easy to see what the Reich is losing by the operation. What is not at all easy to see is what it could possibly hope to gain from it. The financial mess is such that Herr Stresemann found it necessary to appoint an extraordinary commissioner for currency, *Währungskommissar,* Dr. Hjalmar Schacht,[2] who is said to be more than usually competent and honest. But what powers does he have? He can prevent measures being taken, but he can't require them to be taken. He has no authority over the Rentenbank. Has he any more power over the Reichsbank? No. Questions of taxation do not fall within his competence, but are the responsibility of the ministers of finance and economics. The backing of the gold loan and other similar possible issues concerns the whole cabinet and does not concern Herr Schacht. Budgetary savings are the sole province of the minister of finance. But what then are the powers of the new commissioner? I've no idea. It could be another Berlin joke: "Do you know Dr. Schacht's powers?"

Before being appointed, Dr. Schacht had insisted on all the dangers involved in the issuing of the Rentenmark and he had proposed remedies that were apparently serious. This Utopian had asked that measures should be taken to insure against the corporate-capitalist character of the management of the issuing bank; that steps be taken to prevent a new inflation which, thanks to the old credit mechanism, would again become a source of enormous profits for certain circles; that the mortgage taken by the issuing bank on private assets should be distributed equally, without shady schemes; that measures should be taken so that the Rentenmark was not monopolized by speculators as the gold loan had been... He went so far as to ask that in making economies they should remember that "the physical existence of the citizen must have priority over reason of state," in other words that, on economic grounds, they should try to avoid condemning millions of poor people to permanent starvation (according to Leopold Schwarzschild in *Montag Morgen*). Is it not amusing to find a bourgeois journalist quoting these cruel suggestions by a bourgeois financier? So the Rentenmark scarcely permits any illusions...

...And the wages-mark carries on with its work. A professional worker who is a friend of mine, "very well paid" in his own words, had the following misadventure just last week. He learned on Wednesday that his earnings for the week were fixed at seven billion. He was satisfied. Since that day the gold mark was worth two billion, that meant he had 85 gold marks for the week. But when he collected his seventeen trillion on Friday, November 12, the gold mark having risen in the meantime to 600 billion, the sum was now worth only 27 marks... This Friday many workers for their part received only 7, 8 or 9 trillion, roughly a French five franc piece from before the war,[3] for a week's work, to live for a week! But from November 10 to 16, while the rate of the dollar rose only by 166 percent, the cost of living rose by 224 percent. The new inflation—that of papers with real value—continued.

---

3 Before the outbreak of war in 1914, engineering workers in Paris earned around 1.20 francs *per hour*.

Calculated in gold, the cost of living had gone, in those six days, from 104.6 percent to 127 percent (the cost of living in 1914 being represented by 100) and the cost of food from 152.6 percent to 183.2 percent. I have taken these figures from the main paper controlled by Stinnes, who certainly doesn't produce it to help Communist propaganda. They prove just how much harm is done to the worker paid in wages-marks by the issue of paper money with "real value."

Let's conclude. The looting of Germany, the robbery of the working classes and the middle classes, the systematic starvation of the proletariat are continuing. These are the results of class politics carried out very consciously. The task is to carve up and degrade the nation, to sacrifice its unity, to wreck its culture, and to injure its deep vital energies in order to save the capitalist order.

On November 23 Stresemann finally resigned. On the same day the KPD was made illegal. Correspondance internationale *did not appear between November 20 and December 13; its Berlin offices were closed as part of the repression against the KPD and the journal moved its headquarters to Vienna. To cover this period an article is included from* Bulletin communiste, *weekly journal of the French Communist Party, which frequently reproduced Serge's articles.*

Wanted: a chancellor

Bulletin communiste, December 6, 1923

Berlin, November 29–30, 1923.[1]

---

1 According to his *Memoirs,* Serge had already left Berlin for Prague by this date. His article often carried false place names to fool the authorities.

I'm writing these lines on the evening of November 29. In formal terms the cabinet crisis has already lasted since November 23, but in reality it has been going on much longer, and in "well-informed quarters" there is not the slightest hope of finding a satisfactory solution to it. Herr Stresemann has resigned. After a lot of beating about the bush, president Ebert had entrusted one H. Albert with the job of forming the new government, leaving aside all party motives. Although H. Albert had made known his intention to leave most of the retiring ministers with the same portfolios, and to give Stresemann the foreign affairs ministry, his scheme collapsed when faced with the dissatisfaction of the parties. In fact, heavy industry and the landowners have had enough of transitional solutions.

We should simply note which "unpolitical" figure president Ebert had chosen. Doctor Albert—with whom the author of these lines, who is not happy at sharing the name, has nothing in common!—a senior civil servant of the pre-war regime, who during the war, at the most difficult times, was the closest collaborator of Herr Helfferich. He drew up the economic clauses of the imperialist treaties of Bucharest and Brest-Litovsk. He was obviously qualified to interpret the Treaty of Versailles.

There is also a von Kardof plan. But Herr von Kardof, a member of the German People's Party of Stresemann and Stinnes, has not found much support in his own party. Just this morning there was talk of a government headed by Stegerwald, leader of the Christian unions—which are continuing to abandon him—and of the right wing of the Center Party, a government which would include the German National People's Party (monarchists and revanchists[2]), the German People's Party (Stinnes), the Catholic Center and the German Democratic Party. Another failure, this time caused by the in-

---

2 Advocates of military revenge against the victorious powers of World War I.

transigence of the DNVP, who demanded the break-up of the Great Coalition in Prussia, with the clear aim of immediately proceeding to take advantage of their presence in the Reich government to carry out the *Bavarianisation* of Prussia. (To use their own words: "Purge of the administration, reorganization of the police, etc., in a national spirit...") Finally there was talk of a Jarres government, which would have been merely an dubious substitute for a Stresemann government. Now they're talking of a Marx government (Catholic Center).

We shall not waste time examining all these wretched parliamentary combinations. It is more important to draw the general conclusions from this long crisis. In reality, the present Reichstag can no longer constitute a viable government, since it no longer represents the real forces confronting each other in the country. The DDP and the SPD still have more than 230 seats. The parties of the extreme left and the extreme right are weak there, while in the country all real power—money, army, authority—belongs to the big industrial and landowning capitalists; all the real resistance to reaction, the resistance of the proletariat and of the proletarianized middle classes, tends to concentrate around the KPD. Heavy industry and the proletariat, the forces confronting each other are immense; parliament realizes it. Quite unable to come to an agreement, the parliamentary groups which represent—very, very badly—the contending classes cannot either find grounds for agreement or decide on clear solutions that might unleash forces which the big bourgeoisie is rightly afraid of.

All the parties and president Ebert hesitate in face of a dissolution of the Reichstag, their only constitutional expedient. For then they would either have to violate the constitution by postponing the elections, or call them within sixty days on the basis of universal suffrage. Now there are many indications, notably the recent local elections in Bremen, which have revealed the mood of the electorate. A regroupment of parties would work simultaneously to the advantage of the most open reactionaries and of the most energetic proletarian action, and to the detriment of the DDP and above all the SPD. And since nothing entitles the reactionary parties to count on a parliamentary majority, the new chamber might well be nothing other than a civil war parliament...

So a chancellor is needed. They need an eloquent and flexible minister, who at one and the same time would serve the interests of the big monarchist landowners, of the tycoons of heavy industry, of the generals anxious to restore order—which is disturbed by the hungry—and of the most cowardly of social democratic parties, solely concerned with saving republican appearances... While they look in vain, the real German government is doing deals with French imperialism, signing profitable capitulations, economically detaching the Rhineland and the Ruhr from the Reich, and confirming the legal cancellation of the eight-hour day. The Rhineland industrialists Stinnes, Vögler, Krupp and Wolff have signed agreements with the MICUM.[3] They have made peace with the French enemy. They have got their 48 percent. They have the support of the French bayonets against the Rhineland proletariat. An official note passed to all the newspapers has observed that the 1918 demobilization decrees which established the eight-hour day in Germany have not been extended. The SPD did not bat an eyelid. And this ending of the eight-hour day, the only serious gain made by the workers in the 1918 "revolution," seems to us much more important than the cabinet crisis.

---

3 Mission Interalliée de Contrôle des Usines et des Mines: Interallied Mission to Control Factories and Mines. An agreement of November 23, 1923, made a temporary, five month settlement of the reparations question.
4 Striking evidence of the ultra-leftism that was widespread in the KPD.

The Communist Party legally illegal

On the very day when the KPD was dissolved by order of General Seeckt, a party member said to me with a smile: "This changes nothing. We were already illegal; our press had already been suppressed; our central committee was already in hiding... This situation has now had a legal ratification. We used to be in a way *illegally illegal*—now we're *legally illegal...*"

He added: "For my part I can see only advantages.[4] The situation is clear now. All comrades will have to exercise prudence and revolutionary guile, whereas previously their old habits of social democratic legality still often had a pernicious influence. Our education as conspirators will be speeded up and made more systematic on a large scale. Our slightest moves which, when legal, might have gone unnoticed amid the minor events of political life, will at last take on a revolutionary significance and will be noticed by the bourgeois press. And finally, it will no longer be possible to exercise any supervision over our party's activity..."

The fact is that the harsh measures taken by General von Seeckt, wittily nicknamed the last mainstay of the Republic and the last hope of the monarchy—scandalous in a democratic republic, absolutely without precedent (we should recall that the decree of dissolution also lays down the confiscation of all the property of the KPD and the Third International in Germany), seem totally pointless and totally unworkable. The illegal publications of the KPD, even in Berlin, are plainly continuing to appear; the Communist organizations have not been impaired in any way. The central committee has been dissolved; it has been replaced by a directory[5] which

---

5 A small, clandestine committee. The term goes back to Babeuf's conspiracy of 1796.
6 A major thoroughfare in central Berlin.

"is based abroad." In formal terms, the members of the CC, who no longer hold office, should not need to be in hiding, so paradoxically the dissolution of the party could be an advantage for them. To top it all, on Wednesday, November 28, it was necessary to mobilize all the police and army in Berlin to prevent a big Communist demonstration...which they failed to prevent.

At noon on that day, an alarming statement from police headquarters informed the population of Berlin that the police had been instructed to show the utmost ruthlessness against any attempt at a Communist demonstration. At 4:00pm the Reichstag was surrounded by a heavy police cordon. An impressive array of police were gathered in the Wilhelmstrasse area, around the residence of President Ebert. Armored cars crossed Unter den Linden.[6] Despite the efforts of the police of the social democrats Weiss, Richter and Severing, at 5:30pm, in the Lustgarten,[7] there were more than 30,000 Communist workers singing the *Internationale*. This crowd which, in various places, had to fight the police to get to the assembly point fixed by the party, stood up to several charges by mounted police. In a neighboring street, they erected an improvised barricade. They took away their wounded, who numbered about a hundred; then they finally dispersed through the prosperous districts, despite the police brutality. This deserves to be reported. On the evening of the demonstration it was sufficient to appear on the thoroughfares of central Berlin badly dressed—that is, dressed as a worker or an unemployed person—to be pursued by the municipal police with truncheons. In the Lustgarten, the mounted police charged, armed with a new weapon, a whip with a short handle and a long lash. Its proper name is Russian—*nagaika*.

---

7 The former Royal Pleasure Grounds.

Ebert and von Seeckt are installing the rule of the *nagaika*.
They are still playing their role. Nonetheless, according to *Die
Tribune*, the banned KPD was able to bring onto the streets of
Berlin, on this bleak, cold winter evening, some sixty thousand or-
ganized, combative demonstrators.

Acts of white terror

The social democratic prime ministers of Saxony and Thuringia,
Frölich and Fellisch, together with the left social democratic deputy
Kurt Rosenfeld, brought before the Reichstag on November 23
some damning reports of the outrages committed by the soldiery of
von Seeckt in the two workers' states of central Germany. Harmless
people, suspect not of communism but of democratic sympathies,
mayors, municipal councillors, students, arrested without rhyme or
reason, imprisoned in barracks, insulted, thrashed with rifle butts,
stripped naked to be beaten up, thrashed, etc. A large number of
such facts were cited. We know of others. Despite the denials of the
Reichswehr minister, Herr Gessler (DDP), who has been exposed as
a blatant liar by the deputies from Saxony and Thuringia, the
solemn admission of these acts of white terror has just been formulated by General Müller, dictator at Dresden. In an order to his
troops, General Müller has reminded them that "it is dishonorable
for soldiers to harass unarmed populations." And he has recognized
that "regrettable excesses" have taken place. We learn that a number
of Reichswehr officers and NCOs have been pensioned off as a dis-
ciplinary measure.

This is a formal confession. Despite the silence which followed
the revelations made on the floor of the Reichstag, the scandal is
obvious. And we don't think the confessions of General Müller
will diminish their impact.

We must note the attitude of *Vorwärts* in this context, for it is worse than odious. *Vorwärts* said virtually nothing about the indignant protest of the social democrats Frölich, Fellisch and Rosenfeld in the Reichstag. It published none of their evidence; but it devoted fifty lines to the embarrassed response of minister Gessler. So that must be their political line. Was not *Vorwärts* indignant, a few days ago, at the fact that the nationalist press had accused Ebert of still being subject to Marxist influences? Imagine the anger of the editorial staff of *Vorwärts* at the idea that anyone could still take Ebert for a socialist! Finally, did not *Vorwärts* publish a statement from the central office of the SPD in which this party solemnly dissociated itself from the "anti-constitutional" actions of the Communists? They have picked their time. German social democracy remains true to itself, that is, to its cowardice, its treachery, its endless servility to bourgeois dictatorship…

Herr Severing's opinion

Herr Severing's opinion on the current political situation in Germany, and in particular in Prussia, is interesting to discover. Citizen Severing, social democratic minister of the interior in the Great Coalition government in Prussia, has done remarkable service for the bourgeoisie. He played a notable role in the provocation which led to the Communist rising in March 1921. He then and subsequently allowed a certain number of workers to be murdered. In Prussia he dissolved the workers' hundreds and the central organizations of the factory committees. His contribution is therefore considerable in the eyes of the reactionaries. The DNVP nonetheless demanded his removal from the Prussian cabinet in recent days, as well as that of the other SPD ministers. For they don't think this Socialist minister is

---

8 Jungdeutscher Orden.

reactionary enough yet. They think that from now on they can do without the Socialist lackeys of bourgeois power.

Two days ago Herr Severing granted a long interview to a journalist from *Der Abend* (The Evening), of which we shall give a summary of the main passages:

—In Prussia two military organizations, the Young German Order (*Jungdo*[8]) and the *Stahlhelm* (Steel Helmet), dissolved on Herr Severing's instructions, *have just been given authorization to function by the Reichsrat.* All the armed reactionary associations were encouraged by this. "The danger of an extreme right wing coup in Prussia and at Berlin cannot be considered as completely excluded. In the area around Berlin, a large number of officers from General von der Golz's *Baltic* troops have taken refuge on the estates of large landowners. At the beginning of November we found out that General von der Golz and his friends were actively considering a plan to march on Berlin."

"A right wing government would at the very least tolerate the armed organizations of the extreme right, which would enable them to import Bavarian methods into North Germany."

Citizen Severing thinks that for the SPD to leave the Prussian government would be a disaster, for the consequence would be an acute intensification of the class struggle in Prussia. So the socialism of the Second International has nothing to do with class struggle, does it?

Citizen Severing does not think that the German Republic needs to be defended by private organizations such as exist, for example, in Austria. Here are his reasons: "Everything depends on the attitude of the Reichswehr. If the Reichswehr defends the constitution and the republic, then all the attacks on them will easily be repulsed. If the Reichswehr turns against the Republic, then the republican population, which is more or less disarmed, cannot win.

Thus if the Reichswehr is for the Republic, then the Republic has no need of other defenders; if the Reichswehr is against it, then nobody can now save the Republic."

I've translated this word for word. So the Prussian social democratic minister, in his horror at class struggle and revolutionary action, thinks that the German bourgeoisie needs no more than a hundred thousand reactionary soldiers to impose on eighteen million people in humble circumstances, who now face ruin, any ostensibly republican regime in which the monarchists are pulling the strings, or even an undisguised dictatorship or restored monarchy.

Citizen Severing puts all his hopes—as does president Ebert; that is no secret—in the inscrutable General von Seeckt. And he says so quite clearly to the *Abend* journalist, Herr H. Frei:

"General von Seeckt's attitude will have a very considerable importance. Von Seeckt is an extremely intelligent man, politically realistic and clear-headed. It may be said that for as long as Germany's internal regime has to reckon with external difficulties, then General von Seeckt will see no possibility of modifying the established order…"

Shall I take the liberty of interpreting this sentence which is scarcely ambiguous? As long as the governments in Paris and London, or at least one of them, have not indicated their acquiescence in a restoration of the monarchy in Germany, then the cautious General von Seeckt will not throw into the scales his sword which is heavier than the will of a whole proletariat, of the best organized proletariat in Europe.

In these statements by minister Severing, social democrat Severing, there is nothing but double dealing, admission of impotence, admission of betrayal, awareness of the weakness of social democracy. Few contemporary documents seem to us to be more revealing of the state of mind of a great workers' party in degeneration.

A Marx government

Today a Marx government is being formed, headed by one of the leaders of the Catholic Center Party. The new chancellor expects to govern with the support of the center parties and the benevolent neutrality of the DNVP. Herr Stresemann and Dr. Jarres remain in his cabinet, as do Gessler of the DDP and the former member of the German National Party, Baron Kanitz. Herr Marx offered the ministry of economics to the general manager of the Stinnes companies, Minoux, who refused it.

The new cabinet, not much different from the old one, whose policies it will continue in every respect, is a cabinet in which bourgeois interests are concentrated. It intends to hold elections, but in a few months—a few long months, during which an effort will be made to disarm the proletariat and to eliminate from the administration of the nation the social democratic element, which despite its servility is unreliable in the eyes of the leaders of heavy industry and agriculture.

The latter are setting out their plans so clearly that Herr Hergt has just written to president Ebert to ask him to form a right wing government in which the DNVP would have the place it deserves!

And the SPD?

Vorwärts this morning (November 30) makes flattering advances to Herr Marx, praising his "reasonable character," his positive spirit, and his honesty, and promising him the benevolent neutrality of the VSPD, doubtless on condition that his way of serving reaction is not too shocking to the democratic circles who are determined to make any capitulations that are in the slightest

---

9 Established November 10, 1918.

degree respectable.

In the same issue of *Vorwärts*, citizen Dittmann, who now signs himself "former member of the council of people's commissars"[9] of the German Republic—who would have guessed it? — has discovered a completely forgotten law, promulgated on November 12, 1918, by the people's commissars, which legally established the eight-hour day. The official point of view of the German government is different. And the "former people's commissar" must be very naïve to imagine that digging up a scrap of paper, signed by himself and other colleagues of the same quality, will impose on Stinnes, Krupp, Wolff, von Seeckt, Marx and their associates any respect for the eight-hour day which they claim is legally canceled!

This was Serge's last "report from Germany"—in fact he had already left the country. On November 30, Wilhelm Marx had formed a government based on a coalition of the Center Party, the DDP, the DVP and the Bavarian People's Party. The SPD remained outside, but voted for the government which did not have a majority without it. The new government did in fact overcome the more dramatic aspects of the short term economic crisis. But the long term crisis of German capitalism remained, and the next ten years were to see its fateful outcome.

The balance sheet: formidable powerlessness

Correspondance internationale, December 19, 1923

Is there still a parliament in Germany? Under chancellor Marx the fiction of a democratic regime is based only on wearisome combinations of parliamentary arithmetic, which, moreover, are so unreliable that they give the present government no stability and no strength and do not even succeed in concealing some brutal realities...

True executive power is concentrated in the hands of the social democrat Ebert and General von Seeckt, but there is no question of them having equal amounts of power. For, in the opinion of social democratic minister Severing himself, it is the attitude of the cautious general—who is doubtless no republican, but who rejects adventurism—which is decisive.

The likes of Ebert and von Seeckt, like Marx, merely carry out orders. Behind them act, or dictate their will, the men of money, of trade and industry, for whom Germany, looted, ravaged, starved and battered by their own hands, is nothing but a sick hunted animal that must be kept out of the hands of the revolution—and cured: for a slave who is too sick cannot work.

These true masters of the hour have got rid of the costly weapon of fascism, since social democratic treachery enabled them to fulfill their task without civil war. Their politics has two faces: high treason and repression.

High treason, the capitulation of the Rhineland and the Ruhr—which consumed the last resources of the Reich—in the face of French imperialism. High treason, the "legal" separation of the Rhineland destined to form immediately an autonomous state "within the framework of the Reich" (they're not asking much!) High treason, the alliance of heavy industry with French imperialism against the workers of Rhineland-Westphalia. High treason, all the shady plots whose threads stretch between Berlin, Cologne, London, New York and Paris, constantly tightening the links of the international capitalist plot against world peace and the elementary rights of labor!

Repression, the closure of mines and factories in order to starve workers into submission. Repression, the closing down of the Communist press and the dissolution of the KPD. Repression, the outrages of the soldiery in Saxony and Thuringia, the thousands of arrests, the murders of poor people by the troops. Repression, the scandalous measures taken by the military authorities against strikers. Repression, the brutal campaign against the eight-hour day, backed up by shootings and sackings.

In the face of this cruel German reality we are left disconcerted. How was it possible? They have dissolved a revolutionary party of at least 400,000 members, followed by two million vigorous proletarians! They have closed down a working-class press that had nearly 40 daily papers! They have rescinded the eight-hour day, which was the result of a revolution, the collapse of an empire and four insurrections! Starved, trampled under foot, this proletariat, the best organized, the most educated in the world, which has fourteen million trade unionists!

We must begin by saying that all is not over. The revolutionary struggle in Germany may be only just beginning. Stinnes and his menials Ebert and von Seeckt are well aware of it. If you want proof, just ask them to put a—genuine—end to martial law!

But this enigma of a proletarian giant laid low by gnomes whose spines he could break with the back of his hand does have an explanation:

The "formidable powerlessness of German social democracy." The phrase is an old one; it comes from Jaurès, and I got it from a friend of Jaurès. Formidable powerlessness, there is no better way of putting it. This great party has been deadened and bureaucratized, piling up cowardice on top of disloyalty, and disloyalty on treachery so that it may be kindly allowed to keep up an appearance as a loyally passive opposition under an ultra-reactionary regime. This great emasculated party is now almost the sole obstacle to the German revolution, the only bulwark of a bourgeoisie which for years, in order to stupidly enrich itself to the detriment of the nation, has been pursuing a suicidal policy...

...This great powerless Socialist party is so contemptible that even the bourgeoisie that it is rescuing doesn't show it the least gratitude!

Unemployment, a revolutionary problem

German capitalism has survived the fearsome November deadline. Granted. But is it saved? It would be naïve to think so.

In its calamitous present situation, nothing is more serious within the country than the problem of unemployment. In many German cities the unemployed have taken on the role of revolutionaries or of insurgents. If the number keeps on growing, while all the other causes contributing to the disintegration of bourgeois society in Germany continue to act in parallel, then will not German capitalism soon find itself in even more critical situations than those it has just extricated itself from in a rather botched fashion?

Take Berlin. We have precise figures concerning unemployment in Berlin, from October 15 to November 17. Here they are:

	No. of unemployed	Unemployed receiving assistance
October 15	185,730	123,932
October 20	195,300	135,500
October 27	210,586	144,315
November 3	223,181	158,554
November 10	247,432	174,860
November 17	255,841	189,600

Note that Berlin is not in a more critical situation than the majority of industrial centers in non-occupied Germany. What is striking in these (official) statistics is the regular growth of unemployment, from week to week. Must it go on?

The financial problem is not resolved. Germany enjoys no credit abroad and has no currency quoted on foreign exchanges. The cost of living—and hence of production, despite low wages—is higher than anywhere else. Its international political situation is that of a country with which its enemies can't even do a deal because the government is so blatantly powerless. So there is no plausible reason for thinking that unemployment is likely to fall during the coming weeks. On the contrary, everything combines to lead us to predict its indefinite extension from the present point. Now today, in Berlin alone, 66,000 unemployed are receiving no assistance. How do they survive? The combined efforts of International Workers Aid, Austrian Aid, the Salvation Army and various charitable organizations don't reach such a large number of the poor. Workers who have been derisorily paid and undernourished for years have been unemployed in Berlin for months. On the days of demonstrations called by the dissolved KPD they appear, with their threadbare grey military tunics—and no underwear beneath, on these cold December days—haggard, with eyes deep in their sockets and jerky movements. They appear and the green police chase them with coshes through the crowds of well-dressed passers-by on the main thoroughfares. Is that a solution? How many million unemployed will there be in Germany before the end of the winter? When they demand bread, when the red flags of the banned Communist party show them the way, what will Ebert, von Seeckt and their master Stinnes be able to do? For after all, if it is sometimes possible to replace bread with lead, this time far too much would be needed!

Humor

I should like to set before the eyes of the reader a recent issue of *Simplicissimus,* one of the old humorous journals of Berlin. In these few pages normally filled with puns, rather innocent political satires and smutty jokes, there is now expressed a deep bitterness and a profound despair.—The humor of a people reveals a lot about its mentality, and, above all since the war, humorous publications, exploiting a very understandable need to forget, expressing the irony, spite, incredulity and sarcasm of the crowds, have sometimes been an easy way to get rich.—But today German humor is no more than an embittered grin.

In this one issue of *Simplicissimus* I was struck by five tragic cartoons:

—A queue of poor people, in the dark street outside a shop. Someone says: "A bit of luck! We'll get in quicker: two people in front have just fainted." I've seen so many of these pitiable queues in the suburbs of Berlin that I don't find any shocking exaggeration in this painful joke...

Two pictures. The mother at home without bread, surrounded by anxious children: "Relax, kids, Dad's coming home with some spuds!" But Dad will never come home: he is writhing on the cold ground, in a potato field, with a bullet in his body. It's true: some such "thieves" have been killed...

On another page: coming back from market two fat peasants are commenting on the decision of the doctor who has become a vet. "He says a pig is worth more than man!" Good God! Much more. The skin of an unemployed person is worth nothing. But pigskin is expensive. Very expensive.

Two final cartoons: one is mocking the bureaucracy of the sickness insurance fund (where the doctors, who have been on strike once, are threatening to do it again); the other shows the spectre of civil war looming over the starving town.

...It's important to be acquainted with this underlying bitterness and despair which in Germany poisons even the mercenary laughter of "comic" papers, in order to understand that social peace has not been established in Hamburg, Berlin and Dresden, despite the exploits of the Reichswehr of the socialist Ebert...

◆

*By way of conclusion to this collection, there are three articles written by Serge
for the French journal* Clarté, *which was close to, but not formally controlled
by, the French Communist Party, and to which he contributed regularly. These
are more analytic than the news reports for* Correspondance internationale,
*and also offer a broader picture of life in Germany. In the following article
Serge examines the question of nationalism, which posed major problems for
the KPD in 1923. Germany, as defeated power in World War I, was the
victim of rival imperialisms. Yet, as Serge shows, the real enemy of the
German proletariat was its own bourgeoisie.*

The Rich against the Nation

Berlin, October 1923

Clarté, November 1923

The present crisis in Germany, it seems to us, has finally made
clear, to any careful observer who is not dominated by outdated terminology and the interests of a servile bourgeois existence, the inex-
orable decline of the capitalist order. It is the final proof, perhaps
more convincing than the first: for between the two, there could be
room for a return to reason (if reason had anything at all in common with the underlying laws which govern the capitalist order).

In 1914, European civilization had reached the peak of its
prosperity. A century of remarkable scientific, technological and
industrial development was ending with Europe's conquest of the
globe. The planet was explored in all directions, carved up and
colonized; for the great industrial nations it was no more than a
magnificent estate inhabited by hundreds of millions of slaves
with black, brown, copper-colored, sallow and yellow skins... A
whole intellectual aristocracy could nourish the soothing dream of

a prudent evolution towards socialism on the part of the great democracies—towards a pink socialism summed up in the fully and harmoniously balanced clauses of the orators. The average inhabitants of the big cities, even if poor, enjoyed a degree of comfort that was more real than that of the average French lord at the end of the reign of Louis XIV.[1] This peak of civilization came to an end on August 2, 1914. A whole age of human history died along with the first soldiers slaughtered on the frontiers of France and Germany.

The causes of the cataclysm were the same as those of the prosperity of the old European world. Capitalist production—anarchic at first, even in its details, subsequently monopolized by oligarchies of financiers—created powerful rival coalitions which confronted each other; they were armed by science and technology; the division of the world, once completed, obliged them to fight for a new carve-up... The law of exploitation which is the essence of capitalist "order" ended up with war for colonial markets, in other words for the exploitation of the defeated peoples...

The war cost Europe (according to statistics accepted by German experts) and the world 10,200,000 soldiers killed; an increase in civilian deaths of 6,000,000; a reduction in births estimated at 20,850,000. In total, *37 million human lives...* More—for blood and money are added together under capitalism—760 billion gold marks... 16,600,000 tons of ships, naval or commercial, were sunk, 8,850 airplanes brought down. Amid this entire massacred population how many people of genius, how many talents, how many intelligent producers were there, who could have led humanity to new conquests which have now become unthinkable? The huge amount of wealth squandered in gunpowder and smoke, crushed

---

1 1715.

brains and crippled flesh, could have served as the basis for a new society and a new culture. This effective suicide of a universe proves to what extent the system of which it was the logical conclusion has pronounced its own death sentence...

No less extensive in its consequences, the German tragedy has proved and confirmed this first verdict of history. Capitalist Germany is not simply dying of the disastrous consequences of the Treaty of Versailles. One of the great *internal* causes of its collapse lies in the inner contradictions which are inherent to states dominated by capitalist oligarchies. It has been killed by the effect of the very same laws which, today, are producing the prosperity of such capitalist nations as the United States and France.

While the war revealed to us what insoluble international contradictions exist between the vital interests of groups of imperialist powers (and, on another level, between the imperialist powers and the interests of civilization), the collapse of Germany has revealed to us the incompatibility of the interests of the big bourgeoisie and other social classes in the framework of a single nation (and, on another level, the incompatibility of the bourgeois regime with the interests of the nation considered as an aggregate of labor and culture).

◆

These thoughts, inspired by the situation of Germany, seem to me all the more correct because a strict parallel can be drawn between the present role of the German bourgeoisie and that of the Russian bourgeoisie between 1915 and 1922. In both cases, the former dominant class appears as a cause of national disintegration. The bourgeois "nation" has had its day, at least in these two European countries. I have just read in a report from the Reichstag that during the session of October 9—during the separate negotiations between the Ruhr industrialists and General Degoutte—the DNVP deputy

Wulle declared that the industrialists of Borkum Island (West-phalia)[2] were determined to ask for *protection from the Netherlands* against "Communist terror." And I remembered a date: on September 20, 1792, at Valmy, the soldiers of the French Revolution—of the revolution of the third estate—defeated the Duke of Brunswick with the thundering cry, heard for the first time on a battlefield, of *"Long live the nation!"* Until then, people had fought only for kings. There had not been national armies; the relatively small royal armies were made up of professional soldiers who were recruited, hired or forced. The French revolution replaced dynastic, feudal and noble interests with an invincible living reality: the interests of the bourgeois masses who had come to power, and who had just expropriated the court, the nobility and the clergy. The bourgeoisie became the cement of the nations that it was going to establish as states, then as predatory states... Now the Russian bourgeoisie have sold the Black Sea fleet to France and the arsenals of Vladivistok to Japan; German plutocrats, having subjected their country to unrestrained looting, are now working on dividing it up. A historical epoch has come to an end.

◆

For anyone observing events in Germany, the fact is obvious. In Germany today there is no longer any linen, any shoes, any guaranteed bread for the great mass of the population. The consumption of meat has fallen by three-quarters in comparison to pre-war figures, the death rate has gone up, and the birth rate has fallen. The majority of children from the common people are tubercular, the middle classes are dying of hunger.—Production is declining

---

2 Borkum is one of the East Friesian Islands off the north coast of Germany near the mouth of the Ems.

rapidly or has stopped. Goods produced are much inferior to those from abroad and are more expensive. There are 160,000 unemployed in Berlin, more in Saxony, a few less in Hamburg; there are food riots everywhere. State revenue is virtually non-existent; it must be no more than one hundredth of its real expenditure. The monetary inflation which has automated the plundering and starvation of the masses of the population has reached such proportions that a billion marks has become the basic unit; you need several to buy a pound of margarine.

It would be wrong to put the blame for all this on M. Poincaré, whose policies have only precipitated the situation. They are the results, basically quite natural results, of five to six years of bourgeois power in a militarily defeated country.

Back in 1918, the flight of German capital began. How many billions in gold were taken out of the country in every imaginable fashion? We can mention the sale, pure and simple, to foreigners, of industrial establishments, goods or shares, in order not to have to pay the proportion due for reparations and not to run the risk of impending social struggles. My friend Höllein assured me, long ago, that six to eight billion gold marks were expatriated in this way...

As early as 1921, the whole industrial, commercial and financial bourgeoisie of Germany had made a system of speculating on the fall in value of the mark. The constant fall in value of paper money issued by the Reichsbank enabled "imperceptible" cuts in wages, making German competition unbeatable on almost all the world's markets. In the long run, the inevitable result was a reduction of the energy of labor, through undernourishment and overexertion of the workforce, wearing out of the plant and a lack of technological improvement. But after all, they were doing excellent business. Profits from Germany were converted into dollars, pounds sterling, yen and pesetas, and invested profitably and securely in South America—or elsewhere.

The passive resistance in the Ruhr was another source of scandalous profits. The most bourgeois German press *(Kölnische Zeitung, Berliner Tageblatt, Germania)* has not been able to remain silent about the enormous extent of the scandal. Half the remaining gold reserves of the Reich, about half a billion marks, is thought to have been used to finance the passive resistance; in fact, in some cases the Ruhr industrialists were able, thanks to this unhoped for source of wealth, to renew their plant, buy stocks of foreign currency (thus contributing to the fall in value of the mark), and greatly increase their political power. The state has emerged ruined from the Ruhr war. The plutocrats of heavy industry have emerged enriched, arrogant and all-powerful.

The attempts to stabilize the mark made by Messrs. Cuno and Hilferding were profitable only to them. The Reichsbank put foreign currency on the market to make up the difference between supply and demand; the plutocrats bought it all. On the Berlin Stock Exchange you could see cunning financiers at 4:15pm taking advantage of the—fictitious—fall of the dollar brought about by the intervention of the Reichsbank and buying up cheaply currency which two hours later they sold again at a higher price...

Thus for some years any weakening of the state, any increase in national poverty, have been necessarily accompanied by an enrichment and increase in the power of the industrial and financial oligarchy.

Now the drama has reached the final act. The program for reconstruction, put forward by the class of plunderers who have put the country in this situation, is known under the name of the Stinnes program. In the recent political struggles—fall of the first Stresemann government, obstruction of parliamentary government by the industrialists, Stinnes' campaign for dictatorship and martial law—what was at stake was merely its application. It can be summed up in the following four points:

- ♦ Expropriation of the state (transfer of all publicly controlled companies to private industry, and abandonment by the state of any right of control over industry).
- ♦ Taxation policy exclusively directed against the working masses.
- ♦ Ten-hour working day.
- ♦ Dictatorship.

The logic of this program is to replace the rational organization of labor by intensive exploitation. Without dictatorship, it obviously cannot be applied.

This chapter of the contemporary history of Germany can be entitled: "the Rich against the Nation." And the whole present problem is posed, more or less, in these terms:

Will the class of bandits who are responsible for the terrible poverty of the German people—and for the ruin of German culture—succeed in imposing on the proletariat by force, if necessary with the aid of French or Senegalese bayonets, its law of all-out exploitation? This problem will probably not be solved except by civil war which at this moment seems imminent. In this case the dialectic of events will impose on the proletariat, as a basic condition for defending its vital interests, the seizure of power; and, fighting for its class power, the German proletariat will appear by the necessary course of events as the ultimate defender of a great nation of producers, of a wonderful culture—which has been more or less put to death—and of European socialism.

In the second Clarté *article Serge examines the state of German culture in 1923. He gives a broad definition of "culture"; as well as the arts and sciences, he considers the role of the press and many facets of everyday life. Serge can be accused of being too pessimistic about cultural decline in post-war Germany; doubtless he was too busy to notice the Bauhaus and the early Brecht. However, he did recognize the outstanding qualities of Käthe Kollwitz and Georg Gross.*

The Rich against Culture
Writers and Artists
Clarté, December 1, 1923

Berlin, November 14, 1923

I shall never forget the painful impression that Germany made on me at the end of 1921, at a time when it had reached—in comparison with present times—the peak of its post-war prosperity: the mark was worth 20 centimes.[1] In Berlin I felt a confused sense of oppression and almost of despair. On analyzing it, I soon discovered the causes. Already, you could see everywhere in this starving metropolis the indications of a profound cultural decline. A shamefaced poverty still rubbed shoulders in the streets with the blatant bad taste of the newly enriched. From the poster to the comic song, from the shop window to the hairstyle of passing ladies, from the illustrated magazine to the art exhibition, everything bore the

---

1 Five marks to a French franc. Serge is here writing specifically for a French readership.

indelible mark of a defeat of civilization, of a *diminution of culture*. I noticed some young writers and poets. They had just published a remarkable anthology, under the significant title: *Dämmerung der Menschen* (Twilight of Humanity).[2] I noticed thinkers; some coteries of dreamers or snobs were discussing the Buddhist wisdom of Count Keyserling, other, the anthroposophical mysticism of Rudolf Steiner—the philosophy of all decadences, recalling the intellectual corruption of the last centuries of Alexandria.—Above all they were discussing a great pessimistic book, steeped on every page with reactionary assertions, by Oswald Spengler, called *The Decline of the West*.[3] The decomposition of the capitalist regime meant a heavy fate was already hanging over the whole people. Those for whom culture is the most precious result of societies' efforts were living under the influence of a heartbreaking obsession with decadence...

What do they think today? It is difficult to find out amid the general demoralization. There are hardly any new books appearing. Today you couldn't begin to publish Spengler or the despondent poets. The book trade is one of the industries worst hit by the crisis. Thinkers and artists are silent. Nothing is heard but the voices of demagogues. On the stage of Munich, a Hitler, a long-winded NCO, proclaims himself dictator of the Reich after shooting six rounds into the ceiling of a beer hall. In the main thoroughfares of Berlin you hear shouts of "Kill the Jews!" just as they used to be heard, in the days of the Russian hangman, in the small towns of

---

2 Theodor Daebler, Iwan Goll, Walter Hasenclever, E. Lesker-Schuller, L. Rubiner, René Schickelé, etc. The same writers had previously published—in 1919—a fine volume filled with revolutionary hopes—the title of which was just as expressive: *Comrades of Humanity*. [*Serge's note.*]

3 *Untergang des Abendlandes*. The literal translation of this title is even more significant: *The Decline of the Land of Evening*. [*Serge's note.*]

Bessarabia, three centuries behind western culture. People are gnawed by hunger. A lawyer, famous thirty years ago, has starved to death. An old scholar has committed suicide... Those who want to live or just to survive face constant hard work. I know an old engineer in his seventies who has become a cobbler. Clever people speculate, buy, sell and resell dollars, banknotes from the gold loan, rare books and postage stamps. Think, write, read? We have to eat tomorrow. This evening we must spend the paper money which we were paid this morning, for fear it will be worth nothing tomorrow. On Sunday evenings near the approaches to the railways stations you can see elderly intellectuals coming back from the suburbs bent under the weight of sacks of potatoes.

I know people lived through a similar famine in Russia: but there it was in order to proclaim a new truth to the whole world, in order to lay, amid toil and blood, amid snow and anguish, no doubt, the first stone of a new Society. And everything that was really alive in the vast territory of Russia knew it: otherwise, the Revolution would have died long ago, and we should not be observing the admirable rebirth of Russian literature which is perhaps the only victory for the future amid the stagnation and general decomposition of European culture.

Just recently I visited the Autumn Exhibition of painting and sculpture at the Academy of Fine Arts. None of the feasts of color normally offered to our gaze by French or Russian painters. An overall impression in greyish black tones. No harmonious sculpture, no pure lines, no light. Torment, suffering, weary effronteries, above all ugliness, sadness, a psychology of neurotics. The artists I believe to be the best—Kokoschka, Barlach, Albert Birkle, Max Klewer—share with their more mediocre contemporaries the fact that they *know nothing of joy.* On the other hand, there are some who, it seems, cannot and will not see anything but darkness. Barlach makes wood carvings of heavy, thick-set, obstinate, contorted, ill-natured

peasants whom one would guess to be sorcerers, spell-casters, arson-
ists, insurrectionists, Vendeans,[4] straight out of the hallucinated
landscapes of a Verhaeren.[5] In thirty drawings Käthe Kollwitz[6] reveals a different obsession. The haggard working-class girl, her belly
swollen with pregnancy, seems to embody for her all the suffering of
our time. The Mother, the Child, Hunger, Death: Käthe Kollwitz's
art combines these four characters into a never-ending *danse
macabre*. And I can understand this artist. Does she not live in the
north of Berlin, in the middle of a poor working-class suburb? Her
studio is next to her husband's surgery; he's a doctor in a poor district. Looking at other works, by the most varied artists, a question
forced itself on my mind: "Is this man, this misshapen freak, that we
find on all the canvasses, in all the sketches; is this grimacing, contorted mask the human face?" And I was forced to conclude: Yes,
Behold the man! That's exactly how the decadent[7] art of a dying civilization represents man. Defeated. Mutilated. Degenerated.

Two general features: the absence of joy, the absence of force.
A double result: ugliness and despair. The only one of the German
artists today in whom one finds constantly a tone of vigor is Georg
Gross—a revolutionary.[8] But for him, man, the man of the ruling
classes—has strength only because he is essentially a brute who
kills, stuffs himself and fornicates…

---

4 The peasants of the Vendée in Western France launched a counter-revolutionary
rising in 1793.

5 Emile Verhaeren (1855-1916), Belgian poet.

6 Käthe Kollwitz (1867-1945), painter and sculptor, first woman elected to Prussian Academy of Arts; remained in Germany till her death, ignored but not persecuted by Nazis.

7 Serge was using the term "decadent" before it was corrupted by misuse in the period of Stalinism and fascism.

8 George Gross (1893-1959) joined the KPD in 1922, but resigned the same year
after a visit to Russia.

Way of life

The culture of a people is embodied in its way of life rather than in the works of its intellectuals. From this point of view, the spectacle of Germany today is even more painful to observe. A whole series of major social facts, which have been continuously accelerating for some years now, characterize its decadence. They are:

♦ The pauperization of the middle classes, who have often fallen lower than the proletariat, because they are less equipped for the daily struggle. The development of fascism is merely a consequence of this. If we take account of the fact that the middle classes in Germany, numerous, educated and respected—before the war—were the true guardians of "respectable bourgeois behavior," we then see what are the serious results of their proletarianization.

♦ The development of corruption and speculation at every level of the social scale.

♦ The development of begging, prostitution and crime.

♦ The decline in the intensity and quality of labor which results, in the long run, from the decline in physical and nervous energy, as well as the demoralization of productive workers: the slackening of work discipline.

There is a corollary common to all these four facts: the deterioration of public health. About half the schoolchildren in most working-class centers are undernourished and tubercular. The diseases of poverty are making progress; the birth rate is falling and infant mortality increasing.

But to give the reader a more precise sense of these things, I want to refer to how they affect some of the details of daily life. In Berlin taking a bath has become a luxury which only the rich can indulge in. The public baths have all closed down. The bathrooms in petty bourgeois homes serve as lumber rooms; people are happy to be able to fill the bath with potatoes. For fuel is prohibitively expensive. In boarding houses you have to pay for *a glass of hot water!* Another luxury item is the newspaper. This morning I paid 50 billion for mine with the official exchange rate of the dollar at 620 billion. That puts a single issue at a price of 1.50 francs. In recent days the average price was 70 centimes. Manual and office workers can now only read newspapers when they are displayed in shop windows. There you get crowds of people hanging about all day. The end of the circulation of newspapers has had the effect of considerably livening up life in working class districts; people come to get the news. Whatever the weather, large groups hang around, from dusk till the dead of night. The lack of reliable information gives currency to the most bizarre rumors. Not an evening goes by but you hear of some coup being announced for the following day.

The streets in Germany—in the working-class districts—have completely changed their appearance in a few months. Until the great hunger, they had preserved their respectable, impassive, petty-bourgeois appearance. In Germany, you pass along the streets; you don't live in them as they do in Latin countries. Now it seems as though the greyness of the desolate houses has got darker. The windows are dirty, and so are the pavements (they're saving money on cleaning). Outside bakeries, grocers' shops, dairies, there are queues of sometimes a hundred or more persons, standing there for an indefinite period of time, however bad the November drizzle. There are queues outside the kitchens run by the Salvation Army or the local council; queues at the milk carts; crowds, thousands of people, outside the squalid offices where they pay unemployment benefits; crowds wandering in the evenings, along badly lit thoroughfares, at a loose end, bitter and anxious. Berlin has no less than 200,000 unemployed, and if you add to this figure the wives and children of the unemployed, that is some 500,000 people almost completely without resources. What happens to them in the evening? The cold, unlit house with no bread is uninhabitable. They go out onto the street, gather in groups, wander aimlessly, listen to the nationalist agitator, read the anti-Semitic leaflet that is being given out... In a Baltic port, as freezing drizzle was falling, I saw the quaysides in the evening covered with a crowd of motionless men, almost silent, waiting like this, with faces of cold anger, for the pointless evening to pass...

The frequent looting of bakeries seems to me to demonstrate the vigor of the hungry rather than their brutality. I've been told of cases of orderly, calm, "decent" looting, during which, taking only what was necessary, the poor didn't dream of touching money or expensive articles! It's among other elements of the population that we can see a new outbreak of brutal and indeed depraved behavior. In one year, the Berlin police know of 2,000 cases of children who have been ill treated. In France, the mainstream press have reported details of the anti-Semitic pogroms in Berlin. We know less about what the Bavarian fascists are capable of; during the wretched coup of Hitler and Ludendorff on November 7, they wrecked every item of furniture belonging to the social democrat Auer and terrorized his family for hours on end. I've just read that in the surroundings of Chemnitz, uniformed Nazis thrashed Communist workers who had been arrested till the blood ran... Twice, in recent days, at Altenhausen, near Coburg, and at Munich, they set up sham court-martials, in one case to condemn Jews to be hanged, and in the other case to tell SPD and Communist municipal councillors they would be shot...

Civilized behavior has, in short, been rapidly disintegrated by generalized poverty; the reactionaries, in a conscious effort to take the nation backwards, have added to the demoralization of the masses with elements of brutality, cruelty, obscurantism and sadism.

The arts and sciences...

European culture is a whole and you can't remove any part of it
without impoverishing thereby all the peoples and all the minds of
Europe. Can we imagine French thought today without Kant, Ni-
etzsche, Wagner, Haeckel, Marx, Einstein? There is no sphere of
European intellectual life where German intelligence has not contributed its achievements: Avenarius, Mach,[9] Ostwald, Helmholtz,
Einstein in physics; Wundt and Freud in psychology; Max
Müller, Max Weber, Cunow, Sombart, Eduard Fuchs[10] in sociol-
ogy; Bebel, Hilferding, Franz Mehring, Rosa Luxemburg in socialism; Hauptmann, Wedekind, Dehmel, Stefan George, Stefan
Zweig in literature; Richard Strauss and Mahler in music; Böck-
lin, Sleevogt, Liebermann, Corinth, Max Klinger in painting...[11]
Here are European names, contemporary but already classic,
which no "good European" can now ignore. I could mention
many more, but I'm not making a catalog of great men. I haven't
mentioned any of the representatives of the young Germany of
today, because, incarcerated in their "defeated" country, they belong only to the Europe of tomorrow.

...In the country of these laborers of civilization it is no longer
possible to print new books; no longer possible to publish sheet
music; it is no longer possible to maintain the old laboratories or to
buy or make precision instruments. Museums are no longer heated

---

9 The philosopher Richard Avenarius (1843-1896) and the physicist Ernst Mach
(1838-1916) were two of Lenin's main targets in *Materialism and Empirio-criticism*
(1909). That Serge lists them among the great names of German thought shows
how far he was from the dogmatism of the Stalinist era.

10 Eduard Fuchs (1870-1947), subject of the essay "Eduard Fuchs: Collector and
Historian" in Walter Benjamin's *One-Way Street,* was also an activist of the KPD;
in *Memoirs of a Revolutionary* Serge describes contacts with Fuchs.

11 Mach, Freud, G. Mahler are Austrians, which makes no difference. *[Serge's note.]*

in winter; many are closed; in any case it is impossible to add to their stock.—Dr. Georg Schreiber, from Münster, has just published a short book on the *Poverty of Science and Brain Workers in Germany.* I've taken the following data from him:

Institutes of scientific research that for years have been pursuing studies of specialized problems, such as the Institute of Epidemiology and the Institute for the Study of Cancer (Berlin), the Institute for the Study of Tropical Diseases (Hamburg), the Institute of Occupational Medicine and Hygiene (Frankfurt-am-Main), are having to reduce their expenses to a ridiculous minimum—or close down altogether. Taken all together, the scientific libraries of Prussia had, in 1922, a budget of 17 million marks (the exchange rate of the dollar was 4,000), while a single Scandinavian University, Upsala, had 135 million marks for the year. The Berlin Public Library, which before the war received copies of 2,300 foreign journals, now gets no more than 200. The gaps made in its collections by the blockade have not been filled. German scientific journals, like all the others, are disappearing. The Museum of Printing in Leipzig, in a desperate situation, has decided to sell abroad a valuable Gutenberg[12] Bible; only spontaneous donations from German artists enabled it to avoid resorting to this extreme measure.

What is happening to intellectuals amid this collapse of culture? Some, who are worse paid than workers, become workers. The majority vegetate, embittered. A composer said the following to me, which I quote more or less word for word:

"In a few years, nothing but the memory of the rich musical ave to write scores for operettas in order not to die of hunger...

---

12 Johannes Gutenberg (1400-68), regarded as inventor of printing from movable type, produced a 42-line Bible (c. 1455).

On the revolving stage of the great theater built by Reinhardt,[13] a boxing ring has been set up. The *Volksbühne,* the people's theater, in Berlin, is on the road to bankruptcy...

If Pasteur were working in Germany today, he would not be able to do anything for humanity. If Wagner were alive, he would have to write scores for operettas in order not to die of hunger...

So that *Herr Raffke,*[14] newly rich and one of those who has profited from the collapse of German culture, should have music with his supper...

The Stinnesation of intellectual life

Stinnesierung: "Stinnesation." The term is in current use. It is derived from the name of Herr Hugo Stinnes, a plutocrat, richer than Vanderbilt and Carnegie, who owns five or six world shipping lines, a large number of mines, factories and banks, who is one of the kings of coal, one of the kings of electricity, one of the kings of gold in Europe, who is considering putting at the head of a dictatorial government of the German Republic the general manager of his companies, Herr Minoux. Now he wants to make a monopoly of intelligence as well. His press trust, whose influence extends to a good fifty daily papers, uses in various capacities all those well-known intellectuals who don't want to resign themselves to poverty; and he is using them to implant in Germany a fascist ideology that is much more coherent, more elaborated, than that of a Hitler or even of a Mussolini. In the course of the last few months the scholars and journalists on Herr Hugo Stinnes' payroll have published

---

13 Max Reinhardt (1873-1943), theater director famous for spectacular productions; left Germany in 1933 and went to Hollywood.
14 *Raffke:* a current slang term for profiteer.

hundreds of articles, demonstrating the historical necessity of a re-actionary dictatorship and (to quote the *Deutsche Allgemeine Zeitung* word for word) that "the belief in the advantages of the eight-hour day is based on crude scientific errors." The press trust, a powerful enterprise devoted to winning over public opinion in favor of the owners of heavy industry, is not the only element or even the most important one in the "Stinnesation" of intellectual life. In the universities, in the management of large factories, in intellectual circles closely connected to industrial circles, the reactionary thought of present-day Germany is being elaborated, the philosophy of action of a possessing class, determined to make a final effort to survive the national and cultural catastrophe of Germany—that is, to survive its own crime.

At the turning point

Thus German capitalism, which first reached full maturity, then a decline hastened by military defeat, has become, after having been a factor of national organization, a factor of national disintegration, and it is fulfilling a comparable function in relation to European culture which it first developed—directly by means of the development of industrial technology—and which it is now murdering…

In the battle that has been joined between the upper German bourgeoisie and the revolutionary proletariat, between a class which is the cause of the current bankruptcy of culture and a class which, as is proved by the amazing cultural renaissance of Russia, is capable of giving a new impulse to culture, what could be the consequences of even a very temporary victory of the former?

The decadence of which we are witnesses is already the fruit of a temporary victory of counterrevolution. Joy, as I have said, is dead in this Germany of mourning and poverty: its best sons are dead too. Fifteen thousand proletarians—it is the accepted figure—died defeated in the social battles of 1918-19. Fifteen thousand members of an elite, the builders and soldiers of a new order, who had reached a sufficiently high level of class consciousness to try to move, at the cost of their lives, from verbal socialism to socialism in practice. What was their cultural value in a country already impoverished by war? Did they not represent one of its last reserves of civilizing energy? Moreover, the intellectual elite has been struck *in the head* by the counterrevolution. Liebknecht was not just a popular orator but above all a scholar; Rosa Luxemburg was one of the richest and most powerful Marxist minds of our time. Gustav Landauer, whose skull was crushed with hobnailed boots[15] (in Munich, in 1919, after the fall of the soviets), was an artist and a philosopher, one of those anarchists who belonged to the dying lineage of the likes of Reclus and Kropotkin.[16] They have also killed the socialist idealist, Kurt Eisner,[17] Ernst Toller is still in prison, Erich Mühsam, a poet and thinker, is also still in prison, but he, by a singular injustice, is almost forgotten…

What could a new victory of counterrevolution mean to Germany? Some reign of white terror, Horthy-style,[18] with an endless stream of murders, internments, fraudulent trials, executions and pogroms… Think of von Kahr's Munich, from where they are driving out the Jews, as they did in the thirteenth century. A complete "Stinnesation" of any surviving intellectual life. The ten-hour day,

---

15 He was beaten to death in prison by reactionary soldiers.

16 Élisée Reclus (1830-1905), geographer and communard and Prince Peter Kroptkin (1842-1921) were leading anarchist theorists who had greatly influenced the young Serge.

17 Kurt Eisner (1887-1919), USPD prime minister of the Bavarian Republic from November 1918 until February 1919, when he was murdered by a reactionary aristocrat.

18 Miklós Horthy established an authoritarian conservative regime in Hungary in 1920, after the overthrow of the Hungarian Revolution.

arms production, the triumph of the desire for military revenge, perhaps a restoration of the monarchy, certainly, in a few years, war. A perfected form of war, aerial, chemical, bacteriological...

Let us even admit, although it scarcely looks probable, the possibility of a new stabilization of democracy and the return of an economic conjuncture in Germany which is favorable to the bourgeois order. We've already been through it. It would merely be a continuation of decadence: and however long it might last, no other great hope than that of revolution could grow up in the population. By defending its class interests, by preparing to take power, the German proletariat today, in its sector of the front, is defending European culture.

This two part article gave Serge an opportunity to reflect on the failure of the KPD to carry through a revolutionary bid for power in 1923. Obviously for reasons of security he could not tell all he knew, but it was an honest attempt at self-criticism of the sort that would soon be impossible in the Comintern.
Lenin had died in January 1924; despite his warnings to the Fourth Congress of the Comintern in 1922, the new leadership under Zinoviev was imposing "Bolshevisation" on the Communist Parties of the world, paving the way for Stalin.

A 50-Day Armed Vigil

Clarté, February 1 & 15, 1924

In September, October and November in Germany, we have just lived through a profound revolutionary experience, which is still little known and often little understood in other countries. We have been at the very heart of a revolution. The armed vigil has been a long one, but zero hour never came... A drama that was almost silent, almost unbelievable. A million revolutionaries, ready, waiting for the signal to go on to the attack; behind them millions of unemployed, hungry, battered, desperate people, a whole suffering population, murmuring: "We too, we too!" The muscles of this crowd were already taut, their fists already gripping the Mausers they were going to use against the armored cars of the Reichswehr... And nothing happened, except the bloody clowning in Dresden, a corporal followed by four armed ruffians driving from their offices the workers' ministers who had made bourgeois Germany tremble, a few pools of blood—sixty dead in all—on the streets of the industrial cities of Saxony; the jubilation of a bankrupt social democracy, which emerged from the massive but passive adventure dully faithful to its old betrayals. None of those who lived through all the expectations of this fifty-day armed vigil knows all the details, everything that went on behind the scenes: for two whole classes were measuring their strength against each other, embodied in their vanguards, masked, in the shadows that are necessary for conspiracy. Of what everyone knows, not everything can be said; for revolutionary preparation is continuing under a military dictatorship. In this letter I should simply like to give you some impressions, some detailed observations, and suggest a few conclusions to you...

The march towards civil war

It was around September 15 that we felt the harsh approach of decisive events. The Great Coalition, including the party of Stinnes and Stresemann as well as the SPD, had taken power on August 12, as a result of the general strike. The blood of seventy workers killed in the strike sealed the pact of collaboration made between Stresemann, former agent of the Saxon industrialists, a monarchist in 1918, and Rudolf Hilferding, formerly a left wing Independent Social Democrat, Marxist author of *Finance Capital*. Contrary to what was later believed in the International,[1] the remarkable August general strike which drove Herr Cuno from power had been only a substantial success for the working class, but not a brilliant victory. The railway workers had scarcely taken part; in Berlin, traffic in the streets and commercial life were scarcely disrupted. Already social democratic passivity obstructed from the outset a powerful spontaneous mass

---

1 In the debate on the German failure, Radek, Zetkin and others argued the real revolutionary opportunity had come earlier than October.

movement. The hasty vote by the Reichstag, on August 10, right in the middle of the strike, for taxes on property, and the pathetic collapse of Herr Cuno bore witness to the anxiety of the bourgeoisie, faced for the first time with the consequences of its looting of the nation, rather than to the vigor of the workers' offensive, led by a strong minority, but sabotaged by a powerful majority. At this moment, the most perceptive minds in the enemy classes were led into error. The intelligent bourgeois, impressed by the ample spontaneity of the movement, exaggerated the immediate force of the revolutionary wave; they were afraid. Meanwhile, the revolutionary workers were fired with enthusiasm for the popularity of the KPD (to which, in various places, the strikers deliberately offered the leadership of the movement), then for the political success achieved, and thus began to overestimate their own strength and to underestimate the "formidable powerlessness" of the social democracy.

The bourgeoisie quickly got over its mistake. A month later, in the first week of September, all the concessions it had made to the social democracy in order to form the Great Coalition were seen to be null and void; large-scale industry had begun its campaign against the working class. Every day the question of extending the working day came up. At this moment the derisory but pernicious role of the SPD in the cabinet became obvious. The idea of an inevitable resort to force imposed itself on the masses of workers, just as it did on the big employers, the plutocrats and the old military caste. Two preparations for battle would now develop in parallel until the first week in November, which both camps soon seemed to adopt as a final deadline: for the anniversaries of the German Revolution (November 7 and 9) and of the Russian Revolution (November 7) had profound significance. And then, you can't make a revolution or a counterrevolution in wintertime.

Germany was evolving towards civil war. A race for power. Reaction and revolution both needed strategic bases. Reaction had

Bavaria: on September 16, Herr von Knilling made threatening remarks. There Hitler's gangs were arming feverishly, financed by the very rich industrialist Hugenberg, and, it is said, by Mr. Ford, a citizen of the United States.[2] The Communists tried to give the proletariat governmental positions in Saxony and Thuringia, where on their initiative "workers' governments" under Zeigner and Frölich were formed. In this use of governmental power for civil war almost all the advantages went to the bourgeoisie. The people in Munich were supported by Berlin. The workers' ministers in Dresden were under constant threat of action by the Reich. The people in Munich—though divided between separatists and Pan-Germanists, monarchists and popular nationalists, between Wittelsbach and Hohenzollern, between big industrialists and manufacturers, between advocates of an offensive and of delay—were unanimous on one point: that an end must be put, by force, to the red danger. At Dresden and Gotha, only the Communists were determined, knew what they wanted; the left social democrats hesitated; the leadership of the SPD plotted against them; the unemployed, the workers on short time, were burning with desire to act; but a number of social democrats still nourished the sweet dream of a revival of parliamentary democracy. In short, neither in Saxony nor in Thuringia did the Communists succeed in making the left

---

2 The claim that Ford was financing Hitler first appeared in the *New York Times* (December 20, 1922), which contained an account of a visit to Hitler's headquarters: "The wall beside his desk in Hitler's private office is decorated with a large picture of Henry Ford. In the antechamber there is a large table covered with books... published by Henry Ford. If you ask one of Hitler's underlings for the reason of Ford's popularity in these circles he will smile knowingly and say nothing." At Hitler's trial in 1924 evidence was given that "the Hitler movement was partly financed by an American anti-Semitic chief, who is Henry Ford." In August 1938 Henry Ford received the Grand Cross of the German Eagle, a Nazi decoration. (See A.C. Sutton, *Wall Street and the Rise of the Nazis* (Sudbury, 1976), pp91-93.)

social democrats adopt a really revolutionary attitude. Were they, as certain Communists claim (the left of the party[3]) wrong not to foresee this situation? It is easy to "have predicted" after the event. One way or another, I think an experience was necessary to show what a destructive influence social democratic inertia had even on the healthiest elements in the social democracy.

In October, the two permanent conspiracies came face to face. On the one side, the Reichswehr, and behind it the "black Reichswehr," organized at great expense with the support of Herr Cuno and the "Aid to the Ruhr" funds, Hitler's gangs, plus a hundred thousand men, massed in Bavaria, the Stahlhelm in Central Germany, the ex-servicemen's leagues in Mecklenburg and Pomerania, the disciplined organizations of Ehrhardt and Rossbach. On the other side, the Communist Party, feverishly pursuing its technical preparations. Who would take the decision? The most powerful social group on the enemy side, which felt itself being pushed towards dictatorship: heavy industry. In the first crisis of the Stresemann cabinet, Herr Stinnes simply wanted to measure his own strength and the weakness of the legal government. What would the decision be? If it were necessary to fight, and it would be necessary if the working class resisted the systematic encroachments of reaction on the streets, then heavy industry would only in the last resort use the murky fascist elements, whose arms cost it dear, and whose demagogy was displeasing. The centralization of power in Bavaria, in the hands of Herr von Kahr, partly had the aim of forestalling an untimely initiative by the demagogues, impatient elements and mercenaries mobilized by Hitler. The Küstrin incident (October 1)

---

3 The fact that Serge can refer in a non-party publication to the different currents within the KPD shows how far the Comintern still was from the monolithism of the Stalinist epoch.

showed how overheated minds had become in the vanguards of the enemy. Major Buchrucker hoped to give the signal for a nationalist rising. The Reichswehr remained faithful to its leaders who, for their part, were faithful to the very judicious masters of heavy industry.

On the threshold...

Losschlagen!

Losschlagen means: strike the blow you had been holding back, trigger off action. This word is on everyone's lips, on this side of the barricade. On the other side, too, I think. In Thuringia, outside semi-clandestine meetings where a Communist is due to speak, workers—whom he doesn't know—plant themselves in front of him. A railwayman asks, coming straight to the point: "When shall we strike? When?"

This worker, who has traveled fifty miles by night to ask this question, understands little about matters of tactics and timing: "My people," he says, "have had enough. Be quick about it!"

The young Communist you meet on the street tells you in a confidential tone: "I think it will be next week," and looks at you with his square forehead, his tough gaze, to which any lie is alien.

October is cold. Drizzle, rain, grey streets where we hang about for a long time, in the working-class districts. Drivers, housewives, those without work—who are also without shirts and overcoats—are discussing. They shout abuse at the nationalist student. In these nervous groups, huddled together at gloomy crossroads, far from the well-lit squares where the police look after the well-being of the profiteers who are engrossed in schemes for currency exchange, I often hear people insistently talking about Russia..."Over there!" he says, "over there..." And while he takes breath, I think that in the dark sky of these poor people, at least one star has risen. Women often speak in these improvised little meetings. I heard one of them upbraiding a National Socialist student: "Ah! You want to march on Berlin, do you, patriots! It's easier, isn't it, than driving the French out of the Ruhr!... Will you bring me some bread?" The man in his helmet encircled with the green and white ribbon of his scholarly guild, vainly tried to explain: "We'll throw all the tiles from the rooftops onto you!" they shouted.

Mist, drizzle, rain, first cold of October. Homes with no bread and no fire. Shops guarded by the green police, besieged, from dawn to nightfall, by cheerless crowds of women; the police go rushing, their short rifles slung crosswise, through the thoroughfares in working-class districts; suddenly trucks go by, bristling with guns and shining peaked military hats; thin, surly faces at every door in the feverish evening; reports in the newspapers: "Seven dead at Beuthen... twelve dead at Sorau... fifteen dead at Düsseldorf... six dead at Cologne..."

What is to be done when hunger drives crowds to lose their respect for the law? The police are afraid. They are hungry too. But they weren't made to provide bread. To resolve the social problems posed in the streets, they have only bayonets, bullets and handcuffs...

As you read the paper, it's no longer possible to add up those murdered during the day. There are too many, and information is confused. The comrade I've met tells me: "I've just seen a bakery looted..." "At the X factory, the wages haven't been paid, and vanloads of police have arrived." "It seems there has just been shooting in Neukölln..." The bakers pull down their iron shutters. Others, hypocritically calculating, put up notices in their windows saying: "Here you can make donations for the unemployed!" The customer's philanthropy is invited to pay for the bread they give: insurance against looting, at the neighbors' expense. Just about every day, prices double. The week's wage is fixed on Tuesday after the official inflation index is published; it is paid in two installments;

interim payment on Tuesday and the balance every Friday. From Tuesday to Friday, it loses two-thirds of its value.

After this anger, this desperation, this tenseness in the street and the home, it is good to find oneself from time to time gathered round the same table with some men whose brows show that they know what lies behind these things and who reinforce their will by contact with unlimited hope. One evening there were half a dozen of us, but one had returned from a long journey: a few hours earlier, he had been in the hands of the green police in the Ruhr. A young voice, calm and restrained: "We already have whole divisions…" Arms, it is true, are in short supply; we shall go and get them from the barracks. The map of Germany is present in all our minds: "Saxony, Thuringia, Berlin, Hamburg will hold… Russia!" "Radek has written…" I've noticed that the intellectuals—I'm one of them—are the most suspicious about how things will turn out. They weigh and weigh again the difficulties at length with overintellectual arguments that sometimes have a very debilitating effect. A friend cuts our commentaries short, saying: "I believe in the revolution, because I want it; because I live among people who want it." He is a district organizer; he works night and day.

Losschlagen! Losschlagen!

Chemnitz, Munich

The blow has not been struck.

The raised fist of the German proletariat has been slowly and peacefully lowered. All those who have lived through the events know that from many points of view it would have been much easier to act than not to act. We didn't act.

The decisive turning point for us was between October 15 and 21. The Reichswehr had entered Saxony. The right to strike had been abolished there. Military law was ruling this red state shamelessly. Nothing was left to the Saxon proletariat except a general strike—illegal—with the immediate aim of paralyzing, and then driving out, the Reichswehr; hence it would become an insurrection. The rest of Germany must support it. The signal was awaited from one hour to the next. Zeigner was governing in Dresden, with three Communists: Brandler, Heckert, Böttcher. Each day General Müller progressed further into the working-class centers. In reality the defeat, our defeat, occurred suddenly on October 21, at the Chemnitz conference. Left social democrats, Communists, non-party delegates from the factory committees were discussing action there, despite the military dictator, under the protection of the workers' hundreds whose heavy step hammered through the silence in the corridors. *Losschlagen!* The Communists proposed immediate action. "Everything is at stake," Brandler had just written. The—left—social democrats, who had followed them up to this point, replied, after many evasions: "No!"

They weren't ready. It wouldn't be legal. The conference was not formally authorized to decide. Wait. Set up a committee. What is it?

It was the failure, at the crucial moment, of the leaders of half the forces of the revolution, the workers' front broken in the face of the Reichswehr, disarray in minds, distrust returning among the proletarians who had already come to feel that they were brothers in arms. The precious moment, the one moment, wasted. After this, reassured, Herr Stresemann could act, had to act, and act quickly to take advantage of the situation. On October 28, the Berlin government addressed its ultimatum to Zeigner. (In short, it demanded the exclusion of the Communists from the government). Zeigner who, personally, wanted to get rid of our comrades, resisted out of a sense of dignity. The troops turned him out of his office. The initiative for operations passed to the enemy class.

Up to this moment, everything had depended on the attitude of the working class. It was in an attacking position. After the

Chemnitz failure, the worker's fist was lowered, giving up the chance to strike; the fist of reaction was raised.

Losschlagen. Reaction also wants to *losschlagen!*

The Munich tragicomedy resolved all the internal difficulties of the reactionaries. On November 7, Ludendorff and the demagogue Hitler made their coup, and took on the dictatorship of the Reich in a Munich beer hall. For a moment we were carried away by hope. *They were going to oblige the proletariat, which was incapable of taking the offensive, to engage in a counterattack which, with the aid of Communist will, could go a long way.* Such was not the intention of heavy industry, led by far-sighted people who were rather more serious than the Kaiser's former chief of staff.[4] Heavy industry didn't need a civil war. Even less did it need complications with foreign governments. Since Chemnitz, it was more confident about the combativity of the working class. Nothing was now opposed to its legal dictatorship. Henceforth it wouldn't give a halfpenny to Hitler's gangs, who in fact were quite dangerous. For the moment Hitler has come to the end of his career in a comfortable prison where he has been placed by his accomplice von Kahr.

The KPD criticizes itself

The German proletariat arrived at the threshold of revolution, but did not cross it. Is it the fault of the KPD?

To talk of mistakes after the situation has been wound up is all too easy. But it must be done. We need constant, vigorous, detailed self-criticism. For us yesterday's retreat is never anything but a roundabout route to tomorrow's action. We leave to the old

---

4 i.e., Ludendorff.

democratic parties the cult of irresponsibility. Let us ask the question clearly: does the responsibility for the October retreat fall on the leaders of the KPD, and to what extent? We shall see in a moment how the central committee of the KPD itself replies.

German militants readily take the blame for having underestimated the force of inertia of the social democrats in general, and for having overestimated the extent of Communist influence on the left social democrats. Their duty is to be hard on themselves. And yet! Was it possible to foresee in advance the failure of the left social democrats? These Saxon workers with their old-style socialist education, bureaucratic and stuck in a rut, have nonetheless already given the party of the revolution a number of excellent fighters. Didn't they seem at last to be committing themselves all the way? Was it not reasonable to hope for a decisive awakening on their part? And if so, was it not right to gamble on the greatest hope, that is, to show daring?

No, that wasn't the mistake, or if it was a mistake, it was certainly not the fundamental one. Did the fault lie in not acting in spite of everything? That is the thesis of certain comrades from the left of the party. I don't think they are correct. Alone in the face of all the forces of bourgeois society—Reichswehr, police, black Reichswehr, fascists, civil servants, servile social democrats, more than a million reactionaries with better weapons—the Communists could not count on any serious chance of lasting success.

We should take into consideration the party's technical inadequacy. "This technical inadequacy," it is said, "became apparent only at the last moment." Indeed, and that is what is serious. Here we have found the weak point. That indicates defective intelligence, presumptuousness and lack of foresight, at least as far as concrete preparations were concerned. But let's try to be fair. Never, whatever its state of organization, will a revolutionary workers' party before the insurrection be, not better armed, but even as well armed as a modern army. In any circumstances, we must expect a substantial technical inadequacy. Arms could have been taken from the enemy. If the mass movement had developed in the desired proportions, the inadequacy would have been remedied by emptying the arsenals of the Reichswehr...

On the eve of the October Revolution, Lenin recalled the elementary rules of revolutionary strategy, already formulated by Karl Marx. One of the most important of these is: "Concentrate a *great superiority of forces* at the decisive point and at the decisive moment."[5] The extreme decentralization of Germany, as well as its geographical position, make the application of this rule very difficult—hence a certain loss of confidence in everyday action. That must be taken into consideration.

The October retreat seems to me to have been perfectly justified. Nonetheless it is true that in social war, as in all warfare, the defeated leaders—whatever their talents—are usually removed. A new majority has been formed on the central committee of the KPD which has, in "Theses on the October retreat and the present tasks of the KPD" (*Correspondance internationale*, January 3, 1924), specified in severe terms its opinions on the errors of the Party:

a) The party failed to recognize in time the scope of the great mass actions of the proletariat in the Ruhr, in Upper Silesia, and throughout Germany (general strike against the Cuno government) and as a result failed to adapt its tactics to the situation that these struggles had created [...]

b) The party did not begin its preparations for armed uprising at the very moment when it observed the decay

---

5 "Advice of an Onlooker," in *Collected Works XXVI* (Moscow, 1964). Lenin was referring to *Revolution and Counter-Revolution in Germany*, originally published under Marx's signature, but in fact written by Engels.

of democracy (at the time of the Cuno government and the invasion of the Ruhr), but only a few days before the reactionary dictatorship came on the scene. Hence short-term military preparations, made hastily, inadequate arming of workers in the decisive days.

c) The party tried to hold back unprepared mass movements that occurred before the October events, in order to postpone them until the moment when the decisive blow was due to be struck [...] The party failed to closely link its ultimate aim, the dictatorship of the proletariat, to the demands of the transitional period and to partial actions.

d) The party failed to recognize the role and nature of the leaders of the left of the SPD [...]

e) Although it could have done so, the party did not take advantage of the advanced positions it held in the governments of several German states, in order to bring the mobilization of the masses to a successful conclusion with a view to organized resistance.

f) The gravest error in the strategic plan of the party, however, consisted in not making preparations for anything other than the "last fight" for the conquest of political power, while refusing and even opposing the organization of partial actions or sustained actions for partial demands with less aggressive means and methods of struggle.

g) This cardinal error was taken as the basis for an abstract calculation of the forces confronting each other, without taking the trouble to recognize and examine the true situation in this respect. But the study of forces confronting each other can be done usefully only in the course of the action, on which the date fixed for the final offensive will also depend. Thanks to this purely theoretical false strategy, struggle was always evaded.

h) Finally, during the decisive days for the party, excessive importance was attributed to the number of rifles while there was an underestimation of the subjective strength and enormous spirit of sacrifice that the proletarian vanguard brought to the struggle. (See the lessons of the battles of Hamburg.)

i) The rigid plan which conceived of the decisive action as developing solely from the defense of positions in central Germany was based on a false calculation. The consequence, after the reactionary forces entered central Germany, was a complete disorientation of the way comrades saw things.

We must insist on one point: a workers' combat party, at a turning point such as the one Germany is going through, is obliged to be very harsh with itself. From these detailed paragraphs set out like a legal verdict I think we should pick out in particular the following points:

The revolutionary situation developed more rapidly than the party. Despite its revolutionary experience, richer than any except the Russian proletariat, the KPD was not able to adapt to a collapse of German capitalism so severe that within six months it found itself on the threshold of revolution. Overall, it will be seen that these criticisms apply to the general tactics of the party much more than to its attitude at the very moment of the German retreat.

In Chapter III of the same theses it is said that "retreat without fighting was a mistake" because it disoriented, and somewhat demoralized, the most combative of the German proletariat. The mistake of "retreat without fighting" extends over the whole period of struggle that goes from the fall of the Cuno cabinet to the

Chemnitz conference. The mistake of the German revolutionaries was to lack initiative, to fail to continually harass the enemy, to fail to resist the enemy at every step with the maximum of energy, but rather to bide their time for a great final offensive, conceived in a rather abstract fashion… Such, at least, is the judgment suggested by the most qualified among us.

The objective revolutionary situation has ripened much more rapidly than the class consciousness of the majority of the German proletariat. The organized elite of this proletariat—the KPD—was not at first able to adapt itself to the increased speed of events, and subsequently, carried away by its faith and enthusiasm, did not have a clear awareness of the enormous weight of the social democratic mass which had to be shaken… For my part I shall offer only these conclusions.

The retreat is not a defeat

It is nonetheless true that over a period of six weeks to two months, the KPD has made an extraordinary effort. Not a single one of its three to four hundred thousand members remained inactive. There was not a town in the land where they did not prepare for battle with the conscientious concern of people determined to give everything for their cause. Not a day without bitter toil, not a night without its special task. No problem was neglected. I know comrades who for weeks on end did not have a full night's sleep. I have seen faces furrowed with overwork. The stubborn eyes never lost their burning intensity. It was magnificent. In what country (apart from Russia) has anything similar been done? We are not afraid to assert that the German Communist Party *has given the world proletariat the new and precious example of the awesome process of preparing for a revolution.*

That also of the greatest devotion of proletarians to their class. Each time it was necessary, in Saxony, Thuringia, the Rhineland,

Westphalia, Hamburg, to mobilize the workers' hundreds for action, everyone was at their post. Nobody deserted or hesitated. There was absolute unanimity in the voluntary accomplishment of duty. Now each of the workers called to service by his hundred always knew that he was risking his liberty, his life, the last piece of bread of his family. If the signal had been given, the whole KPD would have marched as one person, despite the objective opinions of some individuals as to the probable outcome of the struggle, despite internal disagreements, despite the inadequacy of arms—despite everything.

This party has been dissolved.[6] Its 40 daily papers have been suppressed. Its leading committee is on the run. Its assets have been seized. Ebert's police are offering up to fifteen thousand gold marks for the capture of some of its activists. Some of its arms have been seized. Some of its men have been killed. How many of its comrades are in prison? They can be counted in thousands. But nevertheless...

All the branches of this party are alive and active. The circulation of its illegal press is growing week by week. On several occasions it has put tens of thousands of demonstrators onto the prosperous thoroughfares of Berlin. It has kept its arms and that is no secret. It continues its preparation. It has huge broad-ranging departments (prisoners' aid, ambulances, liaison, research), training schools, a complex and flexible network of organization against which the military dictatorship has shown itself to be powerless. Is this a defeated party?

The October retreat was not a defeat. The rulers of Germany know this better than anyone. They do not enjoy the security of true victors. And that is what preserves, in Germany, a last remnant of the Republic...

---

6 The KPD was made illegal on November 23, 1923; the ban was lifted on March 1, 1924.

The situation is still revolutionary

The threshold has not been crossed. We have even taken a step back. But we are still at the threshold.

The situation in Germany remains profoundly revolutionary. While the military dictatorship gives the upper bourgeoisie some significant strategic advantages, it offers merely possibilities of salvation. In a very few days everything may be called into question again for the German bourgeoisie. The unity of the Reich is a political myth. Neither the Rhine, nor the Ruhr, nor Bavaria, accept the authority of the central government, to which the working-class centers show scarcely greater respect.. Parliamentarism, democratic institutions, constitution, citizens' rights are pure fictions which no longer deceive anyone. The financial situation has never been so serious as today. The gold loan and the credits in Rentenmarks granted to the Reich have been exhausted. State employees, reduced to real starvation pay, can be paid each fortnight only thanks to the invention of new expedients. In December, the cost of living, despite the stabilization of exchange rates and wages, showed a rise of at least 25 to 30 percent. The dilemma facing the state is now whether to resort immediately to a new inflation of vast proportions or to stop making payments of all kinds. No rapid tax collection can get it out of this situation, since no tax can produce sufficient sums. The country people fear that the Rentenmark will fall in value, and since they are still obliged by law to accept paper marks, they are raising their prices, and restricting the sale of foodstuffs. The winter months will very probably not go by without bringing further grave crises of food supplies for the towns, and in their wake food riots, looting and the massacre of the hungry. The aim of heavy industry is at all costs to impose on the country a resumption of intensive production, at the expense of the workers alone. That's their road to salvation. But the German plants are old and worn out, except in the Rhineland regions, where the great plutocrats have intelligently maintained them; but these are regions lost to the Reich, for that very reason (Stinnes, Vögler, Wolff, Klöckner and Krupp are concerned not to have in tow behind them a national industry which is in a very bad way; they would rather plunder it). Everywhere, even in the Rhineland, the labor force is worn out by years of hunger, overwork and acrimony. Finally, German production has become strictly dependent on the international situation; for all the great industrial powers of Europe, its revival would mean the reappearance of a competitor. It will scarcely get any help. In these circumstances, will not the tycoons of industry try to continue a policy which is in some senses feudal, merely enriching their own firms from the general ruin? The endless poverty of the working masses is well-known, the extent of unemployment too (one million, five hundred thousand unemployed, two and a half million on short time). Now proletarianization is attacking new layers of the middle classes, state employees who until now were the most reliable supporters of the social order. The problem of unemployment is insoluble: the state cannot, in the immediate future, either feed the unemployed or promise them work. The states, towns and districts are bankrupt. Fascism in the strict sense, a movement of the impoverished middle classes, armed and utilized by the big employers, is in decline, eroded by disappointment. The disintegration of the democratic parties is continuing. It would be a very big mistake to imagine that the SPD will emerge strengthened from the November crisis. It is obvious that at the next Reichstag elections, it will lose—to the advantage of the Communists—a large part of its vote.[7] Whole regions are slipping away from its influence. Dittmann recently noted

---

7 An example of Serge's overoptimism; the KPD improved its position in the May 1924 election, getting 9.6 percent of eligible voters, as against 1.6 percent in 1920 (with 14 percent for the USPD), and 62 deputies; but the SPD got 15.7 percent (nearly two million more votes than the KPD) and 100 deputies. The SPD had the largest percentage of the vote for any single party at every election from 1919 to 1930.

in Vorwärts "that a handful of young Bolshevik journalists are setting the fashion for Saxon social democrats." The party's unity, and its power, are myths, like the unity and the power of the Reich. The ADGB, the big reformist trade union organization, can no longer pay its full-timers and sees its membership melting away before its eyes. The SPD itself is living on the generosity of the British Labour Party. It scarcely any longer represents an active political factor: it is still significant as an inert mass. Its power lies solely in inaction, and it can no longer either require respect from the bourgeoisie or block the progress of communism.

This internal situation in Germany, a revolutionary one, will necessarily last for at least a few months. With the support of foreign capitalism, by means of a clever and cruel class dictatorship, and by agreeing to pay a major part of the expenses itself, the German bourgeoisie may in the end succeed in consolidating its positions. Our comrade E. Pavlovsky,[8] an experienced observer of economic affairs, admits this is true. For the moment the hostile classes remain confronting each other. On their level of consciousness, their will, their intelligence, still depends the outcome of the struggle in which social democratic inertia gives the victory to the reactionaries in October and November.

At this moment we need to remember that social revolutions need, in order to ripen and be completed, not weeks and months, but years: the French Revolution stretched out, with leaps forward, stabilizations and political storms, over about fifteen years. Prepared beforehand by long struggles, the Russian Revolution joined its first great battle in 1905 and only completed its victories in 1920-21.

---

8 A pseudonym of the Hungarian economist Eugene Varga.

Postscript

Brandler and Thalheimer, the most authoritative representatives of the former majority on the KPD central committee, in their theses, accuse the Executive Committee of the Communist International and the KPD of an "erroneous estimation of relative strength of the forces confronting each other." In particular they claim that the Comintern Executive did not take sufficient account of the observations of the KPD. The International will not fail to clear up this point.[9] The left of the party, of which Ruth Fischer[10] is one of the best-known leaders, has a diametrically opposite point of view. It considers that it was possible to take power in October, but criticizes the party for having failed, before the discussions in Moscow on the German question, to make preparations for revolutionary action. Its opinion is that "the party should have taken on the struggle even at the risk of defeat, for this would have given the German proletariat fine revolutionary traditions attached to the name of the KPD, in this way preparing a future victory." This point of view seems to me to be difficult to maintain. A Communist rising crushed in Germany by the military dictatorship and the fascist bands would, it seems to me, have provided the German bourgeoisie with a sense of security and victory which it is far from having at present. The losses it would have inflicted on the working class would not have been easy to make up for, despite the reputation for heroism which would have remained for the KPD. There are irreparable losses: we need only name Liebknecht and Rosa Luxemburg, leaders whom the German Revolution has not yet replaced, although it is justly proud of their magnificent memory.

---

9 Serge, who knew and despised Zinoviev, the dominant figure in the Comintern now Lenin was dying, may well be using gentle irony here.
10 Ruth Fischer (Elfriede Eisler) (1895-1961), became KPD leader with Zinoviev's support in 1924, but was replaced by Thaelmann and then expelled in 1926.

The 1871 Commune also made an impression of epic proportions on history: but the bloodshed inflicted by the Versailles forces on the working people of Paris nonetheless weakened it for many long years. However convinced we may be of the ultimate victory of the working class, we cannot maintain that all its defeats are necessarily stages towards victory. It may be claimed of certain defeats after having soberly assessed the consequences; it is very rash to talk in the same way of a hypothetical defeat, one which would certainly have been very bloody, very expensive, and very much exploited by an enemy prepared to stake everything.

Further Reading

For those who want to know more about the revolutionary period in Germany, Chris Harman's *The Lost Revolution* (Haymarket Books, 2003) provides an indispensable narrative account and political analysis of events from 1918 to 1923. (Indeed, ideally Harman's book should be read before Serge's articles.) For those who want more detail, see Pierre Broué's monumental *The German Revolution, 1917–1923* (Haymarket Books, 2006), first published in English in 1998 by Porcupine Press. W. Guttmann & P. Meehan, *The Great Inflation* (Saxon House, 1975) gives a lucid and lively account of the economic processes and social consequences of the 1923 inflation. Ian Kershaw, *Hitler, 1889–1936: Hubris* (W.W. Norton & Company, 1998) provides much material on the activities of the extreme right. *Revolutionary History, Vol. 5, No. 2, Spring 1994,* contains some interesting documents and analyses on 1923.

There is now a considerable body of Serge's work available in English, including several novels. His *Memoirs of a Revolutionary* (NYRB Classics, 2011) contains a chapter "Europe at the Dark Crossroads" describing his experiences in Germany; it is interesting to compare his later view with what he wrote at the time. Other writings from his period as a Comintern activist include *Revolution in Danger: Writings from Russia, 1919–1921* (Haymarket Books, 2011) and his essay "Lenin in 1917" in *Revolutionary History*, Vol. 5, No. 3, and available online at http://www.marxists.org/archive/serge/1924/xx/lenin.html. There are some interesting essays on Serge in S. Weissman (ed.), *The Ideas of Victor Serge* (Critique Books, 1997). Bill Marshall, *Victor Serge: The Uses of Dissent* (Berg Publishers, 1992) contains an extensive bibliography of Serge's writings.

Key Figures

BERNHARDT, Georg (1875-1944): Editor of *Vossische Zeitung*.

BÖTTCHER, Paul: Printer, SPD member, joined USPD 1917; joined KPD 1920. Minister of economics in Saxon government; expelled from KPD as rightist 1929; in Switzerland during Nazi period; on return to East Germany arrested and deported to Russia; later returned to East Germany.

BRANDLER, Heinrich (1881-1967): Building worker, veteran Spartacist; KPD leader 1923; scapegoated for 1923 failure, expelled from KPD 1929.

BUCHRUCKER, Bruno Ernst: Involved in Kapp putsch; commanded Black Reichswehr 1923; planned putsch at Küstrin barracks; imprisoned but soon pardoned; later in Strasser's Black Front.

CUNO, Wilhelm (1876-1933): Shipping magnate; Chancellor November 1922-August 1923.

DEGOUTTE, J. M. J. (1868-1938): French General; head of French forces occupying Rhineland from 1919; led occupation of Ruhr 1923.

DITTMANN, Wilhelm (1874-1954): SPD from 1894; secretary of USPD;

rejoined SPD 1922; went to Switzerland 1933.

EBERT, Friedrich (1871-1925): Saddlemaker, leading SPD activist; President of Reich from 1919.

EHRHARDT, Hermann (1881-1971): Leading organizer of Freikorps; supported Kapp putsch; ran Organization Consul; responsible for murders of Erzberger and Rathenau; fled Hitler 1934; lived in Austria.

FRÖLICH, August (1877-1966): Head of workers' government in Thuringia.

GESSLER, Otto (1875-1955): Defense minister 1920-28. Lived as private citizen under Hitler, seven months in Ravensbrück.

HECKERT, Fritz (1884-1936): Building worker, veteran Spartacist; member of Saxon government 1923; Stalinist in 1930s; died in Moscow, reportedly executed by GPU, but ashes placed in Kremlin wall.

HELFFERICH, Karl (1872-1924): Economist; member of DNVP, militant opponent of Versailles Treaty.

HILFERDING, Rudolf (1877-1941): Member of USPD 1918-22; edited party daily *Freiheit*. Rejoined SPD; Finance Minister August-October 1923; left Germany 1933; executed by Gestapo in Paris.

HORN, Rudolf von: Reichswehr general.

KAHR, Gustav von (1862-1934): Civil servant; joined Catholic Bavarian People's Party 1918; prime minister of Bavaria 1921; Bavarian General State Commissioner 1923; executed 1934.

KAUTSKY, Karl (1854-1938): Chief theoretician of SPD and Second International before 1914, known as "Pope of Marxism"; failed to oppose war; joined USPD 1917; strongly anti-Bolshevik.

KLÖCKNER, Peter (1865-1940): Leading industrialist.

KNILLING, Eugen von (1865-1927): Member of Bavarian People's Party; prime minister of Bavaria 1923.

KRUPP von Bohlen und Harbach, Gustav (1870-1950): Industrialist; key role in World War I; named as war criminal but never tried; involved in rearming Germany before 1933; key role in backing Hitler and preparing World War II; used slave labor during World War II; named as war criminal but never tried!

LEVI, Paul (1883-1930): Close to Luxemburg before war; joined USPD 1917, Spartacus League 1918; president of KPD; expelled from Party 1921 for public criticism of March Action; formed Kommunistische Arbeitsgemeinschaft (Communist Study Group); in 1922 joined the USPD, which later that year was reunified with the SPD.

LOSSOW, Otto von (1868-1938): General; Chief of staff of Reichwehr's Bavarian Division 1921; District Commander of Bavaria 1922; Member of Bavarian ruling triumvirate 1923.

LUDENDORFF, Erich (1865-1937): Successful general World War I; imposed Brest-Litovsk Treaty on Russia; involved in Kapp putsch; collaborated with Hitler 1922-24.

MARX, Wilhelm (1863-1946): Chairman of Center Party; chancellor 1923-24 and again later in 1920s; denied pension by Hitler.

MÜLLER, Alfred (1866-1925): Reichswehr commander in Saxony and Thuringia.

MÜLLER, Hermann (1876-1931): SPD member from 1893; chancellor March-June 1920, 1928-30.

NOSKE, Gustav (1868-1946): Veteran SPD right winger; minister of war 1918-20; Chief civil official of Hanover till 1933; dismissed by Nazis, arrested 1944 but never tried.

POINCARÉ, Raymond (1860-1934): French president 1913-1920; prime minister 1922-24 and 1926-29; ordered occupation of Ruhr 1923.

RADBRUCH, Gustav (1878-1949): Academic, joined SPD 1918; justice minister 1923; returned to academic life; first academic removed from office by Nazis.

RADEK, Karl (Sobelsohn) (1875-1939): Revolutionary in Germany and Poland before Russian Revolution; Bolshevik leader; important role in Germany on behalf of Comintern 1919-23; Left Opposition till 1929, then capitulated to Stalin; imprisoned after 1937 Moscow Trial; died in concentration camp.

REINHARDT, Walter (1872-1930): General; held highest military appointment in defense ministry; conflict with von Seeckt; remained in Reichswehr till mid-1920s; considered "father of the republican army."

REMMELE, Hermann (1880-1939): SPD from 1897, involved in anti-militarist activity; founder member of USPD 1917; joined KPD 1920, member of *Zentrale;* KPD leader till 1932, then opposed Thaelmann; emigrated to Moscow 1933; arrested 1937.

REVENTLOW, Graf Ernst zu (1868-1943): Naval officer, then Pan-German journalist; joined Nazis 1927.

ROSSBACH, Gerhardt (1893-1967): Freikorps leader; involved in Kapp putsch; joined Nazis, involved in "beer-hall putsch," then fled to Austria; served in Abwehr in World War II; after 1945 helped re-establish Bayreuth Wagner Festival.

RUPPRECHT, Crown Prince (1869-1945): General, son of last Bavarian King.

SCHEIDEMANN, Philipp (1865-1939): SPD from 1883; chancellor 1919; lord mayor of Kassel 1919-25; fled Germany 1933.

SCHMIDT, Robert (1864-1943): SPD member; minister of economics on several occasions in 1920s; Vice-Chancellor in Stresemann cabinet, August to October 1923.

SEECKT, Hans von (1866-1936): General in World War I; involved in Freikorps; advised creation of Black Reichswehr; granted dictatorial powers after "beer-hall putsch" till February 1924; supported Hitler after 1933 despite having Jewish wife.

SEVERING, Carl (1875-1952): SPD right winger from 1893; Prussian interior minister for most of period of Republic; hostile to Nazis, jailed briefly; active in SPD after 1945.

SOLLMANN, Wilhelm (1881-1951): SPD from 1907; interior minister in Stresemann government; fled to USA after 1933.

STINNES, Hugo (1870-1924): Industrialist with interests in coal, steel, electricity, etc. Member of DVP.

STRESEMANN, Gustav (1878-1929): founded DVP in December 1918; Chancellor August-November 1923; foreign minister till 1929; Nobel Peace Prize 1926.

THYSSEN, Fritz (1873-1951): Industrialist, son of August Thyssen; financed Nazis from 1923, main business leader to back Nazis before 1933; joined Nazis 1933, but broke 1938; fled to France 1939, spent 1940-45 in various camps; went to Argentina 1948.

VANDERVELDE, Emile (1866-1938): President of Belgian Workers' Party and Second International; joined Belgian government of national defense 1914; several times minister in Socialist-Catholic coalitions.

WULLE, Reinhold (1882-1955): One of founders of Deutschvölkische Freiheitspartei—conservative nationalist German Racial Freedom Party.

ZEIGNER, Erich (1886-1949): SPD from 1919; prime minister of Saxony March 1923 till deposed October 1923; withdrew from politics after being jailed for corruption; repeatedly jailed by Nazis; after 1945 lord mayor of Leipzig (East Germany).

Appendix

Anyone comparing this book with Pierre Broué's edition of *Notes d'Allemagne* will observe considerable differences in the dating and arrangement of texts. *Correspondance internationale* appeared in both a weekly and a twice weekly edition. In most cases I have presented the articles as they appeared in the weekly edition. (It should be remembered that *Correspondance internationale* was produced under difficult and dangerous conditions. Because of police seizures the editorial office did not even have a complete file to make up an index for 1923.) To assist anyone working on the material, the following table shows how the 29 items in this book correspond to the sections of Broué's book and the dates he gives—generally referring to the twice weekly edition of *Correspondance internationale*. Many of Serge's pieces were reproduced, in whole or part, in *Bulletin communiste*, a journal of the French Communist Party. I also give dates when all or part of an item appeared in *BC*. All dates 1923 except where stated.

Item	Broué	*Correspondance international* **dates**	*Bulletin communiste*
1	-	-	-
2	-	-	Apr 29 (1922)
3	I	Jan 3	-
4	II	Jan 10	-
5	III	Feb 9	-
6	V	Jul 1	-
7	IV	Jul 13	-
8	-	-	-
9	VI	Jul 30	-
10	VII	Aug 7	-
11	VIII	Aug 15	-
12	IX, X	Sept 5, 7	Sept 13
13	XII, XIII	Sept 11, 14	-
14	XI	-	-
15	XIV, XV	Sept 28	Oct 11
16	XVI, XVII	Sept 30, Oct 4	Oct 11
17	XVIII	Oct 12	Oct 18
18	XIX, XX	Oct 16, 19	Oct 25, Nov 1
19	XXI, XXII	Oct 25, 26	-
20	XXIII, XXIV	Oct 30, Nov 2	Nov 8, 15
21	XXVII, XXV	Nov 9, 15	Nov 15
22	XXVI, XXVIII	Nov 13, 17	Nov 22
23	XXIX	Nov 20	-
24	-	-	Dec 6
25	XXX	Dec 13	-
26	-	-	-
27	-	-	-
28	-	-	-
29	XXXI, XXXII	-	-

About Haymarket Books

Haymarket Books is a nonprofit, progressive book distributor and publisher, a project of the Center for Economic Research and Social Change. We believe that activists need to take ideas, history, and politics into the many struggles for social justice today. Learning the lessons of past victories, as well as defeats, can arm a new generation of fighters for a better world. As Karl Marx said, "The philosophers have merely interpreted the world; the point however is to change it."

We take inspiration and courage from our namesakes, the Haymarket Martyrs, who gave their lives fighting for a better world. Their 1886 struggle for the eight-hour day reminds workers around the world that ordinary people can organize and struggle for their own liberation.

For more information and to shop our complete catalog of titles, visit us online at www.haymarketbooks.org.

Also from Haymarket Books

Revolution In Danger • Victor Serge

The German Revolution • Pierre Broué

Rosa Luxemburg • Paul Frölich

Essential Rosa Luxemburg: *Reform or Revolution* and *The Mass Strike* • Rosa Luxemburg, edited by Helen Scott

History of the Russian Revolution • Leon Trotsky

The Comintern • Duncan Hallas

Witnesses to Permanent Revolution: The Documentary Record
Edited and translated by Richard B. Day and Daniel F. Gaido

Ours to Master and to Own: Workers' Control from the
Commune to the Present • Immanuel Ness and Dario Azzellini

CPSIA information can be obtained
at www.ICGtesting.com
Printed in the USA
JSHW010747310123
37097JS00003B/3

9 781608 460854